D1103815

ONE RARE FAIR WOMAN

Thomas Hardy by William Strang, 1893

ONE RARE FAIR WOMAN

Thomas Hardy's Letters to Florence Henniker

1893–1922

edited by

Evelyn Hardy and F. B. Pinion

University of Miami Press

Coral Gables, Florida

*As for one rare fair woman, I am now but a thought of
hers,
I enter her mind and another thought succeeds me that
she prefers;
Yet my love for her in its fulness she herself even did
not know;
Well, time cures hearts of tenderness, and now I can let
her go.*
                                        'Wessex Heights', 1896

She *has always been a sincere and affectionate friend to
him, staunch and unaltering — and, I am glad to say, she is
my friend too. There was never any idea of his letting her
go — for he, too, is true and faithful to his friends, but the
poet wrote that.*

                                Florence Hardy to Lady Hoare,
                                        9 December 1914

Contents

List of Illustrations

Facsimiles of a letter by Mrs Henniker and a postscript by
    Thomas Hardy appear on pages xxvii and 17)

1. The earliest known portrait of Hardy.
2. Both Mrs Henniker and her husband preferred the shorter form
to the full family name.

Acknowledgements

Miss Evelyn Hardy gratefully acknowledges the permission of the Hardy Estate Trustees to publish these letters and the receipt of a special Research Award from the Leverhulme Trust for her share in this work.

The editors are indebted to the following for their generous assistance: the late Marchioness of Crewe for making available to Miss Hardy the Marquis of Crewe's reminiscences of his sister, and for supplying information which led to discoveries elsewhere; Mr Gerald FitzGerald, Fellow of St Edmund's House, Cambridge, for his valuable recollections and for permission to quote from his aunt's letters to Thomas Hardy; Lord Henniker, for his ready assistance on a number of occasions; the Trustees of the Hardy Estate and the Curator of the Dorset County Museum for enabling us to transcribe Hardy's letters to Mrs Henniker and consult other unpublished ones; the University Library, Cambridge, Colby College Library, the Brotherton Library, Leeds University, and the County Archivist, Trowbridge (and Mr H. P. R. Hoare and the National Trust), for allowing the use of information and brief quotations from letters in their possession; also the British Museum and its Newspaper Library, Colindale, and the University Library, Sheffield, for their ready co-operation in our researches.

We are grateful to the following for the useful information they have been able to supply: Mr Douglas Matthews, Deputy Librarian of the London Library; Mr Ralph Malbon, City Librarian, Portsmouth; Mr John Townsend; Miss E. M. Samuel; and Mrs Madeleine Stewart-Mackenzie. We should like also to acknowledge the patience and courtesy of many to whom inquiries, which proved to be insoluble, have been addressed.

Illustrations are included by courtesy of the National Portrait Gallery (Thomas Hardy by William Strang), the National Library of Ireland (Vice-regal Lodge), the London Library (Mrs Henniker, from *Outlines*), Mrs M. Stewart-Mackenzie (Lady Jeune), Lord Henniker (Major-General Henniker), and Mrs Bellows (Edmund Gosse and Thomas Hardy, photograph by William Bellows). Manuscript facsimiles have been kindly provided by Mr R. N. R. Peers, Curator of the Dorset County Museum.

We are grateful to Constable & Co Ltd for permission to quote from Viola Meynell's edition of J. M. Barrie's letters, and to Peter Davies Ltd for allowing the inclusion of passages from James Pope-Hennessy's biography of Lord Crewe.

Thanks are due to Mrs Pinion for advice on the editorial text, and for assistance in checking the text of the letters, as well as in proof-reading.

When references to bibliographical sources are not given in full, this implies that the details are provided in Appendix IV, p. 213.

E. H. and F. B. P.

Preface

I

The Honourable Florence Ellen Hungerford Milnes was born in December 1855, and was named after her godmother, Florence Nightingale, whom her father, Richard Monckton Milnes, first Baron Houghton, had persistently tried to marry. Her mother was Annabel, younger daughter of John, second Lord Crewe, who could trace his descent in Cheshire and the north of England from the twelfth century. Florence had an older sister, Amicia or Amy, who was to become Lady Gerald FitzGerald, and a younger brother, Robert, who became second Lord Houghton, and subsequently Earl, and then Marquis, of Crewe.

In a letter to a friend, her father describes Florence as a child:

> The second little girl has developed into a verse-writer of a very curious ability. She began theologically and wrote hymns, which I soon checked on observing that she put together words and sentences out of the sacred verse she knew; and set her to write about things she saw and observed. What she now produces is very like the verse of William Blake, and containing many images that she could never have read of. She cannot write, but she dictates them to her elder sister, who is astonished at the phenomenon. We, of course, do not let her see that it is anything surprising; and the chances are that it goes off as she gets older and knows more.[1]

She was not yet seven years old. We catch glimpses of her in 1872, when, at the age of sixteen, she accompanied her father to Paris. He was the guest of M. Thiers, the President of the French Republic, and took her at the President's invitation to dinner with the Thiers at Versailles. She sat next to the President, and thought it 'delightful'. 'Florey enjoyed her first outing (dining thrice with Thiers, with Lord Lyons and the Rothschilds), and behaved with great simplicity and *convenance*', Lord Houghton wrote to his wife eight days later.

1. Reid, II pp. 85–6.

Madame Thiers thought Florence 'very distinguished'. That
there was more than breeding and proper behaviour in this
young girl is evident from a previous letter in which Lord
Houghton tells his wife that 'Florence was quite struck' with
the 'brilliant talk' of M. Renan, the persuasive Breton writer
of *La Vie de Jésus*.[2] Her nephew, Mr Gerald FitzGerald,
states that when Florence accompanied her father on this or
another visit she caused him embarrassment by turning and
studying the faces of the people in the street. This curiosity
reveals a characteristic which she inherited from her father
and which stood her in good stead as a woman and writer –
her interest in human nature, which qualified her to become a
successful novelist, to act as hostess to, and attract, a remarkable number of men and women in different walks of life –
soldiers, statesmen and writers.

Her father, noted for his extravagant hospitality, was in the
habit of giving large breakfast and evening parties, attended
by politicians, poets, men of letters, artists, actors, explorers,
foreign visitors, and members of titled and fashionable society.
At one of these Florence, when she was twenty, had a disturb-
ing encounter with Swinburne, then only thirty-eight.

> Swinburne [she writes to her brother], in a very excited
> state, came in in the evening ... He is madder than ever, to
> my astonishment he *flopped* down on one knee in front of
> me, and announced that my hair had grown darker. This
> was rather embarrassing, and he is also so deaf now, which
> does not make it easier to talk to him.[3]

One wonders whether, in their later acquaintanceship,
Florence Henniker ever described the scene to Hardy, Swinburne's close literary friend, pilloried like him over the years
for his perverse agnosticism and obstinate unconventionality.
It is amusing now to read that Florence was considered
rather 'fast' by the members of the older Victorian set, who
looked with disapproval upon the spirited precursors of the
Edwardian era. In another letter to her brother she describes
how, at Taymouth in a New Year rag, the young people 'ran
the lifts up and down, broke the windows, baited old Alistair
Murray nearly mad, sugared the top of his bald head and

2. ibid., II pp. 266–9.   3. Pope-Hennessy, p. 5.

generally raised him finely'. In yet another Scottish household
she wrote that,

> on going to bed, in the passages – Lord Melgund bounced
> out upon us in a cocked hat and cloak and mask and Amy
> [her elder sister] nearly went into hysterics and fled down
> into the hall where she encountered Lord Minto and Sir
> H. Smith, who naturally were a little surprised to see her.[4]

In those days girls with original minds did not marry
quickly; intellectual gifts in women caused suspicion. Florence
and her older sister remained what James Pope-Hennessy calls
'resolute spinsters' until their middle twenties. In 1882, when
she was twenty-seven, Florence married the Honourable
Arthur Henry Henniker-Major, a somewhat impecunious
younger son of the fourth Lord Henniker of Thornham Hall,
in Suffolk. The seat, Tudor with later additions, had descended to his father through two heiress sisters, the Duchess
of Chandos and Baroness Henniker of Worlingworth Hall. But
good blood and ancient lineage were not enough for Baron
Houghton. What he had wanted for his pretty, eligible daughter was *money*. He sourly confessed that he had been paid
back for his mercenary motives. Gifted, exacting, irritable and
extravagant, he was forced to admit that he had been disappointed over Florence's marriage settlement.[5]

Arthur Henniker, 'Arty' to his relations and intimate
friends, was the same age as his bride, and a mere adjutant in
the Coldstream Guards at the time of his marriage. Soon
afterwards he was on active service in Egypt, the first of many
separations which his duties necessitated. Florence Henniker's
brother, Lord Crewe, gives the details of his subsequent military career:

> A popular officer in the Coldstream Guards, and a staff-
> college graduate destined for military distinction, he held
> various regimental and staff appointments until the out-
> break of the South African War, in which he successively
> commanded a Battalion, a mobile column, and then a
> District until the declaration of peace. Until his promotion
> as Major-General he commanded the Guards Brigade at

4. ibid., pp. 14–15.   5. ibid., p. 19.

Aldershot, receiving active employment until his death from an accident, in February 1912.[6]

In 1894 Hardy dined with the Major at the Guards' Mess, St James's. He recorded in his *Diary*, 'After dinner went round with him to the sentries with a lantern'.[7]

On the eve of his going to South Africa Hardy wrote to him that he had long considered him 'the most perfect type of the practical soldier that I know'.[8]

That he should have married a girl of an intellectual cast of mind is perhaps surprising, and there is an amusing anec- dote about Arthur Henniker in the days of early courtship, in a letter of Thomas Hardy's:

> The Major (who is really a very good fellow) was very amusing – describing the only time ever he studied poetry: when he was getting engaged to Mrs H [enniker] – at which time he bought a copy of Byron, and read him manfully through. He then got married, and has never read any since.[9]

She was of medium height and erect carriage, with chestnut hair (darkening as she grew older), and grey-blue eyes. Her expression was alert, 'like one ready to be amused. *I do not ever remember seeing her ill-tempered*', her nephew tells me. He stresses the fact that, although she was sincerely and con- ventionally religious, she was also gay and worldly, to the extent of liking pretty clothes and accepting, if not courting, admiration. While she had many devoted women friends she enjoyed the minds and company of men, which is perhaps natural when one remembers how her father had made com- panions of his children, and especially of his daughters. 'She enjoyed the robust humour of her soldier husband.' An especial characteristic was her horror of brutality: 'She felt acutely the amount of suffering in the world.' (This, and her power of entering into the feelings and thoughts of others, which made Hardy sum her up on meeting her as 'a charming, *intuitive*

6. From unpublished reminiscences.

7. *Life*, p. 266. Henniker was a thorough soldier. His men, when on duty, 'never knew where he might be met with, day or night'; they said he 'could see through a brick wall' (*Arthur Henniker*, arr. Florence Henniker, 1912, p. 96).

8. Letter dated 19 October 1899.

9. Weber, p. 36.

woman apparently',[10] were sufficient to ensure his attraction to her.)

> In literature [her nephew comments], tragedy, drama, and pathos made a strong appeal to her. She did not appreciate Jane Austen nor care for the work of Meredith.[11] In spite of her enjoyment of humour and gaiety she had, in some ways, a pessimistic outlook – insisting on the unhappiness of so many marriages, although her own and that of her nearest relations were singularly successful. She felt acutely the amount of suffering in the world, *although she was not censorious*. It would be unjust to estimate her qualities on her novels and stories alone, for in some ways she displayed her weakest side in her writings.

I am indebted to the Marchioness of Crewe for some unpublished reminiscences of his sister by the late Lord Crewe, who corroborates this closing remark on Mrs Henniker's character and writing. 'She was one of those whose personality outshone her achievements.'

With memories of her childhood and girlhood in her father's open houses, in Upper Brook Street, London, and Fryston, Yorkshire (where a lock of Keats's hair was preserved among other literary relics), which Swinburne, Browning and Carlyle, Richard Burton, Trollope and Herbert Spencer, Mrs Gaskell, Dean Stanley, and John Morley visited with easy familiarity, it was to be expected that Florence Henniker would one day have a coterie of her own literary and political friends, inheriting, as she did, many of her father's tastes and characteristics. Mr Gerald FitzGerald gives the names of some of them: 'Before the South African War she had made many friends among the Irish M.P.s – T. P. O'Connor, Dillon, and Swift McNeil. John Burns, who represented the Labour element in Mr Asquith's Cabinet, was another of her unexpected friends.' Among others, her brother, Lord Crewe, tells us, were 'Lord Wolseley, Sir John French, Lord Grenfell, and Sir James Grierson, as well as Generals Plumer, Smith-Dorrien, and Monro. But with the writers – with Rhoda Broughton, Mrs W. K. Clifford, Edith Sichel, Edmund Gosse, George Russell, W. E. Norris, Bret Harte, and not least of all

10. *Life*, p. 254.
11. Like Hardy; see the letters, pp. 138–9 and p. 192 n.

Thomas Hardy, she also maintained a close relation of friendship.'

We see Florence Henniker in her *salon* in the pages of the
Reminiscences of Justin McCarthy, one of her friends who
appears in these letters:

> There is one house in London ... [where] one had a chance
> of meeting ... in a small congenial company.... I am speak-
> ing of the house which had for its gifted and charming
> hostess my friend Mrs. Henniker.... Mrs. Henniker is, as
> everyone knows, an authoress of rare gifts, a writer of de-
> lightful stories ...; like her brother she inherits from her
> father a rich poetic endowment. She is also one of the
> hostesses, not very common in our days, who, if she had
> lived in Paris at a former time, would have been famous as
> the presiding genius of a *salon* where wit and humour,
> literature and art, science and statesmanship found con-
> genial welcome.[12]

McCarthy had relished meeting Bret Harte at Mrs Henniker's
house, and her letters to Hardy indicate that Harte's descend-
ants did not forget her hospitality.

In her thirties Florence Henniker published three novels,
and a volume of short stories. Other novels and short stories
followed, as well as a four-act comedy, *The Courage of Silence,*
which was published in 1905. In 1896 she was elected President of the Society of Women Journalists. During her lifetime
her work was extravagantly praised by her father's old friend
Gladstone, and by the professional literary critics: it was
compared to that of Balzac, Maupassant and other French
writers, as well as to Dickens; and it was described as 'power-
ful', 'pathetic', 'fascinating', 'vigorous', 'sympathetic', 'fresh',
'vivid', and 'poignant'. One critic dwells on what he calls 'the
sustained pity and sweetness of her work'. Her style was said
by one critic to be 'easy and graceful', and by another 'simple
and graphic'. She was called 'a keen and sympathetic observer
of life and human nature'. As the following letters show,
Hardy himself paid her compliments more than once, both on
her style and her originality.

He was tireless in his efforts to prosper her writing. He read
and criticized her work. He introduced her to agents. He

12. Justin McCarthy, *Reminiscences,* London, 1899, ii pp. 69–70.

urged her work on editors. He even wrote a short review of it, anonymous for propriety's sake, for his friend Clement Shorter, in which he defines 'her note of individuality, her own personal and peculiar way of looking at life' as 'that of emotional imaginativeness, lightened by a quick sense of the odd, and by touches of observation lying midway between wit and humour'.[13]

Lord Crewe sums up her ability when he says that her 'gift was genuine, but not of the highest distinction'. He is, however, careful to emphasize that the claims of her husband's career, of her family and of her numerous friendships, 'joined to somewhat uncertain health, detracted from the exercise of her proper abilities'. Nevertheless, in the space of fourteen years Florence Henniker published six novels, three collections of short stories, and many uncollected tales, as well as the play referred to above. The chief characteristic of her work is compassion, joined with the habit of looking ironically at institutions, current social conventions, and attitudes of mind. One is not surprised to note that she has the ability to draw the characters of men more readily than those of women.

She met Thomas Hardy in Dublin at the Vice-regal Lodge in May 1893, possibly earlier, but we lack proof of this. Her brother, then Lord Houghton, and Lord-Lieutenant of Ireland, had been tragically widowed in 1887, and Mrs Henniker acted as hostess for him. The brief record of their meeting is given in *The Life of Thomas Hardy*,[41] together with details of the ten days' sojourn of Hardy and his first wife, Emma, in Ireland. But thereafter Mrs Henniker, save for scant references, is excluded from Hardy's autobiography until her death in 1923, thirty years later, when a note like a sigh taken from his journal is set down.

The invitation which led to the Dublin visit was a long-standing one, and Hardy himself is careful to point out in his letters that he has been, so to speak, a friend-by-proxy for many years. He had met Mrs Henniker's father some time in the 1870s, and been invited by him to Fryston in 1880,[15] an invitation he had been unable to accept because of sudden, serious illness. Her father had earlier remarked, 'I think I know every

13. The review is given on pp. 209–10.
14. pp. 254–6.   15. *Life*, pp. 145–6.

man of letters now whom I want to know, except one'. The
exception was Thomas Hardy, for whom he felt 'a great
admiration',[16] shared by his children. Thus Mr and Mrs
Hardy were invited to Fryston in 1892 by the second Lord
Houghton, Mrs Henniker's brother. But the death of Hardy's
father, in July, had prevented their going, and it was not until
the following May that the journey to Ireland was made.

It is not to be expected that a man of Hardy's extreme
reticence should confide on paper – either in his private letters
or in his journals – the strong emotion which Florence Henniker instantly aroused in him; we are more likely to find this
recorded in the poems. While it is dangerous to deduce from
the dated poems all that they imply, we have it on the authority of that careful warden of her husband's work and interests,
Florence Hardy, that at least two – 'A Broken Appointment'
and 'A Thunderstorm in Town' – are clearly to be associated
with Mrs Henniker, and there are other significant poems.[17]
The letters, especially the opening ones, corroborate the
poems' hidden meaning. Hardy's careful omission of dates
from the early letters, his eagerness to meet Mrs Henniker at
all costs –

'I have accepted also an invitation to Lady Shrewsbury's
dinner ... but I can throw her over if necessary' –

the frequency of notes and letters in the first six months after
his meeting with Mrs Henniker – there are twenty-four extant letters from June to December – and the suggestion that
he might become her architectural mentor, all bear witness
to a deep attraction which continued for at least another three
years. By 1896 Hardy's ardour was cooling, if we may believe
the penultimate stanza of the dated 'Wessex Heights', placed
at the beginning of this volume. But he remained her devoted
friend until her death.

When the two met in Dublin, Hardy was close on fifty-three,
and Mrs Henniker was thirty-seven years of age. Mrs Hardy's
eccentricities had become more marked, and Hardy was
restive under their display. The barrenness of their relationship in the autumnal days of their marriage is now well
known – how, wounding each other without conscious intent,

16. Reid, II p. 368.   17. See pp. xxxiv–vi.

they strove to protect themselves by barricading their hearts, each against the other's. The perceptive reader of the poems may follow the painful, the 'palpitating drama' imbued with tragic irony. If Hardy was to continue 'to breathe and have his being' it was essential for him to find an outlet for pent-up, starved emotions. As Barrie has said, Mrs Henniker 'took him on holiday from himself', at a time when he desperately needed distraction and refreshment. To put it more poetically, in the words of Hazlitt, she perfectly 'filled up the mould of his imagination'. The craftsman in him turned the double frustration, and the ardour which could never be slaked, into a handful of poems, most significant among them the three black 'In Tenebris' poems,[18] and the prose work *Jude the Obscure*. Hardy himself tells us that three months after meeting Mrs Henniker, 'from August 1893 onwards into the next year', he was writing out the novel 'at full length'.[19] Again we have the important testimony of Florence Hardy that Sue Bridehead, Hardy's most intellectual heroine, was in part drawn from Mrs Henniker.[20]

Florence Henniker's role in their personal relationship remains of necessity conjectural, since most of her letters have been destroyed, probably either by Hardy's own hand or at his wish after his death by his second wife. But she appears to have handled Hardy's vibrant emotion with tactful firmness. There are references, both in his letters and the poems, to some occasion on which she made it clear that she could never return his affection. The 'one-sidedness' of their relationship, which Hardy guardedly emphasizes twice in his letters, would seem to refer to this.

As for the poems, we have statements such as these:

You love not me,

....

— I know and knew it.

18. The second and third are dated respectively 1895–6 and 1896, and are probably to be associated indirectly with Mrs Henniker and a crisis in Hardy's matrimonial life.

19. *Jude the Obscure*, 1895 preface. See the letters, pp. 31 and 36–7, however.

20. Purdy, p. 345.

and:

For then it was
You let me see
There was good cause
Why you could not be
Aught ever to me![21]

Mrs Henniker was happily married. Hardy, 'a time-torn man' who had provocation for separation from his wife, was also indisputably married. There could be no question of a liaison between two people of conscientious character, and little likelihood of one between those of such widely divergent social strata. Yet Mrs Henniker, with a freedom which now a little surprises us, provocatively sent her admirer gifts of books, an inkstand, and other objects – as well as photographs of herself. She was obviously flattered that the leading novelist of the day paid court to her, as befitted her father's daughter. One imagines, too, that she pitied him a little, caught in the net of his matrimonial frustrations. They also had common interests, literary and compassionate, chief among the latter their hatred of vivisection. The full recital of these may be left to the letters.

Their collaboration in the tale 'The Spectre of the Real', and Mrs Henniker's dedication of one of her books to Hardy, publicly marked her out as his literary friend – some thought his disciple – but her good sense and behaviour seem to have prevented their names from being linked more ominously together. It is not clear when Hardy became a friend of Arthur Henniker. Mrs Henniker liked and esteemed both of Hardy's wives, 'entertaining warmer feelings for the second':[22] Florence Hardy became the devoted admirer of her aristocratic namesake. The judicious circle was complete. How far Florence Henniker realized that she was the embodiment of Hardy's life-long fantasy of the lady whom 'the poor man' loves, subject of novel and poems,[23] we cannot tell. Since she was an

21. 'A Broken Appointment' and 'The Month's Calendar'.
22. Lord Crewe.
23. Hardy's first novel (which remained unpublished) was *The Poor Man and the Lady*, the main story of which in an abridged and modified form was published in 1878 as 'An Indiscretion in the Life of an Heiress'. The poem 'A Poor Man and a Lady' (*Human Shows*) recalls an episode in the original story. The theme is repeated in 'In Death Divided' (p. 203) and elsewhere.

astute observer of human nature I suspect that she guessed at it, at least in part, but she may have underestimated the violence of his first feelings for her, as that stanza of 'Wessex Heights' implies.

The letters reveal many things about Hardy the man and writer that we have half surmised. His was a complex, deceptively simple character. Here, for instance, we have the peace-loving man, who deplores war as an unsatisfactory way of settling international disputes, mingled with the warlike, who follows the strategic tactics of the Boer War with an interest almost as avid as that employed in his study of the Napoleonic. Here, too, is that paradoxical creature, morbidly sensitive to suffering, who cannot bear to think of animals for human consumption being improperly transported and killed, who, as a boy, had picked his way between the coupled earthworms along the lane lest they be trodden on, in contradistinction to the old man, nearing eighty, who dwells with seemingly sadistic pleasure on the burning alive of a woman for poisoning her husband in 1705,[24] and, at eighty-seven, on a man hanged through the evidence of a governess.[25] These are only two of the curious anomalies.

There is another characteristic we do not like to recognize, what one might almost call his snobbism. Hardy's recital of aristocratic names in the opening letters looks a little as if he were seeking to ingratiate himself with Mrs Henniker. His easy offer to 'throw over' the Countess of Shrewsbury, his familiar chit-chat about the titled ladies whom he familiarly calls by their Christian names, even by their nicknames – 'Catty' and 'Birdie' – reveal a side of Hardy that does not accord with those other aspects of his nature that have delighted us. We have known since the publication of his autobiography that when he was nearing forty he had begun to mingle with the aristocracy in town, and later in the country.

24. Evelyn Hardy, *Hardy's Notebooks*, pp. 82–3. When Lady Il-chester and her daughter were at Max Gate in February 1919, eleven days after Hardy had written the note referred to above, he persisted in telling the story in all its gruesome details, though Florence did her utmost to stop him when she saw the effect it had on Lady Ilchester's daughter, who turned 'quite white'. She was only fifteen (Meynell, p. 301).

25. His mother had told him the story when he was about six (*Life*, p. 440).

Hardy's introductions by Mrs Henniker's father to the latter's
literary and titled guests brought about the writer's meetings
with peers, and more especially peeresses, who, after the ap-
pearances of *Tess of the d'Urbervilles,* treated him with adu-
lation. In 1880, however, he was only in midstream with his
writing: *The Return of the Native* had been published, together with earlier novels like *Far from the Madding
Crowd,* but not *The Major of Casterbridge, The Woodlanders, Tess,* and *Jude the Obscure;* nor as yet any of the
volumes of poems.

He admitted in a conversation with his old friend Edmund
Gosse that as a young man he had shown 'a wonderful insight
into female character' in his first unpublished novel, *The
Poor Man and the Lady,* adding, 'I don't know how that came
about'.[26] Hence the 'noble dames' of the 1890s — the Duchess
of Marlborough, the Marchioness of Londonderry, the Countess of Ilchester, Lady Jeune and others — found little difficulty
in confiding intimacies of their own and their feminine
acquaintances' lives to this original, intuitive writer. That he
took his place among them easily does not surprise us because
of his native integrity and simplicity of bearing. He himself
was probably living out, with great but unconscious satisfaction, the fulfilment of the youthful dream that had been
induced by the caresses and kisses of the childless Julia
Augusta Martin, showered on him 'almost from his infancy ...
until he was quite a big child', an affection he returned in full,
according to his own admission.[27] Hardy the worldling, with a
sophisticated side to his nature, what someone has called 'a
loose affability', appears in these letters. We find it hard to
reconcile their suavity with Hardy the countryman, who
wrote:

> *Lonely places in the country have each their own peculiar
> silences,*[28]

and Hardy the poet, who was to sweep away the ashes
from those extraordinary fires, banked up beneath an
exterior of 'formal subtlety', after his first wife's death.

26. Sir Edmund Gosse, 'Thomas Hardy's Lost Novel', *The Sunday
Times,* 22 January 1928.
27. *Life,* pp. 18–19.
28. Evelyn Hardy, *Hardy's Notebooks,* p. 36.

Here irony, of which Hardy was a past master, relentlessly pursues him. It has become the fashion for writers on him to over-emphasize his first wife Emma's preference for 'being the niece of an Archdeacon rather than the wife of Thomas Hardy'. Yet here we find him carefully pointing out, on more than one occasion, to Mrs Henniker, and taking pride in, Emma's relationship by blood to the Giffords and by inter-marriage to his new neighbours at Kingston Maurward, [Sir] Cecil and [Lady] Hanbury.

There are slight indications also of Florence Hardy's involvement in that larger irony that wounded her not long after her marriage, when Hardy's heart and mind reverted to his courtship and the idyllic early days of his marriage to his first wife, Emma. In fact, Emma's shadow lay so persistently across the life of Florence Hardy that on one occasion she was forced to record that it was almost unbearable. *The Notebooks* and *The Life of Thomas Hardy* have described those sad journeys westward with Florence, who watched Hardy review, often with pain, the former loved scenes, and inspect epitaphs, memorials and graves in Cornwall and Devon. She accompanied him, too, to Sturminster Newton and other Dorset places where he and Emma had been content, even gay. She wisely recognized that sorrow, even suffering, was an inherent part of Hardy's inspiration; and came, perhaps, to acknowledge that without the spectre that had haunted his first marriage he would not have been the poet that he was. In one of her letters she says that her husband is upstairs writing 'an intensely dismal' poem 'with great spirit'.[29] Restive but submissive, she grew to speak of the Hardy graves, including Emma's, as 'our graves', and, although shocked at Hardy's appearance one morning at the breakfast table wearing a mourning-band and other funereal accoutrements on the anniversary of Emma's death, she accepted the living spectre as well. Florence Henniker had introduced her namesake to the Max Gate household before Emma's death. Florence Dugdale, as she was then, confided later that she had gone down to Dorset expecting to pity Hardy but came away pitying Mrs Hardy (Emma), whose birthday no one remembered except herself.[30] Watching her from a distance, Mrs Henniker must sometimes have been troubled in spirit for this younger friend,

29. Meynell, p. 307.   30. ibid., p. 308.

whom she describes as having 'a beautiful nature, very full of sympathy'.

The literary value of these letters lies in Hardy's comments on dead and living writers – Sappho, Shelley, Meredith, Stevenson, Henry James, Galsworthy and others, wherein we are given added insight into his literary taste; in his revelations concerning details of *Jude the Obscure,* written with Mrs Henniker half in mind; and in his comments on his poems, as they appeared in journals and papers, and then in volume form, and on *The Dynasts,* that great warlike epic threaded with humorous rustic, or shadowy episodes, intermingled with the historical. But the ensuing letters have their personal value in a unique relationship.

Although more than fifteen years his junior, Florence Henniker predeceased Hardy by five years. Her brother, Lord Crewe, who outlived her,[31] tells us that she had undergone 'a long and painful illness' but left 'a memory of undying youthfulness, of observant humour, of earnest faith and of unchanging affection'. The year before her death she willed Hardy's letters to her to his widow.

It is doubtful whether the sequence as now preserved in the Dorset County Museum by the will of Florence Hardy, after her death in 1937, is complete. Mrs Henniker probably burnt some of them. As for hers to Hardy, this also applies: some of her letters are originals, some are in transcript form. They do not begin until 1906, and there is then a long gap. Since they corresponded from 1893 onwards, obviously a great many letters must have been destroyed, either by Hardy himself, or in that great holocaust that went up, by his wish, in the garden at Max Gate after his death.

Soon after Hardy's death in 1928, his widow consulted Sir James Barrie about the advisability of publishing her husband's letters to Mrs Henniker, copies of some of which she sent to him to read. Barrie returned them with the comment:

I have read the letters to Mrs Henniker. ... They show that here was a lady of great charm to him, for whom he had more regard than for any other person in an important time in his life, and it is valuable to the reader to know of her as such ... I rather grudge her being a writer at all, and

31. He died in 1945.

TEL. :
HORNSEY
941.

FAIRSEAT,
HIGHGATE HILL,
N. 6.

2. Hyde Park Square
W. 2

November 9th
1922

I wish all the letters
written to me by Mr.
Thomas Hardy to be
given to Mrs Thomas
Hardy after my death.

Florence Henniker.

indeed I believe he did also. Of course, the pieces about *Jude* and *The Well-Beloved* and the poems are the kind of thing one is searching for. . . . She was delightful and cultured and could take him on holiday from himself (for which I bless her), but she did not in these letters draw blood, so to speak; there is no indication to me that she influenced his work.[32]

About 1930 Hardy's hesitant widow once again contemplated publishing these letters, but the appearance of, and reactions to, Bernard Shaw's to Ellen Terry deterred her. Hardy's letters are therefore presented for the first time here, more than forty years after his death. Interest in them is likely to increase as the date of his death recedes.

No, Florence Henniker did not visibly 'draw blood' from Hardy in the letters, but they show that she influenced him in the writing of *Jude the Obscure*. The poems are stronger, more conclusive evidence of her influence on him. In them, for a brief moment, the writer dared to wear his vulnerable heart on his sleeve.

Evelyn Hardy

32. *The Letters* of *J. M. Barrie*, ed. Viola Meynell, London, 1942, pp. 153–4; letter dated 18 March 1928.

The main purpose of this postscript to Evelyn Hardy's preface is to provide facts and points of view which are relevant in defining the areas of the actual and the probable in the first, somewhat conjectural, stages of the friendship between Hardy and Mrs Henniker. Speculation on their early relationship and its reflection in a number of Hardy's poems, parts of *Jude the Obscure*, and, interestingly but less significantly, in the improbable story of 'An Imaginative Woman',[33] combines with the attraction and interests of the two principal characters to give the letters a special fascination. The more closely one considers them and what Hardy wrote with Mrs Henniker in mind (consciously or otherwise) the more convinced one becomes that these writings contain important clues to much in a critical phase of Hardy's life.

Some uncertainty has been expressed about when this long and enduring friendship began. In the summer of 1880, Hardy met Mrs Henniker's father, Lord Houghton – not for the first time, it appears – and dined with him twice. In 1883, the year after her marriage, he lunched at Lord Houghton's, 'off Park Lane', and there 'met Browning again, Rhoda Broughton for the first time, and several others'.[34] It is possible, though not very probable, that he was introduced to Florence Milnes (Henniker) on one of these occasions; but a meeting would have been more likely had he been able to visit Fryston at Lord Houghton's invitation in the autumn of 1880. In one of his earliest surviving letters to Mrs Henniker,[35] Hardy wrote:

> You seem quite like an old friend to me, and I only hope that Time will bear out the seeming. Indeed, but for an adverse stroke of fate, you would be – a friend of 13 years standing.

He then refers to the protracted and serious illness which occurred during the writing of *A Laodicean* and which made it impossible for him to accept Lord Houghton's invitation. The passage quoted above seems to imply that their friendship is so new that only time can show how lasting it will prove to be.

33. See n. 116, p. 38.   34. *Life*, pp. 138, 159.   35. See p. 13.

The first Lord Houghton died in 1885, and his successor invited Hardy to Fryston in the summer of 1892, stating that as
his sister Mrs Henniker would be staying with him it would
be a great pleasure to see Mrs Hardy as well. It is clear from
this and a subsequent letter that Mrs Henniker, who had by
this time completed two novels and was naturally not without
literary ambition, was especially eager to meet the author
who, after the publication of *Tess of the d'Urbervilles,* was
rapidly becoming the most famous writer of his time. After
the death of Hardy's father, the invitation was renewed for
August. Once again, the anticipated meeting had to be de-
ferred when Lord Houghton accepted the Viceroyalty of
Ireland from Gladstone. In January 1893 Lord Houghton had
a copy of his *Stray Verses* sent to Hardy, who, thanking him in
reply, expressed the hope that Mrs Henniker's novel (*Bid Me
Good-bye*) had 'sold out'. The following April,[36] the Hardys
were invited to stay at Vice-regal Lodge, Dublin, during
Whitsuntide, when Phoenix Park would be 'in full beauty'.
Hardy's notes on this visit are detailed and succinct; his reference to Mrs Henniker, Lord Houghton's hostess, as a 'charming, *intuitive* woman apparently' does not suggest an earlier
acquaintance.[37] Neither do Hardy's tone and approach in his
first letters to Mrs Henniker, where it is evident that he is
anxious to please and do nothing to impair a friendship of
which he is not entirely assured. Hardy himself wrote that the
chief significance of his visit to Dublin was meeting Mrs Henniker, 'who became afterwards one of his closest and most
valued friends'.[38] This statement reinforces the conclusion that
they first met in Dublin in May 1893.

When Mrs Henniker died in April 1923, Hardy wrote in
his notebook 'After a friendship of 30 years'; and such it was,
within a few weeks from that 'romantic' time when they met
in Dublin. It hardly seems likely that doubt would have
arisen on this question but for a note written by Rebekah

36. The invitation, in Lord Houghton's handwriting, is dated
'April 22, 1892'. He recommended crossing the Irish Sea on Friday, 19
May. Hardy took this advice (*Life,* p. 254). This time factor and the
date of Lord Houghton's appointment leave no doubt that the letter of
invitation was inadvertently misdated.

37. *Life,* p. 254.

38. J. O. Bailey, *The Poetry of Thomas Hardy,* Chapel Hill, 1970,
p. 30.

Vice-regal Lodge, Phoenix Park, Dublin, *c.* 1893

Florence Ellen Henniker (the Hon. Mrs Arthur Henniker), 1893

Owen, an American admirer of Hardy who had settled in England. Some time after being taken on 'little' Wessex tours by Hardy at the beginning of September 1893, she wrote in her copy of *Tess of the d'Urbervilles* that the idea of having Tess executed at Winchester occurred to Hardy when he escorted Mrs Henniker to the milestone on West Hill 'whence Clare and 'Liza-Lu saw the black flag'.[39] If this were true, it would mean that Hardy knew Mrs Henniker as early as 1890.

It will be seen in the course of this correspondence that Mrs Henniker was particularly interested in the topography of *Tess* soon after she met Hardy in Dublin, and that she visited Winchester with him only about twenty days before Rebekah Owen heard the West Hill story. It is highly probable that Hardy referred to this visit when he spoke of the place where he [had] thought of Tess's execution at Winchester. The tense he used may have been ambiguous, but it must be admitted that another discrepancy exists besides the chronological. There may have been a second misunderstanding on Rebekah's part, and this could easily have arisen from Hardy's terseness; she noted that Hardy met Mrs Henniker at Winchester, whereas in 1893 he met her at Eastleigh, on the way to Winchester. Without unequivocal supporting evidence, Rebekah Owen's note should be regarded with caution, if not with complete scepticism. Nothing is known to justify the inference that Hardy's acquaintance with Mrs Henniker began before the memorable visit to Dublin in May 1893.

The readiness with which Hardy and Mrs Henniker corresponded and met for some months at the beginning of their friendship betokens an unusual degree of mutual attraction. Each was flattered by the other's immediate response – she, one suspects, mainly for literary reasons at first, and he, mainly for personal. Mrs Henniker was gratified to number among her friends an author whose fame was spreading rapidly; she may also have been tempted to think that the continuing friendship of a novelist with whose genius she was deeply in sympathy could be to her literary advantage. If this were so, she was not disappointed; Hardy gave critical attention to the stories on which she was working in 1893,

39. Carl Weber, *Hardy and the Lady from Madison Square*, Colby College, 1952, p. 85.

submitted suggestions for textual and constructional revision, and advised her on publication. Aid very quickly spread to collaboration. At the end of the year, Mrs Henniker acknowledged her indebtedness by inscribing her forthcoming volume 'To my dear friend Thomas Hardy'. In the meantime Hardy's eagerness to continue the friendship had made him offer to act as tutor in architecture; less prudently, he had insisted that intellectual enfranchisement was imperative for Mrs Henniker's success as a writer. Retrospectively it is clear that, whatever the conscious aims promoting it, this friendship was based from the first to last on high mutual esteem and genuine sympathy.

Hardy had special reasons at this time for seeking compensations from society and a new friendship. His poems and letters, as well as the letters of Florence Hardy[40] (in whom he was to confide more than in anyone else), provide consistent and cogent evidence that his love for his first wife died some twenty years before her death at the end of 1912. Their severance or 'division' is alluded to in 'Alike and Unlike', a poem recalling the drive round Great Orme's Head while on their way to Dublin in May 1893. The MS. indicates that Hardy imagines his wife reflecting on the way in which visual impressions of the selfsame scene were transformed in the minds of two people with different outlooks:

> But our eye-records, like in hue and line,
> Had superimposed on them, that very day,
> Gravings on your side deep, but slight on mine!
> Tending to sever us thenceforth alway.

A fictitious allusion to the tragic change which came over his first marriage approximately twenty years after he fell in love with Emma Gifford and twenty years before her death may be seen in the poem 'The Voice of Things'. The friendship and appreciation of the attractive and *intuitive* Mrs Henniker was certainly unction to the soul of a 'time-torn' man. How much he told, how much she guessed, must be left to conjecture, but his use in the letters of the term 'one-sidedness' with reference to their relations is suggestive. He had discussed it with her; later, he says that it is 'disappearing from the situation'.

40. Especially those to Edward Clodd in the Brotherton Library, University of Leeds.

Possibly this 'one-sidedness' reflected a certain class inferiority, though Hardy's friendship with Lady Portsmouth,
Lady Carnarvon, Lady Jeune, and members of other aristocratic families makes this interpretation rather unconvincing.
It is true that there is a note of flattering inferiority in the
early letters: it is 'such a privilege' to write to Mrs Henniker;
she is his 'valued correspondent' and among 'the most valued'
of his friends, while he hopes to remain one of 'the rank and
file' of hers. It seems more likely that the 'one-sidedness' alludes to the embarrassment which he felt as a result of his
matrimonial difficulties. Mrs Hardy may well have been
jealous and critical, and he could never be certain how she
would receive Mrs Henniker in London. Two letters written
in June 1893 indicate that Hardy pursued a 'plan' or policy
of seeking to forget the 'situation' by turning to entertain-
ments and social distractions, making 'a serious business of
unserious things'. If the 'one-sidedness' were related to the
love which we must assume Hardy expressed for Mrs Henniker in certain poems, and which he there indicated could
never be returned, it seems improbable that he would have
discussed it so much with her, when his 'plan' was to forget
it, or that he would have been relieved to find it disappearing
'from the situation'.

We are told by a more modern poet than Hardy that 'the
more perfect the artist, the more completely separate in him
will be the man who suffers and the mind which creates; the
more perfectly will the mind digest and transmute the pas-
sions which are its material'.[41] There is nevertheless a strong
tendency among modern critics to read poetry as if it were
based wholly on actual experience, and to ignore or minimize
the possibility that the imagination can transmute for artistic
ends. Certainly if we wish to know how Hardy appeared to
Mrs Henniker, our best evidence is in his letters; if we wish
to find the direct expression of the man who suffered, we must
turn to the poetry, and make allowances for the transmuta-
tions of art. Socially, Hardy tended to be discreet and cautious;
except in his poetry, he was generally reserved in the expression of his personal feelings.

The inner life of a poet is not usually identical with the
outer, or apparently of the same quality. This is especially

41. T. S. Eliot, 'Tradition and the Individual Talent'.

B

true of Hardy, with 'his constitutional tendency to care for
life only as an emotion' for artistic ends.[42] None of his poems
conveys a sense of deeper gloom than the brief series 'In Tenebris', in the first of which (alluding probably to the death of his
love for his first wife: 'my bereavement-pain', 'that severing
scene') he echoes a Shakespearian thought to the effect that,
though wintertime approaches, it cannot be turned colder
by friends for him who has none. Hardy was never without
friends, and though the first of the 'In Tenebris' poems is
undated (the other two belong to the period 1895–6), it is
more than likely that it was composed at a time when he could
have written to his 'dear friend' Mrs Henniker, just as he did
at the end of 1896 when, in another bout of inspissated dejec-
tion, he was composing 'Wessex Heights', a poem in which he
expressed the view that he was but a passing thought to her,
and that, after having regarded her tenderly, he could now 'let
her go'.[43] Florence Hardy observed the dualism of the man and
the poet, and, commenting on this passage, wrote to Lady
Hoare in December 1914:

> *She* has always been a sincere and affectionate friend to
> him, staunch and unaltering – and, I am glad to say, she
> is my friend too. There was never any idea of his letting her
> go – for he, too, is true and faithful to his friends, but the
> *poet* wrote that.

Of the poems which have been associated with Mrs Henniker,[44] two – 'The Coming of the End' and 'Alike and Unlike'
– relate to the 'division' between Hardy and his wife Emma.
'The Division' was probably written in London, possibly in
the July or August of 1893 (see letters 11 and 12), and certainly with Emma in mind; the 'hundred miles' is approximately the distance between the centre of London and Max
Gate.[45] 'The Recalcitrants' could refer to Jude Fawley and
Sue Bridehead, but not to Mrs Henniker, as the letters clearly

42. *Life,* p. 87; see also ibid., pp. 53 and 104.
43. See the stanza with which this edition opens.
44. Purdy, pp. 345–6.
45. J. O. Bailey (op. cit., p. 212) suggests that this is the distance
between Max Gate and Southsea, where Mrs Henniker stayed. Southsea is certainly not more than sixty miles from Max Gate.

testify. In 'He Wonders about Himself' Hardy regards himself as a puppet, a plaything of Chance, just as he regarded
Jude. This seems to be the poem referred to in a note of 28
November 1893, 'He views himself as an automaton'; the
date and the incidental allusion in the second stanza may
suggest that he was thinking of Mrs Henniker, though the
poem requires no particular reference. 'Come not; yet Come!'
may be the song of a slightly earlier date,[46] occasioned by those
'beautiful large photographs' of herself which Mrs Henniker
sent to Max Gate, though, if so, it cannot be taken altogether
literally ('deign again/Shine upon this place'). 'At an Inn'
probably recalls their visit to Winchester, though of this we
cannot be certain.[47] There is nothing to indicate whether 'The
Month's Calendar' was written about Mrs Henniker or any
actual person; the dramatic unity of the poem suggests the
neatness of artistic invention, though the ending may have
originated in the realization that Mrs Henniker could not
return Hardy's affection. If so, it shows, like the seventh stanza
of 'Wessex Heights', the disproportioning of a transient or
poetic mood. 'In Death Divided'[48] (dated 189–) may be
accepted as occasioned by Mrs Henniker and Hardy's poor-
man-and-lady obsession. 'Last Love-Word' (also dated enig-
matically 189–) has the air of imaginative dramatization, and,
like 'The Month's Calendar', is inconsistent with the statement in 'Wessex Heights':

Yet my love for her in its fulness she herself even did not know.

By quoting the last two lines of this 'song' –

> *When that first look and touch,*
> *Love, doomed us two!*

– to conclude his valuable note on Mrs Henniker's friendship
with Hardy,[49] Professor R. L. Purdy may have unduly roman-
ticized their relationship. Two other poems were associated
with Mrs Henniker by Florence Hardy, presumably on

46. See the note for 7–10 Oct., *Life*, p. 260.
47. Hermann Lea, who almost certainly acquired his information
from Hardy, simply states that the poem was written at the George Inn,
Winchester (*Thomas Hardy's Wessex*, London, 1913).
48. Quoted fully on p. 203.
49. Purdy, p. 346.

Hardy's admission: 'A Thunderstorm in Town' conveys a momentary impulse or wishful fantasy, and 'A Broken Appointment,' bitter disappointment and perhaps excess of self-pity. In general, though the poems express moods and fancies, they show quite clearly that Hardy harboured feelings of deep affection for Mrs Henniker, which he soon realized could never be returned.

One affirmation in the poems has the ring of conviction. Mrs Henniker had never known how much he had loved her. She could not have perceived it, one suspects, when they met; nor is it apparent in his letters. The later ones denote a durable friendship; the earlier can hardly be described as those of a lover. Their endearing diminutives are almost paternal; her letters are 'little' or 'nice' (an epithet which pleased her, if we may judge from her use of it in her own letters of a much later period). She is his 'dear little friend'. Soon his shaping imagination conceives her in Shelleyan terms; she is 'almost a sister'; in the allusion to the couple who are spiritually united (as far as the man is concerned, he adds) we catch a hint of Mrs Henniker's image in Hardy's eyes when he was convinced by 'mutual influence' they were reading Shelley's 'Epipsychidion' simultaneously. Her outward form is less prized than her nature, which has that 'ethereal intangible' quality he rightly associated with Shelley's heroine and was to include in Jude's 'tender thought' of Sue, 'the sweetest and most disinterested comrade that he had ever had, living largely in vivid imaginings'.[50] Possibly in these words, written in 1894, the feelings of Hardy towards Mrs Henniker are more truly disclosed than in the poems already discussed.

Closer scrutiny of *Jude the Obscure* confirms the view that Hardy's early friendship with Mrs Henniker contributed to the development of the doom-burdened relationship between Jude and his cousin Sue Bridehead. Initially, as the 1895 preface and his *Life* show, Hardy had had his cousin Tryphena Sparks in mind for 'some of the circumstances' in the life of his heroine. To what extent he intended to involve her in his story must remain conjectural, but it is quite clear that after meeting Mrs Henniker Hardy modified his plans. The cousinship remained a critical factor, but the only other features that can be convincingly traced to recollections of Tryphena are

50. *Jude the Obscure*, III ix; cf. 'Epipsychidion', ll. 75–9.

external. Sue's 'vivacious dark eyes', her dark hair, and her 'apprenticeship' as a pupil-teacher under Phillotson at Lumsdon are based on Hardy's memories of Tryphena at Puddletown from 1867 to 1869. Jude's situation and feelings, however, are directly related to Hardy's own unhappy marriage and his new friendship; undoubtedly the thought that 'the one affined soul he had ever met was lost to him' through marriage smote him 'with cruel persistency' in the second half of 1893 when he was making his final preparations for *Jude the Obscure*. 'She was nearer to him than any other woman he had ever met, and he could scarcely believe that time, creed, or absence, would ever divide him from her.'[51] The first thought and its expression cannot be dissociated from the 'motto' Hardy wrote for the title-page of *The Woodlanders* in the summer of 1895; the inclusion of 'creed' in the second quotation is obviously based on Hardy and Mrs Henniker's correspondence of July 1893.

Reference has been made to the Shelleyan idealism with which Hardy invested Mrs Henniker, and which he subsequently transferred to Jude's impressions of Sue. It is characteristic of Hardy that he presented the religious parallelism in reverse: it is Sue whose intellect scintillates like a star and whose views on the First Cause are identical with Hardy's, and it is Jude who considers her 'Voltairean', as the Anglican Mrs Henniker must have regarded Hardy when he tried to modernize her beliefs.[52] Her resistance to his criticism and scientific outlook undoubtedly influenced Hardy when he decided that Sue, after affliction had made 'opposing forces loom anthropomorphous', should turn to ritualistic worship in 'the Church of Ceremonies'. 'It is no use fighting against God!', she said. When Jude protested that it was 'only against man and senseless circumstance', she agreed and admitted that she was becoming 'superstitious'. Her refusal to change made Jude vehement; his outburst, 'You make me hate Christianity, or mysticism, or Sacerdotalism, or whatever it may be called, if it's that which has caused this deterioration in you',[53] is not far removed from Hardy's regret that Mrs Henniker had 'allowed herself to be enfeebled to a belief in

51. *Jude the Obscure*, II vii and III iv. See also note 136, p. 44.
52. ibid., VI iii, III iv.
53. ibid., VI iii.

ritualistic ecclesiasticism' or 'retrograde superstitions'. He
would trust, he wrote, 'to imagination only for an enfranchised
woman', and it was in Sue Bridehead, before her catastrophe
and breakdown, that he portrayed her. Sue is a composite
creation, largely imaginary, and perhaps not wholly convincing: it was Mrs Henniker, more than any other person, who
contributed to her character, and Hardy's rather surreptitious
inclusion of 'Florence' among Sue's Christian names is significant.[54]

Hardy 'sighed' over Mrs Henniker's conventional views,
and was quite certain they would hamper her progress as a
novelist despite her 'sympathetic and intuitive knowledge of
human nature'. A novelist, he affirmed, had to be twenty-five
years ahead of his reader intellectually to command attention.
Yet, though she read J. S. Mill and agreed with him on some
things – to Hardy's astonishment – she remained immune to
the influence of new scientific or Positivist thinking. As a
result of expressing her views more decidedly than she had
done in the early stages of their friendship, she appeared to be
more intransigent as time passed. Hardy noted this in 1896;
she seemed to have changed a great deal from what she was
when she accompanied him to see 'Ibscene' drama in 1893.
Even as late as 1911, he laments that they have drifted 'so far
apart'. Yet their friendship did not suffer; in 1904 she was the
same to him personally, he says, as she was when he met her in
Ireland; ten years later, he addresses her as his 'best friend'.
Their interest in each other's work did not diminish.

All her life Mrs Henniker had many friends among the
upper classes; through her brother, Lord Crewe, she came to
know many leading politicians; through her husband, many
persons of high rank in the Army. She enjoyed company, particularly when she was with her husband – a practical, thorough,
just, and genial soldier, and a versatile and highly accomplished sportsman, who won friendship and admiration
wherever he went. The social world could not have been
completely satisfying to her for long, however. She loved the
country and travel; and she was devoted to literature and
humane causes. The latter were interests she could share very
largely with Hardy, but there were, one suspects, deeper
affinities with his genius and character. Her writings indicate

54. ibid., IV ii.

not only responsiveness to the sunshine and humour of life
but also, to an even greater extent, an underlying awareness
of the sad and tragic vicissitudes which enmesh mankind.

It is not surprising therefore that Emma Hardy did not care
for her, or that only two of the innumerable letters Mrs Henniker wrote to Hardy from 1893 to the end of 1912 have sur-
vived. Florence Hardy expressed astonishment at the first Mrs
Hardy's dislike of two such 'warm-hearted, generous kind
women' as Mrs Henniker and Lady Jeune.[55] She herself had no
cause for jealousy; yet it is perhaps significant that she was less
sympathetic to Sue Bridehead than to Arabella Donn.[56] In his
1912 preface to *Jude the Obscure* Hardy admitted that 'there
can be more in a book than the author consciously puts there'.
Jude's final attempt to break away from Arabella and his
rejection by Sue, now a slave to convention, may have derived
much of its dramatic appeal from yearnings and inhibitions
which Hardy could not escape in times of extreme provocation. Consciously or otherwise, Mrs Henniker may have transferred the situation to 'A Statesman's Love-Lapse', one of the
novelettes on which she was working in the summer and
autumn of 1893. With Hardy charity and the philosophy of
endurance prevailed: 'Nothing can be done. Things are as
they are, and will be brought to their destined issue,' said
Jude. At critical times, Mrs Henniker's sympathetic under-
standing, or his confidence in her, may have helped to sustain
Hardy more than anything else: 'I can say that if we are not to
be the *thorough* friends that we have been, life will have lost a
very great attraction for one who is above all things/Ever sincerely yours', he wrote in October 1893. A friendship rendered more difficult on one side by the very circumstances
which promoted it, and undoubtedly subject in its early
phases to strains and doubts on the other, required an unusual
degree of reciprocal sympathy to survive. Its preservation for
nearly thirty years until broken by death is sufficient warrant
for its continuing 'thoroughness' or integrity. Possibly it was
strengthened by early stresses. The lasting loyalty of Hardy
and Mrs Henniker each to the other argues an unusual affinity,
steady affection, high personal regard, keenly shared interests,
and – perhaps the most critical factor of all in the long run –

55. Letter to Rebekah Owen, Colby College Library.
56. Letter to Lady Hoare, 13 March 1916.

susceptibility to, and respect for, differences of outlook. Their full story can never be known; much evidence remains, however, particularly in Hardy's letters, pointing to one of the most fascinating friendships in literary history.

F. B. P.

NOTE ON THE TEXT

The transcriptions of Thomas Hardy's letters to Florence Henniker follow the originals with the following exceptions. The dates have all been placed on the right-hand side of the page, although this was not Hardy's invariable custom, and titles of his works have been presented with a consistency which he wrote too hurriedly to observe. Hardy's numerous abbreviations have been indicated by brackets; ampersands have been discarded; but his punctuation, which is casual and unrevised, and his rare lapses in spelling, have been left unchanged.

LETTERS

1. 70, Hamilton Terrace,[1]
N.W.
June 3, 1893

My dear Mrs Henniker:

I am glad to get your note, as I was beginning to wonder if you would soon be here, and I much desire to go somewhere with you. I will see about Ibsen[2] immediately, and let you know. I don't think the series is finished yet.

I have already obtained the books, and should have sent them on to you, but that I want to ask you something first. I will accordingly keep them till we meet.

I have nothing to do next week from Monday till Thursday that is of any consequence. But I have a dreadful confession to make. In a weak moment I have accepted an invitation to lunch, to meet

John Oliver Hobbes![3]

She is very pretty, they say, but on my honour that had nothing to do with it – purely literary reasons only.

My little scrap of a play has taken up so much of my time this week – more than it is worth. It is to be produced to-night with 4 others – and I prophesy a *fiasco* for such a heterogeneous

1. It had become Hardy's custom to spend a few months each year in London, and he kept up the habit until late in life. In the spring of 1893 the Hardys rented a London house for the first time, and staffed it with their Dorchester servants. They returned from their visit to Ireland on Monday, 29 May 1893. No time was lost, it will be noticed, before the correspondence between Mrs Henniker and Hardy began.

2. Together with Mrs Henniker and her sister and brother-in-law, Lady and Sir Gerald FitzGerald, Hardy saw *The Master Builder* the following week. In the early part of June he saw *Hedda Gabler* and *Rosmersholm,* the former for the second time. He had seen it in 1891 with his friend Edmund Gosse, who had translated the play and was the first writer to introduce Ibsen to the British public. Hardy, who was one of the earliest members of an association for promoting the production of Ibsen's plays (Rutland, *Thomas Hardy,* p. 252), was obviously quite out of sympathy with the 'blinkered insular taste' which branded them as 'Ibscene'. He saw more of them in 1897 (*Life,* pp. 234, 256, 292).

3. The pseudonym of the novelist Mrs Pearl Craigie (1867–1906). Hardy with reference to the meeting (on 8 June) describes her as 'that brilliant woman' (*Life,* p. 256). She was a friend of Emma Hardy.

collection.⁴ If there should be any kind of success in the performance I will ask you to see it. I have wished so much that you had been in town these last few days so that you might have accompanied me to a rehearsal and given me your opinion.

Many thanks for the book and the letter, which fortunately you had posted.

> Believe me,
> Ever yours sincerely
> Thomas Hardy

2.   Athenaeum Club⁵
                                                    S.W.
                                  Wednesday [June 7th 1893]

My dear Mrs Henniker:

It was very absent-minded of me not to hand over the photograph. Perhaps it will be as well to leave it now till you are again in London.

I went on Monday afternoon to an architectural bookseller's and found the handbook that will suit you. I can post it on, or keep it to make use of in the lesson which I shall have great pleasure in giving. Westminster Abbey, St. Saviour's Southwark, and St. Bartholomew's Smithfield,⁶ contain excellent

4. In April J. M. Barrie had suggested that Hardy should dramatize his short story 'The Three Strangers'. The dramatization was called 'The Three Wayfarers', and produced at Terry's Theatre by Charles Charrington, who played the part of the hangman, on Saturday, 3 June, in a bill which included Barrie's 'Becky Sharp' (a scene from Thackeray), 'Foreign Policy' by Conan Doyle, 'Bud and Blossom' by Lady Colin Campbell, and 'An Interlude' by Mrs W. K. Clifford and W. H. Pollock. *The Times* voted Hardy's 'the best piece of the evening' (Purdy, p. 79), and Lady Jeune (who accompanied the Hardys) and Barrie were delighted over this success.

5. Lord Carnarvon, who died in 1890, had proposed Hardy for membership of this club.

6. For eleven years, from 1856 to 1867, Hardy had been trained as an architect, in Dorchester, then under Arthur Blomfield in London. He was to visit the second of these churches two years later with his former employer, now Sir Arthur Blomfield, to see how the work of restoration was proceeding (*Life*, p. 268). Much of Hardy's work, then and later, had been concerned with church repairs and restoration, and he was particularly interested in Gothic architecture. Whether Mrs

features for study. I want you to be able to walk into a church and pronounce upon its date at a glance: and you are apt scholar enough to soon arrive at that degree of knowledge. Oral instructions in actual buildings is, of course, a much more rapid and effectual method than from books, and you must not think it will be any trouble to me.

Mr Daly has promised to send us tickets for the opening night of his theatre – the 27th of this month – when Ada Rehan[7] will play the Shrew, her finest character. It will be an interesting occasion, and perhaps you will be present? As I go by invitation (if he does not forget) I cannot write for more tickets.

If I can be of any use to you on your arrival please command me by saying when and where.

Reaching home Monday at tea-time who should be sitting in the drawing room but the author of *The Heavenly Twins.*[8]

Always yours sincerely
Thomas Hardy.

3.   Athenaeum Club,
                                            Pall Mall, S.W.
                             Saturday [June 10th 1893]

My dear Mrs Henniker:
Herewith the book, which I should have sent yesterday on receipt of your note if there had been time. Will you please

Henniker was an apt pupil or whether the description is Hardy's, eight lines on architectural features of St Bartholomew's, Smithfield, where the protagonists are married, appear in 'The Spectre of the Real', the tale in which Hardy collaborated with Mrs Henniker. It will be seen that she was interested in other buildings in this area (pp. 205–6).

7. Augustin Daly was manager and proprietor of Daly's Theatres in New York and London. He opened the latter in 1893, after bringing several companies over to London from 1884 to 1891. His greatest actress was Ada Rehan; Hardy saw her in *The Taming of the Shrew* in 1888 and, two years later, in *As You Like It* (*Life*, pp. 211, 228). For the 'Lines' written by Hardy and spoken by Miss Rehan at the Lyceum Theatre on 23 July 1890, on behalf of Lady Jeune's holiday fund for poor London children, see *Wessex Poems*.

8. Mrs David C. M'Fall (1862–1943) wrote under the pseudonym of Sarah Grand. She was Mayoress of Bath in 1923 and from 1925 to 1929. *The Heavenly Twins* (1893) did more perhaps to establish her reputation as a novelist than any other work.

first impress on your mind the elementary facts of date given at pp. 19–20 — (if you are not already familiar with them) and after doing this you can go on to the characteristics of each style. I am sure you will not be a slow scholar: the danger with you lies rather the other way – if I may be allowed to be so critical. Indeed I fancy you write your MSS. a little too rapidly: though *Sir George*,[9] which I have just finished, is a far more promising book than I guessed it was going to be when I began it: and I should like ten minutes conversation with you concerning it when you come to London.

I may possibly run out of town for a day or two Monday or Tuesday next week, or merely for the day – but this is uncertain.

I think *Merely Mary Ann*[10] very good up to the point at which she comes into the dollars. After that I don't care for it.

I wonder if you like my little story in *Scribner*.[11] I see in to-day's papers that a lady-critic[12] is going to drag me over the coals in next month's *Century* for the way in which I spoilt *Tess*. She is an unmarried lady, and I shall be much interested to see how she handles the subject.

The evening of yesterday I spent in what I fear you will call a frivolous manner – indeed, during the time, my mind reverted to our Ibsen experience; and I could not help being regretfully struck by the contrast – although I honestly was amused. Barrie had arranged to take us and Maarten Martens[13] (*sic*) to see B's play of *Walker, London*,[14] and lunching yesterday with the Milmans[15] at the Tower we asked Miss Mil-

9. This was the first of Mrs Henniker's published novels (1891). Gladstone, her father's friend, noted 'real power' in it, and thought the principal character 'a very remarkable delineation'. The assiduity with which Hardy prosecutes his role, first as architectural, then as literary, preceptor, is noticeable.

10. A novel by Israel Zangwill (1864–1926), published in 1893.

11. 'The Fiddler of the Reels', *Scribner's Magazine*, May 1893.

12. Harriet W. Preston. The review appeared, as expected, in *The Century Magazine* (New York), July 1893. It could not have been too displeasing, for Hardy later enjoyed accompanying her on Egdon Heath (Weber, *Hardy and the Lady from Madison Square*, p. 234).

13. Maarten Maartens (1858–1915), born in Amsterdam, was an English novelist and a friend of Edmund Gosse.

14. Barrie's play *Walker, London* was first performed at Toole's Theatre on 25 February 1892. Its original title was *The Houseboat*.

15. On his retirement from the Forces, Lieutenant-General Milman

man to be of the party. Mr Toole[16] heard we had come, and
invited us behind the scenes. We accordingly went, and sat
with him in his dressing-room, where he entertained us with
hock and champagne, he meanwhile in his paint, wig, and
blazer, as he had come off the stage, amusing us with the
drollest of stories about a visit he and a friend paid to the Tower
some years ago: how he amazed the custodian by entreating the
loan of the crown jewels for an amateur dramatic performance
for a charitable purpose, offering to deposit 30/- as a guarantee that he would return them – etc., etc., etc. We were rather
late home, as you may suppose.[17]

Several lords spiritual are near me as I write this letter,
which I would rather be penning than one of their sermons.
I have, by the way, had a sermon sent me about *Tess*, of which
I will if possible get a copy for you. Forgive this disjointed
epistle from

Ever yours sincerely

Thomas Hardy.

P.S. I am afraid my chronicle is mere 'frivol',[18] or a great part
of it: but having made a serious business of un-serious things
I must follow on for the present, to redress by any possible
means the one-sidedness I spoke of, of which I am still keenly
conscious.

I sincerely hope to number you all my life among the most
valued of my friends.

I rush back to Hamilton T[erra]ce where Miss Milman
comes to tea – this afternoon – Miss Preston's (the old maid's)
article is out in the *Century*.

---

had been appointed Major H.M. Tower of London. His daughter
Lena was an accomplished linguist, who later translated some of
Dostoevsky's work.

16. J. L. Toole made his reputation as an actor in comic parts. He
was manager of Toole's Theatre and a friend of Henry Irving, who in
1895 was the first actor to receive a knighthood.

17. The paragraph is included in Hardy's *Life*, pp. 256–7. His letters
were returned after Mrs Henniker's death, and, like many others,
were used in the autobiography which he prepared and checked for
posthumous publication.

18. The word was in vogue at this time. The *Oxford English Dictionary* gives a quotation from *The Saturday Review* almost a year later
on the transition from 'the novel simply frivol to the novel frivol-
philosophic'. See later, p. 100.

4.   Athenaeum Club,
                                     S.W.
                          Tuesday [June 20th, 1893]

I send you, dear Mrs Henniker, the sermon I promised
about *Tess*; but don't read it if you are already burdened
with my sendings. You will, of course, understand, that I don't
endorse all he says.

We are not, so far as I know, on the Marlborough House[19]
list. Not orthodox enough perhaps. Do you remember
Thackeray's satire? 'Literary men are greatly encouraged at
the Court of England. So many as two have been invited to
meet their sovereigns since the reign of Queen Anne', or words
to that effect.

I went to Oxford yesterday[20] – and may be there for an hour
or two to-morrow morning – but I return in the afternoon, and
shall be here every day after lunch. I have nothing to do from
to-morrow, Wedn[esda]y either morning or evening, till the
middle of next week, and if I can be of use in showing you
concrete examples at Westminster of what you have by this
time read in the handbook, I shall be delighted. Saturday
morning, $\frac{1}{4}$ past 10, Sloane Square Station, shall we say? –
if no earlier day.

The lady you met is the wife of my wife's cousin Charley.[21]

19. Marlborough House (set back from the Mall) was designed by
Wren for the great Duke of Marlborough. It was sold to the Crown,
and for many years was the home of Prince Albert Edward (later
Edward VII) and Princess Alexandra. The marriage of their second
son, the Duke of York (later George V), and Princess Mary (May) took
place in the summer of 1893.

20. Hardy was making observations for the Christminster scenes in
Jude the Obscure. The Commemoration proceedings which he viewed
helped him to write chapter VI i of the novel. The visit to Oxford, he
tells us, took place ten days after the visit to the Tower described in
the previous letter. See *Life*, p. 257.

21. See p. 200. Mrs Henniker had been staying with her husband
at Southsea. For three years, from January 1891 to January 1894,
Captain Henniker was on the headquarters staff of the D.A.A.G.
(Southern District) at Portsmouth. From the summer of 1892 to the
summer of 1893, at least, their home was Letcombe, Southsea. Gerald
FitzGerald remembers staying there with his aunt, and thinks that the
house overlooked the Common and the sea.

– who is not the son of Dr Gifford[22] who married Miss Jeune,
but of another uncle of my wife's. Lady Jeune has a dinner on
the 9th July – I wonder if you are to be there. I have accepted
also an invitation to Lady Shrewsbury's dinner on the 29th
[of June] but I can throw her over if necessary. The R[oyal]
Academy crush is on the 27th. Rather amusing: and you
could easily get tickets if they have not been sent, as they
probably have.

Well – perhaps you are right about the story of the two
people spiritually united – as far as the man is concerned.

By the way, if you go to the Ball[23] Friday, you can hardly be
ready Sat. morning so early. Say later if 10.15 is too soon. Don't
fag yourself out at that dancing. Promise you won't.

Sincerely yours
T.H.

5.   Athenaeum Club,
                                                  S.W.
                              Thursday [29th June, 1893]

My dear Mrs Henniker:

It is such a privilege to write to you that I avail myself of
it at the earliest opportunity.

Yesterday was very dreary – the most dreary and melancholy day I have known in London for a long time – the rain
having come at last – though only fitfully. I sat down in the
morning and tried to write a letter – then gave it up; and read

22. Hardy was related indirectly by marriage to Lady Jeune. He and
Emma Gifford had been married at Paddington by Emma's uncle, Dr
E. Hamilton Gifford, Archdeacon of London, whose wife was the
daughter of the Bishop of Peterborough and sister of Lady Jeune's
second husband, Francis. In 1891 Francis Jeune became a Divorce
Court judge; in 1892 he was knighted; later he became Baron St Helier.
Hardy often stayed at the Jeunes', in Harley Street, London, or
Arlington Manor near Newbury. In her *Memories of Fifty Years* (1909)
Lady St Helier described him as 'a delightful companion' and the
most modest man she ever met. She and her children remained his
most affectionate friends, the latter writing to him as 'Uncle Tom'.

23. Possibly at Devonshire House, where the Duke of York and
Princess Mary (May) were the chief guests at dinner on Friday, 23
June.

your novel *Foiled*.[24] It is really a clever book – quite above what I had been led to expect from the reviews. I don't like some of the men in it – though they are truly drawn: and speaking generally I may say that as a transcript from human nature it ranks far above some novels that have received much more praise: e.g. *The Heavenly Twins*. If ever I were to consult any woman on a point in my own novels I should let that woman be yourself – my belief in your insight and your sympathies being strong, and increasing.

I said I would chronicle my doings: and I must therefore in honesty tell you that I *have* entered on my scheme – the plan I spoke of[25] – little pleasure as it has given me, as you will well imagine. Whether I can keep it up is another matter, though I have lunched to-day with a lot of people, dine at Lady Shrewsbury's to-night and lunch to-morrow at the Jeunes to meet a party including Miss Ada Rehan – whom I really do wish to meet – She is a genius, as you would have said if you had been present Tuesday night. Her reception was tremendous. It is so provoking that you are not here; as Lady J[eune], who was at the theatre, asked if you could also come to meet Miss R[ehan].

After the theatre we went on to the Academy crush – where, of course, we met a great many vain people we knew – One amusing thing occurred to me.

A well known woman in society, who is one of those despicable creatures a flirt, said to me when I was talking to her: 'Don't look at me so!' I said, 'Why? – because you feel I can see *too much of you*? (She was excessively *décolletée*). 'Good heavens!' said she, 'I am not coming to pieces, am I?' and clutching her bodice she was quite overcome. When next I met her she said bitterly: 'You have spoilt my evening: and it was too cruel of you!' However I don't think it was, for she deserved it. She was not H. B. by the way, though one of that sort, and an acquaintance of hers. Saturday night is the date of the Lord Mayor's dinner to literature. I accepted in an

24. Mrs Henniker's third novel, published in 1893 and dedicated to Bret Harte. *The Speaker* drew attention to its 'unforced pathos and bright little touches of satire', and H. D. Traill in *The New Review* noted 'a rare faculty of observation and an extensive knowledge of the world'.

25. This may be related to Hardy's 'one-sidedness' (p. 5). See p. 11.

inconsiderate moment; it is usually a lively, dyspeptic entertainment: and I hear it will be very crowded.

I wish so much you could see Miss Rehan as the Shrew, if
you have not already. Could you fix any evening next week,
for certain? I could get stalls if you will go – my reason for
wishing you to see the play being purely an artistic one.

Yours very sincerely
T.H.

6. Athenaeum Club,
Pall Mall.

30.6.93

My dear Mrs Henniker:

I have posted to you to-day the Summer number of the
Illustrated – in case you might like to see the story:[26] but
don't read it carefully, as it is of the slightest.

Mrs Moulton[27] is a friend of mine, and she has pressed me
to go to see her Tuesday afternoon. As you will (I presume)
have to get to her by underground from Sloane Sq[uare][28] to
Portland Road, I may be of service in conducting you. If so,
please don't mind telling me, as it will be no trouble.

I suggest your seeing Miss Rehan without reflecting that it
might be difficult or awkward, if your time is short. There is
a great rush for places, but Mr Daly has just written to me to
say I can have seats for any night. I cannot go Wedn[esda]y.

The idea of writing the true names of the places in your
Tess[29] is a very pleasing one. I have never yet done it for anybody, but you may not think it any objection in the future
that you will possess the only copy thus marked.

26. 'Master John Horseleigh, Knight' (later included in *A Changed
Man*) first appeared in *The Illustrated London News*, 12 June 1893.
27. Louise Chandler Moulton, an American writer and reviewer, was
a frequent visitor to London, where she met Hardy in 1889. She sent
him copies of her poems in 1900 and earlier.
28. Mrs Henniker would be staying with her sister, Lady FitzGerald,
in Cadogan Gardens, near Sloane Square. See p. 6.
29. *Tess of the d'Urbervilles* was published in volume form in
November 1891. Hardy had made a few entries of this kind in a copy
of *The Mayor of Casterbridge* belonging to an American admirer,
Rebekah Owen (Weber, *Hardy and the Lady from Madison Square*,
pp. 58, 237).

I may possibly make the party too large at Hertford House?

Yes – I dined with Lady Shrewsbury last night. My partner at the table was Lady Gwendolen Little, Lady S's daughter – by far the brightest woman present, as I found afterwards, on sounding them all round. The lady the other side of me was Lady Julie (?) Wombwell – to whom I did not say 3 words the whole dinner time – although I meant to.

It is very pleasant to think you are coming to London again so soon. I am happy to say my engagements are getting less. We are asked to a big party at Lady Ardilaun's Monday night the 3rd; but may possibly not go. I dine out Wed[nesda]y night – and lunch with Mr Pinero[30] Friday the 7th. It is so warm here to-day that my hand is almost too hot to hold the pen.

Yours sincerely
T.H.

7.
Athenaeum Club,
Pall Mall, S.W.
Sunday [July 2nd 1893]

My dear Mrs Henniker:

I have received your card, and shall be much pleased to conduct you through the pestilential vapours of the Underground to Mrs Moulton's; your sister may be sure you will be in safe hands. To-day I lunched with Douglas[31] at the Conservative Club. Both he and I, although we each have two

30. Arthur Wing Pinero (1855–1934) began his career as a playwright with a series of comedies. He came to the fore in 1893 with *The Second Mrs. Tanqueray*, the first of a number of realistic tragedies. It was in this play that the actress Mrs Patrick Campbell first won great acclaim.

31. Sir George Brisbane Douglas, who became fifth Baronet in succession to his father in 1885, lived at Springwood, Kelso, and had been a devoted friend of Hardy since their first meeting in 1881 at Wimborne, where George Douglas was visiting his brother, who was studying land-agency there. Hardy consulted George on Farfrae's Scottish tongue in *The Mayor of Casterbridge*. For his impressions of the Hardys on their visit to Scotland in 1891 (*Life*, p. 239), see G. B. Douglas, 'Thomas Hardy: Personal Reminiscences', *The Hibbert Journal*, April 1928. Hardy's letters to Douglas are preserved in the National Library of Scotland; an article on them by W. M. Parker is to be found in *English*, XIV, Autumn 1963.

clubs on the line of the wedding procession,[32] have drawn
blanks for ladies' places (which were balloted for). Thus we
have two places each for ourselves though we can only use
one, and don't want either: and not one for a lady. All the
clubs are very selfish this time – the incursion of women on
the occasion of the last procession having irritated crusty
members – D[ouglas] and I, if we look at the show at all,
are going to stand in the street, and walk through the crowd,
which is by far the most interesting feature. There is an
illumination in the evening, which must be viewed on foot
I believe, as I hear that all vehicular traffic will be suspended.

What beautiful translations those are! I like the two verses
from the Spanish best.[33] You are a real woman of letters:
and must be invited to the next Mansion House dinner to
literature. It was lively there last night: but many ladies
did not come, I am told, because their husbands were not
invited. So much for their independence.

Duse[34] and Miss Rehan you must certainly see. There is
an absurd paragraph in last night's *Globe* about my being
interested in Miss Rehan's performance, and intending to
write nothing but plays in future, etc., an entire invention of
some kind friend.

I adhere desperately to my plan, with poor results; but
time may help it. I am glad to hear you enjoy the air, and
take walks and drives. I sleep hardly at all, and seem not to
require any.

If you knew the name of the German paper we might find
it (I mean the paragraph about you). When you have any
definite information about your writing and publishing send
it to me: I am continually asked for paragraphs.

Miss Milman is going with my wife to a party at Alma

32. The marriage of the Duke of York and Princess Mary took
place on 6 July 1893.
33. Mrs Henniker also translated verses from the French and Italian.
34. Eleonora Duse (1859–1924), an Italian actress, was at the peak of
her fame at this period. Hardy attended performances by her and Ada
Rehan (*Life,* p. 257), but whether with Mrs Henniker or not is unknown. Eleonora Duse was one of the many actresses, including Mrs
Patrick Campbell, Ellen Terry, and Sarah Bernhardt, who asked Hardy
for the part of Tess in a stage version of *Tess of the d'Urbervilles* (*Life,*
p. 265).

Tadema's[35] Tuesday night: but I don't think of joining them.
Believe me

Sincerely yours
Thomas Hardy.

8.   Max Gate,
                                            Dorchester.
                                         July 13, 1893

My dear Mrs Henniker:

I have just packed up, and will send off to-morrow, the
promised books. The edition is a poor and tasteless one; but
I hope some day to send you the novels[36] uniformly printed
and in better style.

Lady Jeune will be much disappointed if you do not go to
her dinner. It is indeed a pity, as you would meet some
interesting people. She has asked me to think of some guests
for her, and I have thought of Lena Milman – whom I fancy
she knows: you will say I have not thought far. You could,
of course, go at the last moment if you chose, even if I had
asked L.M. in your place.

I am due in Harley St.[37] either on the 19th or 20th as I
choose: and go out with her (M[ary] Jeune) to the dinner to
P[rin]cess M[ay] on the 20th. She (M.J.) has one at her own
house on the 21st: and we go all together to Irving's farewell
performance[38] on the 22nd (Sat). I must stay on in town somewhere till the 26th, for I have promised Sir H[enry] Thomp-

---

35. Lawrence Alma-Tadema, painter (1836–1912), was born in
Friesland. He settled in England in 1873. Edmund Gosse became his
brother-in-law in 1875. Hardy, as his *Life* shows, had met and visited
Tadema several times before 1893. In 1896 Tadema suggested that the
play of Tess be translated into Italian or French for Eleonora Duse.

36. His own.

37. 79 Harley Street, the home of the Jeunes. See letter 11.

38. The famous English actor Henry Irving (1838–1905) had been
associated with the Lyceum Theatre and Ellen Terry for many years.
He was about to leave for his fourth tour of the States. Hardy
returned to London for this performance, and mentions visiting City churches
(*Life*, p. 257); he may have been accompanied by Mrs Henniker.

son[39] to dine with him (men only) on that day, to meet L[or]d
C[harles] Beresford and Mr Chamberlain.[40] A pretty waste
of time, for I have nowhere to go during either day before
dinner, and shall be sure to fritter the minutes away. I would
give Ada Rehan, Miss Milman, Lady G[wendolen] Little, her
sister, Mrs S[tuart] Wortley, or any other of that ilk, lessons
in architecture at astonishingly low fees to fill up the time.

I am so glad you met Julia Peel[41] and had a nice time in the
House of Commons. I like her much. The first night of my
arrival here I slept more soundly than I had done for weeks.
I am also glad I called on you. Afterwards I went on to the
Athenaeum, found what I wanted, and hastened to catch the
train, reaching here about 7.

You seem quite like an old friend to me, and I only hope
that Time will bear out the seeming. Indeed, but for an
adverse stroke of fate, you would be – a friend of 13 years
standing. *A Laodicean* by the way, one of the books I send, was
the novel written during the long illness which prevented my
going to Fryston. I had only got a little way on when Lord
Houghton's letter came, and I, almost simultaneously, went
to bed for 5 months.[42]

I am afraid I am lapsing into a morbid mood; and my
whole letter is very inadequate to the occasion, and to what
should be written to such a valued correspondent.

Believe me, my dear Mrs Henniker,

Yours sincerely

T.H.

39. Sir Henry Thompson (1820–1904) was a distinguished surgeon, a
keen astronomer, and an amateur painter whose work was exhibited at
the Royal Academy. Hardy probably met him first in May 1881, when,
after the protracted illness during which he dictated the greater part
of *A Laodicean*, he and Mrs Hardy called on him for a consultation
by appointment (*Life*, p. 148).

40. Beresford was Lord of the Admiralty from 1886 to 1888, and
later created Admiral and Baron. Hardy had been impressed by
Joseph Chamberlain, the statesman, when he opposed Gladstone's
Bill for Home Rule in Ireland (*Life*, pp. 177–8).

41. This is probably the daughter of the Prime Minister who was
responsible for the repeal of the Corn Laws. Julia Peel died in August
1893.

42. See p. xxix.

9.   Max Gate,
                                            Dorchester.
                                 Sunday, July 16. 1893

It is so good of you, my dear Mrs Henniker, to send the book
of ballads, that I must thank you at once. Also for the promised
copy of Lord Houghton's poems,[43] which I really covet as a
gift from you. It lends such a continuity to one's life.

The notes I put to *Tess* cost me no trouble; and with a map
of Dorset you might now trace her journeyings exactly, if you
cared to.

As to my beginning to write again Heaven only knows when
I shall do it. – I feel much more inclined to fly off to foreign
scenes or plunge into wild dissipation. Next week in London
may bring some change of mood. And though at Lady
J[eune]'s dinner I may be able to fill your place at table with
some new female acquaintance she will certainly not remove
my disappointment at your absence.

I will religiously obey orders about the architectural lessons.
You shall hold the copyright in them. Is not that promise very
handsome of me?

I too have been reading 'Epipsychidion' – indeed by mutual
influence we must have been reading it simultaneously.[44] I had
a regret in reading it at thinking that one who is pre-eminently
the child of the Shelleyean tradition – whom one would have
expected to be an ardent disciple of his school and views –

43. The receipt of these poems by Mrs Henniker's father, the first
Lord Houghton, is acknowledged in letter 17.
44. Shelley was Hardy's favourite poet, the one whom above all
others he wished he could meet. For an idea of the influence of Shelley
on his works and thought, see Phyllis Bartlett, 'Seraph of Heaven',
PMLA, LXX, 1955 and 'Hardy's Shelley', *The Keats–Shelley Journal*,
1955; and Pinion, *A Hardy Companion*, pp. 213–14. Hardy was steeped
not merely in the best known of Shelley's poems; his knowledge of
The Revolt of Islam, for example, was exceptional. There are frequent
references to 'Epipsychidion' in his novels, from his first (represented
by 'An Indiscretion in the Life of an Heiress') to the last, *Jude the
Obscure*, which he was now preparing. In this novel (III ix) Sue Bridehead appears to Jude as did Shelley's heroine to him – ethereal, her
spirit trembling through her limbs; Jude acknowledges that lines
from the poem describe Sue (IV v). It will be seen that Hardy tended
to idealize Mrs Henniker in the same way (p. 39).

should have allowed herself to be enfeebled to a belief in ritualistic ecclesiasticism.[45] My impression is that you do not know your own views. You feel the need of emotional expression of some sort, and being surrounded by the conventional society form of such expression you have mechanically adopted it. Is this the daughter of the man who went from Cambridge to Oxford on the now historic errand?[46] Depend upon it there are other valves for feeling than the ordinances of Mother Church – my Mother Church no less than yours.

I am writing too much as the mentor, and you may ask me for my licence. Well; forgive me, and I will follow Tennyson's advice in future, ('Leave thou thy sister ...'[47]) and trust to imagination only for an enfranchised woman.[48] I thought I had found one some years ago – (I told you of her) – and it is somewhat singular that she contributes some of the best pieces to the volume of ballades[49] (sic) you send. Her desire, however, was to use your correspondent as a means of gratifying her vanity by exhibiting him as her admirer, the discovery

45. These are strong words from Mrs Henniker's 'mentor'. The sequel suggests that, though willing to accept guidance in architecture and the writing of fiction, Mrs Henniker exercised her own judgement and was not prepared to be a free-thinker. It is clear that she opposed Hardy's views more strongly as time went on. Her religious predilections obviously affected the course of *Jude the Obscure*: the shock of events makes Sue, whose intellect made her, like Hardy, fearlessly unconventional in her views, take refuge in 'ritualistic ecclesiasticism' (see *Jude the Obscure*, VI iii).

46. In December 1829, the representative of the Cambridge Union, Milnes, Arthur Hallam (whose early death is the subject of Tennyson's *In Memoriam*) and Sunderland, 'drove manfully through the snow' to Oxford to defend Shelley against the alleged superiority of Byron as a poet. Milnes gives an account of the speakers and their performance in a letter to his mother (Reid, 1 pp. 77–8).

47. From *In Memoriam*, xxxiii, and quoted in *Tess of the d'Urbervilles*, XXVII.

48. Hardy was thinking of Sue Bridehead. He had mapped out *Jude the Obscure* by the spring of 1893, but his early impressions of Mrs Henniker were to change the heroine's character considerably.

49. Letter 59 shows that the 'book of ballads' referred to at the beginning of the letter was *Ballades and Rondeaus, Chants Royals, Sestinas, Villanelles, etc.*, edited by Gleeson White, 1887. It looks as if Hardy had in mind Mrs Arthur Tomson ('Graham R. Tomson'), with whom there is no evidence of his corresponding after 1891. See Michael Millgate, *Thomas Hardy*, London, 1971, p. 302.

of which promptly ended the friendship, with considerable disgust on his side.

Tell me if your cold is better.

Ever sincerely yours

T.H.

10.   Max Gate.
Tuesday [July 18th, 1893]

My dear Mrs Henniker:

This is rather a happy thought, of my coming on to see you, since I shall be so near. My thanks for your kind invitation to lunch with you and your cousins; but it will be more convenient to myself to call afterwards, and as you are going out early I will be there at 2. I afterwards continue my journey to London.[50]

Yes: the opening of *A Laodicean* is generally considered good. But think how I was handicapped afterwards. I had to lie with my feet higher than my head for some time of the 5 months. I forget what point I had reached when the illness began.[51]

That your auditors should have wept over the story is certainly very gratifying; such grief means money – to adopt the sordid views of the Committee of the Society of Authors.

I go on and sleep at the Jeunes to-morrow night.[52]

Believe me,

Your sincerely,

Thomas Hardy.

[A postscript to this letter is reproduced opposite.[53]]

50. Hardy planned to interrupt his journey by rail to call on Mrs Henniker at Southsea.

51. He had been suffering from an internal haemorrhage, and had had to dictate the novel to his wife (*Life*, pp. 145–9).

52. Hardy had indicated the 19th or 20th in letter 8.

53. Hardy had formed a scientific view of the universe, and believed that events were ruled by a network of causes often resulting in the rule of unforeseeable Chance rather than of Providence: the ultimate Cause is neutral or indifferent, 'neither moral nor immoral, but *un*moral' (*Life*, p. 409).

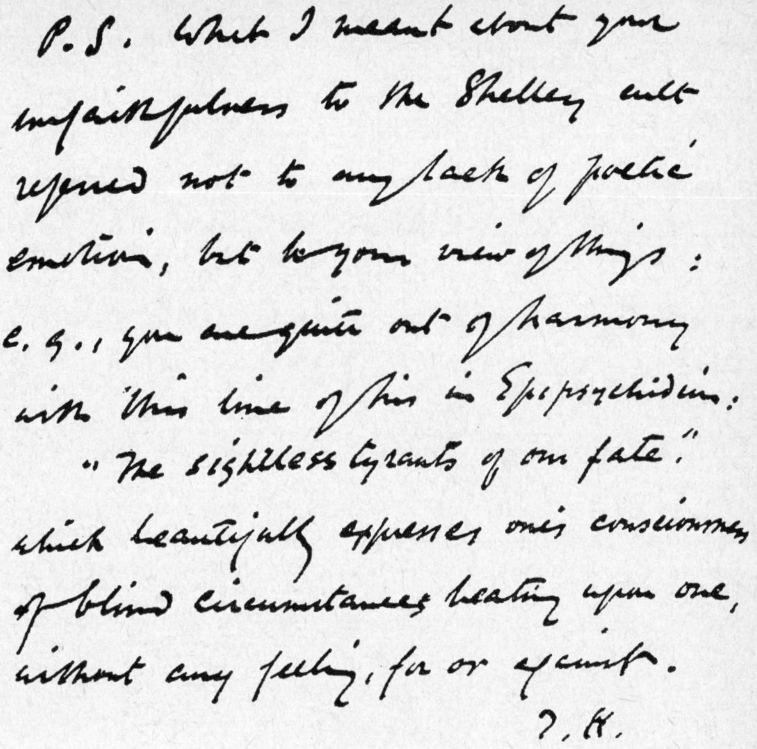

[handwritten letter]

P.S. What I meant about your
unfaithfulness to the Shelley cult
referred not to any lack of poetic
emotion, but to your view of things:
e.g., you are quite out of harmony
with this line of his in Epipsychidion:
" The sightless tyrants of our fate."
which beautifully expresses one's consciousness
of blind circumstances beating upon one,
without any feeling, for or against.

T. H.

11.   79 Harley Street,
                                             W.
                            Thursday [July 20th, 1893][54]

My dear Mrs Henniker:
    It is too wet this morning to go out as yet, and this affords
me an excuse for the pleasure of sending you a letter *apropos*
of nothing in particular. My fellow-lodger is Prince Victor
Albert,[55] the son of Princess Christian, who is reading at my

54. The correctness of this date is borne out in a letter Hardy wrote
to his wife from Lady Jeune's the following Monday (Weber, p. 22).
Here it will be seen that the dinner to Princess Mary was at Mrs
Kennard's, but that the Princess was unable to attend because of a
family bereavement.
55. A grandson of Queen Victoria, and son of Prince Christian of
Schleswig-Holstein. He and his parents had come over for the royal
wedding.

elbow waiting for a train to take him on to Windsor. He is very
genial, and curiously enough we both have a touch of rheumatism from the damp weather of yesterday. As soon as it
stops raining I am going out to hunt up some books, etc.,
among them the *Poems & Ballads*[56] that I am going to give
you. Please keep the volume I lent you, say for a month or two,
marking or annotating anything, and I will do the same in
yours: we can then restore each to each ... I had written thus
far amid interruptions from my acquaintance, who is also
suffering from indigestion; he has now gone: and my peace of
mind is next broken by the entry of a pretty actress, who has
called for an introduction from Lady J[eune] to theatrical
managers, which she is writing at another desk whilst I write
at hers. . . . I have been obliged to talk to the stage lady, who
has now gone off with her coveted letter, leaving me and my
hostess to finish our correspondence quietly.

I cannot help wishing you were free from certain retrograde superstitions: and I believe you will be some day,
and none the less happy for the emancipation.[57]

I will think over the scheme for our collaborating in the
talked of story,[58] and write again. It will delight me much to
hear from you.

Believe me –
Your ever sincere friend
T.H.

56. Probably the first series of Swinburne's *Poems and Ballads,* which
was published in 1866. Hardy in his 'buoyant' years read it with
astonishment and delight. He had yet to learn that he and Swinburne
were to be the most abused of living writers, Swinburne for *Poems
and Ballads,* and he for *Jude the Obscure* (*Life,* pp. 270, 325).

57. This explains the loan of *Poems and Ballads.* For the effect of
Swinburne's poetry of revolt on Hardy, and its likely effect on Mrs
Henniker, see Rutland, *Thomas Hardy,* pp. 70–5.

58. Here we have the first mention of their future collaboration – in
the story which was finally entitled 'The Spectre of the Real'.

12.   Max Gate,
                                               Dorchester.
                                        Thursday morning
                                        August 17, 1893

We are here again, dear Mrs Henniker, after our pleasant
visit to Wenlock.[59] We had intended to go to Gloucester on our
way back, to see the Cathedral,[60] but the heat was so intense
that we gave up the idea. We did get to Ludlow Castle,[61]
however, and spent a good many hours there.

We liked the evenings at Wenlock, after dinner, when we
sat on the lawn in the starlight, and told tales over the coffee –
a horn lantern on the table to light our jokes, the moths flying
round it, and the dogs beneath. Catty can talk the Devonshire
dialect to perfection, and the darkness took away her shyness;
she held forth with a humour and *abandon* which I did not
credit her with till then.

You will have learnt that I may go to Mrs Dugdale[62] later
on – besides the dates fixed she says 'any other time that would
be convenient': so that I must see her some time, if not
immediately.

Douglas writes this morning, hoping I shall spend a little
time with him when I run up to London, where he is, oddly
enough, just now. As I have to go on business I propose to
join him. Unless you write to say you have made any change

59. The Hardys had accepted the Milnes Gaskells' invitation to stay
at Wenlock Abbey. The Rt Hon. C. G. Milnes Gaskell was Mrs
Henniker's half-cousin; Lady Catherine was a daughter of Lord and
Lady Portsmouth, and Hardy probably knew her well, as he had stayed
with her parents more than once. He had sent her a copy of *Wessex
Tales* in 1888. At Wenlock he and she proved to be congenial spirits.
It is strange that Hardy uses the 'pet name' by which Lady Catherine
was known among her most intimate friends, as he detected in it a
'tremor of malice' (*Life*, pp. 258–9).

60. Hardy had to wait until 1911 before he was able to examine what
was traditionally supposed to be the first work in the perpendicular
style of Gothic architecture, in Gloucester Cathedral. See *Life*, p. 357,
and 'The Abbey Mason' (*Satires of Circumstance*).

61. Hardy's visit was occasioned more by literary than by architectural interest: here Milton's *Comus* was performed and Samuel Butler
wrote part of *Hudibras* (*Life*, p. 259).

62. Probably the wife of William Stratford Dugdale of Merevale
Hall, Warwickshire. The Dugdales and Hennikers were friends. See
letter 19.

in your plans I will come, with him, to see you at 5 Saturday,
or at any other time on that day, if you say so. By the way, shall
we take you to church Sunday morning? This of course is pre-
supposing you are *not* going to Merevale on your way to
Dublin. A letter will reach me here if you send it before post-
time this evening – or even to-morrow, as I may not go up till
Sat[urday] morning.

   You allude to the letter of Aug[ust] 3rd. If I sh[oul]d never
write to you again as in that letter you must remember that it
was written *before* you expressed your views – "morbid"
indeed! petty rather – in the railway carriage when we met
at Eastleigh.[63] But I am always your friend

                                                    T.H.

13.   Max Gate,
                                             Dorchester.
                                    September 6, 1893
   I was very glad to receive your letter, dear Mrs Henniker,
and to hear about the stories, and that you received my
scribblings for amendments on their pages without any of the
umbrage you might have felt at the liberty I took in making
them.

   If I may venture to say it, I think you have made a serious
mistake in leaving 'His Excellency' out of the collection.[64] That
little sketch was of value to the series by its contrast of scene

   63. A railway junction where it seems that Hardy met Mrs Henniker
from Southsea on their way to Winchester. On Tuesday, 8 August 1893,
they attended evensong at the Cathedral (K. Phelps, 'Annotations by
Thomas Hardy in his Bibles and Prayer-Book', Toucan Press, p. 11).
The poem 'At an Inn' (*Wessex Poems*) may recall this visit to Winchester, and it could have been on the same day that Hardy escorted
Mrs Henniker to the West Hill milestone where Angel Clare and
'Liza-Lu saw the black flag hoisted to mark Tess's execution, rather
than before that scene was written in 1890, as Rebekah Owen thought
(Weber, *Hardy and the Lady from Madison Square*, Colby College,
1952, p. 85).
   64. *Outlines* (1894), Mrs Henniker's first volume of stories (four
novelettes), was dedicated 'To my friend Thomas Hardy'. The hero of
the first, 'A Statesman's Love-Lapse', finds pleasure in following the
fortunes of men so unlike himself as two of Hardy's heroes, Gabriel
Oak and Giles Winterborne.

and scope, and enlivened those which had preceded it by that contrast. Curiously enough it had a lightness and sureness of touch lacking in some of the others, the character of Hilda being gracefully hit off. She is quite living, though so little described, and her presentation was just one of those things which only a woman can do. The simple and sole fault of the tale was its conventional ending, as I said, which might easily have been remedied by re-writing a conclusion. I enclose for what it is worth a third suggestion on that point, which occurred to me just after dispatching my last letter.

I should call the book *The Statesman's Love-Lapse,* and other stories namely ... (here w[oul]d follow the list *on the title-page.*) Or the words 'and other stories namely' might be omitted, the list being merely given.

It is very warm and dry here still, and the wasps are troublesome.

I am reading Keary's[65] novel *The Two Lancrofts*: very scholarly and truthful, but it does not palpitate with life.

Crewe Hall[66] must be a very nice place. So also must be Howth Castle.[67] I should have liked to see Vanessa's place.[68] I trust your book will have a cordial reception when it comes out: and hope that you are taking the rest that I am sure you needed. Believe me

Yours very sincerely
T.H.

(On second thoughts it is not worth while to enclose the note on the story.)

65. *The Two Lancrofts* by Charles F. Keary, novelist and writer on ancient history and mythology, was published in 1893.

66. Lord Houghton, Mrs Henniker's brother, did not succeed to the Crewe estates until the death of his uncle in January 1894 (see letter 25). Crewe Hall was burnt down in 1866, and the present building, which Lord Houghton inherited, was designed in rich Victorian style by Edward Barry.

67. Howth Castle stands on the rocky peninsula north of Dublin Bay.

68. This was Marley Abbey at Celbridge on the banks of the Liffey, about eleven miles from Dublin. Here lived Esther Vanhomrigh, Swift's 'Vanessa', the rival of his 'Stella', Esther Johnson.

14.   Max Gate,
                                              Dorchester.
                                    Sunday, Sept. 10, 1893

My dear Mrs Henniker:

I send the 'Desire'[69] sketch, with the trifling modification. I think the insertion in red at the end improves it.

The books I do not send (unless you say you want them with you) as it seems hardly worth while to give you the trouble of dragging them over the mountains of Scotland.

I hope 'His Ex[cellency]' will work out well as you plan it. But I fear for the volume: people like quantity in their books. You ought to have consulted me on the point – if you will allow me to say so.

What a thoughtful present you tell me of! Oddly enough I am badly off in inkstands. But really I have done nothing to deserve it. The pleasure, however, will be in thinking that it gave you pleasure to get it for me. Certainly the next big story shall be written from its contents.

I am glad to hear about Up-Cerne.[70] It is only a little way from Minterne, where Tess's walk crosses the high road: and would be a very convenient centre for you – though $4\frac{1}{2}$ miles from a r[ail]l[wa]y station. I have already been making little tours – not to Tess's scenes, but to those of *The Trumpet-Major*, with a young American lady, who with her elder sister is staying at Dorchester. She and I went to the inn (visited by John and Anne) last week, and sat there just as that pair did[71]

69. The first suggested title for the 'joint' story eventually called 'The Spectre of the Real'.

70. A tiny village among the chalk hills near Cerne Abbas and the Dorchester–Sherborne road. Minterne Magna, further north, is near the route followed by Tess from 'Flintcomb-Ash' (south of Nettlecombe Tout) to 'Emminster' (Beaminster) on her fruitless mission to see Angel Clare's parents. Mrs Henniker may have contemplated a visit to Captain Henniker's aunt (see p. 201).

71. For the story of Rebekah Owen and her elder sister, see Weber, op. cit. On p. 85, immediately after the reference to Hardy and Mrs Henniker's visit to the West Hill milestone, Winchester, there is an account of Rebekah's outing with Hardy to Faringdon Ruin, visited by John Loveday, the trumpet-major, and Anne Garland. There is no mention of a visit to an inn in the novel, nor is it clear which scene Hardy had in mind. (Could he have been thinking of Dick Dewy and Fancy Day at the Ship Inn?)

— (I don't mean that we re-enacted the very tender part). She has a Kodak, and takes the spots very skilfully. I am also scribbling away as fast as I can, to get finished a few short things, so as to have a good time in the Midlands a little later on. A friend[72] wants me to stay with him a few days at Aldeburgh in Suffolk on Oct. 7 but I am not sure about doing that. I think I told you of the place. Henry Arthur Jones[73] is going to read a new play next week, called *The Tempter* (a good title) and asks me to come. I suppose there will be a number of stage ladies present. Mrs Patrick Campbell is a friend of some neighbours of ours here I find. I don't know if she will visit them.

I had a nice letter from Catty this week. She is all alone, her husband and son having gone to Scotland. The Dublin paper was amusing. How exactly they have hit off your brother in the sketch. Of course I don't think it conceited in you to send it, nor should I even if you had marked it for me alone. I should not have the least hesitation in sending you the most flattering notice of myself if I had it. An interviewer, by the way, has just written asking if he may come.

You may be thankful to hear that the *one-sidedness* I used to remind you of is disappearing from the situation. But you will always be among the most valued of my friends, as I hope always to remain one at least of the rank and file of yours.

Ever sincerely
T.H.

72. Edward Clodd (1840–1930) left Aldeburgh, Suffolk, at the age of fourteen to become a clerk in London. In 1872 he was made Secretary of the London Joint Stock Bank. He was interested in science and folklore, and wrote many books, including a popular study of evolution. He became a member of the Savile Club (of which Hardy was a member) in 1881. At Strafford House, Aldeburgh, he entertained many eminent Victorians. In 1906 he became Chairman of the Rationalist Press Association. Although they remained friends, Clodd disapproved of Hardy's refusal in his later years to become an outright rationalist.

73. He and Pinero were the main contributors to the realist problem drama which flourished towards the end of the century.

C

15.   Max Gate,
                                                   Dorchester.
                                                   13.9.93
   Your elegant and valuable little present,[74] dear Mrs Henniker, has arrived today, and is being used at once by un-
deserving me. Many many thanks. I particularly prize it for
the initials you have been so thoughtful as to have put on it.
They ought to be an inspiration, and will certainly be an ever-
delightful reminder.
   I don't know where to send this, and thought you might
have written to-day to tell me. I hope you received the skeleton
MS. If you don't like either of the two stories will you be frank,
and tell me? I can send others, as I have several partly thought
out: and it *must* be a good one.
   To-day I have refused to go with my American friend[75] to
the tombs of the Turbervilles – having a hope of conducting
you thither some day, and feeling that you were a nearer
friend – almost a sister – to
                                        Always yours sincerely
                                                   T.H.

16.   Max Gate,
                                                   Dorchester,
                                           Saturday. Sept. 16. 1893
   To-day I send you, my dear Mrs Henniker, *The Woodlanders* and *Desperate Remedies* – which you thought worth
having, though I hardly think so. You will be amused to read
my first venture.[76] Would that I could write all my books over
again: I might make them worth reading.
   I write this with ink from your pretty present; and I have

   74. The inkstand which was gratefully anticipated in the previous
letter.
   75. Miss Rebekah Owen. The tombs referred to are in the Turber-
ville Chapel in the south aisle of the church at Bere Regis, the
'Kingsbere' of *Tess of the d'Urbervilles* (see chapter LII).
   76. Hardy's first venture was *The Poor Man and the Lady*, which was
never published (see Rutland, pp. 111–33 and Pinion, pp. 15–17). His
next novel, *Desperate Remedies*, was published anonymously in 1871.

already jotted down a few notes for the next long story[77] –
which I hope may be big as well as long.

Since you are nice, and a *little* candid in your last, I will be
quite so, and tell you that I was a trifle chilled by your letters
from Dublin and your first from Crewe, and much regretted
having sent the effusive ones to which they were in answer,
especially as you read parts of them aloud. Feeling that something was influencing you adversely, and destroying the charm
of your letters and personality, I lost confidence in you somewhat. I know, of course, that there is nothing in my epistles
which it matters in the least about all the world knowing, but
I have always a feeling that such publicity destroys the
pleasure of a friendly correspondence.

My wife has gone on horseback[78] to a place miles away, near
Weymouth, on the strength of my opinion that it would not
rain. It has now come on heavily, and I fear she will get
drenched to the skin.

Up-Cerne is only about a mile from 'Cross in Hand'[79]
where D'urberville (*sic*) swore never to molest Tess again.

This is the actual name of the spot, which is exactly as I describe it.

I thought you might know that Capt. Henniker[80] and I had
corresponded.

We are much exercised here about enlarging the house. We
have hardly room to do anything: as things are, although I
have given up my original writing-room[81] for a temporary
little one. Yet we hate the idea of the discomfort that alterations will cause. (I have written this so stupidly that it seems

77. Hardy had obviously not completed his planning of *Jude the
Obscure*. The MS. of the novel shows much replanning, and many
changes, in the early chapters.

78. It will be recalled that one of Hardy's first outings with her was
to Beeny Cliff, she on horseback. See *Life*, pp. 71, 75 and 'Beeny Cliff'
and 'Places' (*Satires of Circumstance*).

79. See *Tess of the d'Urbervilles*, XLV. This short stone pillar, of
uncertain age and origin, stands by the road which runs along Bat-
combe Down. For the legend associated with it, see Hardy's 'The Lost
Pyx' (*Poems of the Past and the Present*).

80. This is the first reference to Mrs Henniker's husband. He served
in the Coldstream Guards. See note 21, p. 6.

81. Reference to the alterations which resulted in a new study or
writing-room for Hardy will be found in the note for 13 September
1893. (*Life*, p. 259.)

as if we *were* altering, which of course we are not.

Yes: I *do* sigh a little; over your position less than over your conventional views. I do not mind its results upon the present little story (which please alter as you like) – but upon your future literary career. If you mean to make the world listen to you, you must say now what they will all be thinking and saying five and twenty years hence: and if you do that you must offend your conventional friends. 'Sarah Grand',[82] who has not, to my mind, such a sympathetic and intuitive knowledge of human nature as you, has yet an immense advantage over you in this respect – in the fact of having decided to offend her friends (so she told me) – and now that they are all alienated she can write boldly, and get listened to. 'Fellow Townsmen'[83] is one I thought rather good myself; but it is a story to write *after* you have drawn attention to your work, rather than to draw it with. But, my dear friend, don't let this disturb you.

The photograph is good, of course! As to my having 'contempt' as you suggest, for your rendering of the 'Desire' you know I *never* can have that for *anything* you do.

Always your friend
T.H.

17.   Max Gate,
Dorchester.
22.9.93

Just a note, my dear Mrs Henniker, to acknowledge with a thousand thanks the safe receipt of, first, the really valued poems of L[or]d Houghton:[84] which I don't prize any the less,

---

82. See note 8, p. 3.

83. One of Hardy's earlier short stories, which first appeared in *The New Quarterly Magazine* and *Harper's Weekly* in the spring of 1880, and was later included in *Wessex Tales*.

84. The first Lord Houghton's collected poems were published in two volumes by John Murray in 1876. The copies sent by Mrs Henniker and inscribed 'Thomas Hardy from Florence Henniker, September 1893' are among Hardy's books in his reconstructed study in the Dorset County Museum. Lord Houghton was Keats's first champion and biographer, his *Life, Letters and Literary Remains of John Keats* being published in 1848, and his edition of Keats's poems in 1854. He was a friend of Tennyson and one of the first to recognize the genius of Swinburne.

you may be sure, when I see what somebody has written inside, and passages that somebody has marked. (It is very neglectful of me not to have let you know sooner that they came Monday.)

Second, the photograph. A charming one. Whether I like it as a remembrancer better than Chancellor's[85] I will tell you if you give me liberty to criticize it.

Third, the MS. just received. I am going to read it almost directly. I send this wandering after you on y[ou]r long journey north.

I have been buying photos all the afternoon to illustrate an article of mine on a noted earthwork near here.[86]

My address will be here till Wedn[esda]y, possibly Thursday, morning when we go to London, I to meet Zola.[87] Thence we go to the Jeunes, Arlington Manor, Newbury, Berks – where we are due Saturday – 30th. Thence I am not quite sure where – possibly Oxford.

Ever your friend
Tom H.

18.   Max Gate,
Dorchester.
Friday, 6.10.93

How thoughtful and nice of you to give me these beautiful large photographs! – which have come to me here. Many many thanks. The one with the sweetest expression is, I think, that with the bird-cage; but perhaps Chancellor's recall what is best in your *nature*. I prize them all highly, though they represent only the outward form of my most charming friend!

85. Dublin photographers. Clearly the photograph had recalled Shakespeare's 'Sweet remembrancer' (*Macbeth*, III iv 36).

86. Hardy's descriptive story 'A Tryst at an Ancient Earthwork' (relating to Maiden Castle, and included in *A Changed Man*) was first published in the States in 1885. It appeared as 'Ancient Earthworks at Casterbridge' in *The English Illustrated Magazine*, December 1893, with four photographs by W. Pouncy of Dorchester. See p. 36.

87. Émile Zola (1840–1902) was the principal figure in the French school of naturalist fiction. Whether Hardy was influenced by him in *Jude the Obscure* is debatable; he asserted that he had read little of Zola (*Life*, p. 273).

— which reminds me of Bacon's words: 'The best part of beauty is that which a picture cannot express.'

I enclose with this a letter I wrote at Arlington, having kept it back on the chance of your sending a more specific address. Of the three you have given me I will select Lady Ashburton's,[88] I think — which perhaps you meant me to do? — If not unavoidable, this vagueness is rather wicked of you! Or perhaps you are so engrossed with millionaire sportsmen that you take small thought of a mere scribbler who would not kill a fly!

I did not at all *mean* my last note to be unkind, and am sorry that it seemed so, and hurt you about the MS. The fact is that letters have grown trollish again of late; therefore I propose to drop the subjects we drifted into, which we can explain when we meet. Never would I give *you* pain!

I have several things to ask you on our literary partnership, but I cannot enter into them till a distinct postal communication is re-established between us — or, still better, a meeting is feasible. I wish as much as ever to carry out the joint story. It is unfortunate that just when this scheme rendered it necessary for us to communicate freely and easily you sh[oul]d have rushed off to such outlandish latitudes: otherwise we should almost have been in print by this time.

If I think of a still better story than the 'Desire' — since I cannot consult you on the arrangement of that — and put back the desire (*sic*) for the present, would you mind the trouble of writing it out?

We had a delightful picnic to Savernake Forest from Arlington — a party of about 10 — Lady J[eune] cooked the luncheon at the picnic-house with the dexterity of a *chef*. One evening she played and sang at least a dozen Scotch ballads to me — so kindly — and will she says, at any time that I wish her to. She thinks you may stay with her aunt for some time.[89] Mrs

88. In county Ross, Scotland. It was the shooting season. Captain Henniker was an excellent shot, and Mrs Henniker had almost certainly travelled with him. See p. 30, note 96.
89. Lady Jeune was descended from a Highland family, the Mackenzies of Seaforth. She spent much of her youth with her grandmother at Brahan Castle, Ross and Cromarty. Her first husband was Colonel Stanley, and Tennyson and his wife spent an evening at the Stanleys' home in Upper Wimpole Street to hear Scottish songs and Irish melodies.

C.[90] being a R[oman] C[atholic], and I being a Pagan, we were obliged to go for a walk in the woods on Sunday when the others went to church. Lewis Morris,[91] who was also amongst the guests, wrote off-hand a charming little poem to one of the girls.

There is a remark about Zola and myself in *The World*[92] this week, wh[ich] perhaps you may have seen.

So far from my not forgiving you anything, and not feeling as friendly as ever, I can say that if we are not to be the *thorough* friends in future that we hitherto have been, life will have lost a very very great attraction for one who is above all things

Ever sincerely yours
T.H.

19.

Max Gate,
Dorchester.
Sunday Oct. 22. 1893

I have just written to Watt,[93] my dear friend, to stir him up about your stories. As he has probably engaged in negotiations with publishers about them I think it best not to interfere with his progress, or the reverse, till he says he cannot make satisfactory terms, in which event I will try McIlvaine[94] – who is at the present moment I believe on his way back from New York – and whom I shall probably see soon.

You must remember that in England there is very little to be made commercially out of short tales – and that publishers are as a rule shy of them, except those that are written by people who cannot write long ones successfully – an odd

---

For an account of the visit to the Jeunes at Arlington Manor, Newbury, see Hardy's *Life*, p. 260.

90. Mrs Craigie (p. 1) had become a Roman Catholic. Hardy found her reasons for this step unconvincing.

91. Lewis Morris (1833–1907), poet and Welsh educationist.

92. This London weekly reported (4 Oct. 1893) that Hardy was unable to attend the banquet given by the Authors' Club in honour of Zola.

93. A. P. Watt, literary agent.

94. Clarence W. McIlvaine of Osgood, McIlvaine and Co., Hardy's publishers at this time.

exception! – and have established a speciality in that line. You must not *waste* the stories for the mere sake of getting them printed quickly.

I hope you modified that one of them called 'A Lost Illusion'[95] as I suggested – and did the other things, as the changes were likely to affect a publisher's views.

Now to your previous nice letter. I should have answered it a day or two ago had I not thought it advisable to send mine to Crewe, lest you sh[oul]d miss it at Fasque[96] by leaving. By the way you don't tell me *much* about your doings: still, I am thankful for small mercies in that kind, and am truly glad to know that your health is good amid the bracing air. I would say I much wish to see you again if I thought you wished to see me. Merevale I give up thinking of for the present – perhaps till next summer: but I could of course get there easily on short notice if desirable.

Very well, don't have the 'Milnes'[97] as one of your authornames if you won't. But other women have done the same thing: e.g. 'Ann (*sic*) Thackeray Ritchie' [98] etc.

I could not take the 'Desire' in hand till to-day, having been hunting up the tales I told you of ('Two Ambitions'[99] being one of them). They are now fastened together to be dispatched to the publisher, and I turn to the 'Desire' – which by the bye, is the 'Desire' no longer. – For I have planned to carry out Ending *II* – since you like it so much better: I feel I ought

95. It seems that Hardy was responsible for the concluding irony of 'A Sustained Illusion', the final tale in *Outlines* (1894).

96. Mrs Henniker was staying at Fasque, the home of the Gladstones near Fettercairn, Kincardineshire. It stands just below the eastern Grampians and commands extensive views. As the third Baronet, Sir John Robert Gladstone (a great-nephew of W. E. Gladstone, the statesman) was in the Coldstream Guards and a bachelor, the probability is that the Hennikers were on holiday together.

97. Her maiden name.

98. Anne Isabella Thackeray, the novelist's eldest daughter (1837–1919), married her cousin Richmond Thackeray Ritchie, and wrote novels, tales and biographical essays. Hardy knew her through Leslie Stephen, who had married her sister; she confirmed his misgivings about living in the country by insisting that a novelist must like society (*Life*, pp. 100, 104).

99. Hardy's short story 'A Tragedy of Two Ambitions' appeared in *The Universal Review*, December 1888, and is to be found in *Life's Little Ironies*, the text of which Hardy was about to send to the publishers.

not to force the other upon you – wh[ich] is too uncompromis-
ing for one of the pretty sex to have a hand in. The question
now is, what shall we call it? – 'The resurrection of a Love'?

What name shall I give to the heroine of my coming long
story when I get at it?[100] I don't quite know when that will be,
though it must be this winter. Your remarks on the various
possibilities of the 'Desire' are very thoughtful and good – of
course I don't object to your criticisms: please do any amount
of them, dear fellow-scribbler.

I have got back to a very satisfactory state of health: – how
good you are to be so sympathetic! Mrs Allhusen [101] we know
very well, owing to her husband taking a house near here for a
year or two: I don't know how she c[oul]d have heard of my
knowing you.

I only wished for those sketch-plots you have sent back in
case I had to fall back on one. If you feel you would ever like
to work out the one you have not adopted, please say so.

It *will* be a pleasure if you come to Upcerne (*sic*). Only
think how the lack of motive causes one to lag! For two years
I have been going to add some rooms to this house: [102] and
never till now regretted that I postponed doing it.

Ever your sincere friend
Tom H.

20.   Max Gate,
                                                 Dorchester.
                                          Wednesday 25.10.93

Your letter, dear Mrs Henniker, has come by this afternoon's post. I think that I mostly anticipated your inquiry in
my hurried note of yesterday; but in case I was not clear I

100. The more one studies Hardy's activities during 1893, the less
surprising it becomes that he had not been able to 'get at' *Jude the
Obscure*. He had yet to begin writing the novel at full length, for there
is no change in the heroine's name in the MS. See p. xxxviii.

101. Mrs Wilton Allhusen lived near Lyme Regis. She was most probably an aunt of the Henry Allhusen who married Dorothy Stanley, the
daughter of Lady Jeune by her first marriage, in 1896.

102. The same association of ideas is to be found in a previous letter
(p. 25). It suggests that Hardy looked forward to the opportunity of
seeing Mrs Henniker in Dorset but not at Max Gate.

recapitulate. I know nothing of Hutchinson; but I think that upon the whole I sh[oul]d accept.[103] On any half-profit system the publisher gives you practically what he pleases: yet, as short tales do very much go a-begging, I fear you may lose the chance of early publication if you go elsewhere. Before closing with him, however, ask what he w[oul]d give (on day of publication) for the right to publish the volume for 5 years, in any edition he chooses: and if he offers £50 I advise you to take it.

If he wont give anything, and you agree to half-profits, be sure you stipulate (best) that he is to have the right to publish the library or original edition only. Any cheaper form of the book to be the subject of a new arrangement, or, next best, for, say 5 y[ea]rs any edition. About America etc. I have already written. Also, ask *when* the book is to be published.

Also say he shall have 'the first offer of your *next* new novel' – not of *any* new novel you may write: (or you will be bound to offer him *all* your future books.) You will not, of course, say he shall *have* your next new novel – only the offer of it – wh[ich] means on your terms.

Speaking generally, I think you are not likely to be treated very badly: one reason is that you being a friend of mine would make a publisher remember that you are likely to know the tricks of the trade. Don't part with the copyright – which you would do (or he w[oul]d say so) if you were to agree to half-profits without stipulating *time* or *edition*. I am in the middle of a scrimmage with Macmillan about the very same question.[104]

A word as to our story: in working it out I find it may possibly be necessary to effect a compromise between the two endings: for on no account must it end weakly.

I enclose a German review of *Tess*, some parts of which will interest you.

I must not write now to you for *ages*? I have written so much lately as to bore you, I am sure.

Ever sincerely
Tom H.

103. Mrs Henniker was considering an offer for the publication of *Outlines*.

104. In June 1893 Hardy informed Macmillan that he wished to withdraw *The Woodlanders* and *Wessex Tales* for inclusion in a collected edition of his works. This had been planned since 1890; see p. 42, note 129.

21.   Max Gate,
                                          Dorchester.
                                     Saturday. 28.10.93

You will say, 'What, another letter so soon!' And perhaps
you may add 'Yes – and so prosy too!' Our correspondence of
late might indeed almost have been cut from the pages of *The
Author* (which you ought to take in, by the way).

However, I must let you know that the story is finished virtually, and that the MS. was sent early this morning to Miss
Tigan. I have told her to return me the original (in case I
should want to insert a little more detail from it) and to send
to you direct the type-written copy. Will you please read it
from the beginning (*without* glancing first at the end!) so as
to get the intended effect, and judge of its strength or weakness. It is, as you wished, very tragic; a modified form of
Ending II – which I think better than any we have thought of
before. If anything in it is what you don't like please tell me
quite freely – and it shall be modified. As I said last time, all
the wickedness (if it has any) will be laid on my unfortunate
head, while all the tender and proper parts will be attributed
to you.[105] Without wishing to make you promise, I suggest that
we keep it a secret to our two selves which is my work and
which yours. We may be amusingly bothered by friends and
others to confess.

In reading it over, particularly the bride's doings in the
morning from dawn till the wedding-hour, please insert in
pencil any details that I have omitted, and that would only be
known to a woman. I may not be quite correct in what I have
hastily written, never having had the pleasure of being a
bride-elect myself. If you will then send me the copy I will go
through it for final corrections, and send it off.

The ending, good or bad, has the merit of being in exact
keeping with Lord P.'s character.

---

105. Hardy's forecast proved correct. 'The Spectre of the Real' was
published in the weekly *To-Day*, 17 November 1894. It was revised and
improved for inclusion in *In Scarlet and Grey* (1896). The other stories
in this volume, however, received higher commendation from the
critics; and *The Spectator* concluded that Hardy had hardly been a
'judicious literary counsellor'. Purdy (p. 348) reminds us that this
criticism came after the publication of *Jude the Obscure*, when Hardy
was 'excommunicated' by a section of the press (*Life*, p. 276).

Yesterday's photograph was a charming little surprise: many thanks for your thoughtfulness, dear friend. It is the best, I think, of Lafayettes (*sic*): and is very good as a specimen of his art. Now I suppose it will sound like heresy to say that the profile by Chancellor still *beats all of them* as yet. It has the quality of *charm* in the expression of the face, which Lafayette's have in a far less degree. It is a very mysterious thing that photographers should differ in this point. Chancellor is incomparably the truer *artist,* to my mind. He lets you take a more natural pose, too. When you are in Dublin again *please* have another by Chancellor. If you do decide to put the portrait at the beginning of the volume take my advice and have the profile one – (the first you sent me).[106] Perhaps you won't however, since you won't adopt the 'Milnes' as part of your literary name. If you *don't* have the Chancellor profile the one you now send is next best: the features are sculpturesque.

I will send you back the pages of detail omitted, if you w[oul]d like to have them, as they may be useful. You will *quite* understand that they were not omitted because they weren't good; but because the scale of the story was too small to admit them without injury to the proportion of the whole. I refer particularly to the description of the pool, and the bird tracks; which I *much* wished to retain.

I did not mean to flow over into another sheet with literary affairs, but there are one or two things more to say under that head. One is the title. Our old title was in itself rather good, but as it does not quite apply, I have provisionally substituted 'The Spectre of the Real' – 'The Looming of the Real' is perhaps almost better. I have also thought of 'A passion and after': 'To-day's kiss and yesterday's'. – 'Husband's Corpse and husband's kiss'. – 'A shattering of Ideals'. When you have read the modifications you will be able to choose; or suggest.

This question also arises: shall we print the story in America etc., simultaneously. It will cause a delay of a few weeks perhaps (not so long *possibly*). On the other hand if we

106. Mrs Henniker took this advice, and used the photograph for the frontispiece to her next book, *Outlines,* published by Hutchinson in 1894, and extravagantly praised by critics, who compared Mrs Henniker to Dickens and the masters of the French short story.

sacrifice America for the sake of being sooner out here, we
may lose, say £20 or £25.

Ever yours sincerely
Tom H.

[P.S.] Blathwayt[107] is on tour, lecturing about 'Celebrities' he
has interviewed. I wonder what he says about you and me.
Lady Jeune is writing an article or [']Conversation', for
wh[ich] she is promised £10 she says. Would you like me to
send *The Two Lancrofts*?[108] Also your Swinburne,[109] which I
have by me.

T.H.

22.   Max Gate,
                                        Dorchester.
                              Monday afternoon. 30.10.93
   I have just received your yesterday's letter. Quite right to
bother me.
   I advise you to accept Messrs Hutchinson's offer of half-
profits with conditions as particularized on draft which I enclose with this.
   My reasons are these: it is your wish to get the book out
soon: and there cannot be *much* money got out of it by you
in any case, though you *may* get a great deal of attention and
praise – which are worth more than money to you, in view of
future writing. The having to purchase stock and plates in the
event of getting back copyright is of no consequence, since in
the event of your making a name by that time you will have a
publisher at your beck and call (if not Hutchinson) who will
naturally take the old stock if he republish the book.
   I could not ensure its publication by McIlvaine on better
terms – or I would advise you to refuse the above offer. I
think I could get him to publish it: but there w[oul]d be

107. Raymond Blathwayt, journalist (1855–1935), special correspondent for *Black and White*, interviewed Hardy on 27 August 1892 on
Tess of the d'Urbervilles. His account of the interview is reprinted in
L. Lerner and J. Holmstrom, *Thomas Hardy and his Readers*, London,
1968.
   108. See p. 21.   109. See p. 18.

some delay as he does not return from America till Nov. 15.
I don't know anything against Hutchinson, and he may be a
very respectable man. – Watt, by recommending him in a
way, is a sort of guarantee.

I sent a letter to Crewe yesterday.

I hope you will have left directions there for the type-
written copy of our story to be sent on to you.

Ever sincerely
T.H.

I am writing to Watt this evening about our story, and I will
give him a hint to watch your interests carefully.

T.

23.
Max Gate,
Dorchester.
Dec. 1. 1893

I send you to-day, my dear friend, a vanity – a copy of *The
Sketch* containing some remarks about myself which may
amuse you; and also some portraits of friends of mine, more
or less, in whom the world takes an interest. An article I wrote
on some earthworks near here appears in this month's *English
Illustrated Magazine*: and I am intending to send that too.
The editor[110] has taken it upon himself to identify the spot
with Dorchester, which I did not wish him to do, since it is
just possible that a character who appears in the narrative may
be said to be drawn from a local man, still living, though it is
really meant for nobody in particular.

I am glad to know that Watt sent you your dues – well-
earned – on 'The Spectre'. (£71.15.6 the sum sh[oul]d be i.e.
half the total paid for the story, £159.10.0. less half his com-
mission.) Considering the shortness of the tale – 8000 to 9000
words – the price is a very fair one for serial use only – £18
per thousand words. As to your paying a share of the type-
writing, certainly not; the charge was quite small.

I am not sure that I feel so keen about the, alas, unwritten,

110. Clement Shorter (1857–1926), who edited and founded several
magazines. Hardy had written an anonymous article on Mrs Henniker
as author in his *Illustrated London News*. His present concern arose
from the fact that the archaeologist of the story (see p. 27) proves to
have been dishonest.

long story as I should do. I feel more inclined just now to write short ones. However, as it is one I planned a couple of years ago I shall, I think, go on with it, and probably shall warm up.

Plays are very uncertain ventures[111] – and would – taking merely a commercial view of them – most likely bring less than novels in the long run. Moreover they are distinctly a lower form of art: what is called a good play, receiving a column's notice in the morning papers, being distinctly in point of artistic feeling and exhibition of human nature no higher than a third rate novel. Consider what a poor novel *Mrs. Tanqueray*[112] would make – I mean, how little originality it w[oul]d possess – that sort of thing having been done scores of years ago in fiction

I have read the dedication of *The School for Scandal*. Certainly I did not know that Mrs Crewe[113] was your great-grandmother. How very charming to have such an ancestress! Do you know Fox's verses to her? They are given in Horace Walpole's *Letters*.

It is rather a curious coincidence that in all probability our two volumes of short stories[114] will be published about the same time.

Always your sincere friend
Tom H.

Our friend the Duchess of Manchester[115] wanted me to dine

111. Mrs Henniker may have sought advice on writing a play. She wrote a four-act comedy, *The Courage of Silence*, which was produced in 1905.

112. See the note on p. 10.

113. Richard Brinsley Sheridan's comedy (1777) was dedicated to Mrs Crewe in a long 'Portrait' preceding Garrick's 'Prologue'. She was a reigning beauty of the day, and a friend of Fox, Sheridan, Burke, and Reynolds, who painted three portraits of her. She married John Crewe of Crewe Hall in 1766; he became the first Lord of Crewe. Charles James Fox's anapaestic verses to Lady Crewe are contained in a letter to the Rev. William Mason, dated 27 May 1775. Hardy's knowledge of Horace Walpole's letters is remarkable. As early as 1868 he read the six volumes to Sir Horace Mann; (see Pinion, pp. 209–10, for Walpole's influence on Hardy).

114. *Life's Little Ironies* (published April 1894) and *Outlines*. For the former, see p. 30.

115. Hardy described her as temperamentally like the Julie-Jane of his poem. He dined with her and other celebrities twice soon afterwards (*Life*, pp. 258, 260).

with her last Sunday; but I did not stay in Town. She said she had a lot of interesting people coming.

24.   Max Gate,
                                                       Dorchester.
                                                  Dec. 18, 1893[116]

How pleased I have been to get your notes, my dear little friend! You will be glad to know that, immediately on receipt of this afternoon's request, I packed up the type-written story,[117] and sent it on to Mr Shorter, *without altering a line*. One *letter* I had altered, and did not remember till it was sealed up: in the spelling of 'Gawd' – which is Kipling's, and should decidedly be avoided. But you can restore it in proof if you care to. My defence for having thought of tampering with the sketch is that you said I was to get £50 for it, which of course you will not get as it stands.

I did not suggest to Hutchinson to change y[ou]r title. What a laughable blunder has been made by him. Instead of calling the suggested one 'A Few Cursory *Insights*' he calls it 'A Few Cursory *Incidents*'! Just like publishers.

You are quite right to have the book advertised as by 'The Hon. Mrs H.' I was going to advise it.

I have, after all, been victimised by that interviewer. To my amazement, instead of the *literary* interview in *The Young Man* which I conceded I get a proof of a *political* conv[er-satio]n with Mr T.H., in the *Westminster Gazette*! Fortunately I have been able to correct it: but it consists of some careless remarks I made after, as I thought, the interview was over. I find that these men, out of one visit, will make 4 or 5 interviews, for various papers.[118]

116. It is worth noting that about this time Hardy found and 'touched up' a short story which he called 'An Imaginative Woman' (*Life*, p. 260). In this story certain features recall Mrs Henniker: the Solentsea where the heroine stays is Southsea; like Mrs Henniker, she is interested in Shelley's poetry, and she is the poet's 'ideal She' as Mrs Henniker was Hardy's (cf. p. 39); her husband, like Mrs Henniker's, was most unpoetical and connected with the weapons of war.

117. Mrs Henniker's unconventional and ironic tale 'Bad and Worthless' was published in *The English Illustrated Magazine*, of which Clement Shorter was the editor, in April 1894.

118. The literary interview appeared in *The Young Man* in April 1894.

I hear from the Harpers that Henry H. the head of the firm, will be in London in January. As I know him very well I shall probably dine with him – to talk over business engagements.[119] You may possibly be in London at the same time.

An old acquaintance of mine – Fellow and Tutor of Corpus, Cambridge, is going to dine here tonight.[120]

Of course I shall *never* dislike you, unless you do what you cannot do – turn out to be a totally different woman from what I know you to be. I won't have you say that there is little good in you. One great gain from that *last* meeting[121] is that it revived in my consciousness certain nice and dear features in your character which I had half forgotten, through their being of that ethereal intangible sort[122] which letters cannot convey. If you have only *one* good quality, a good *heart*, you are good enough for me. Believe me, my dear friend,

Always y[ou]rs

Tom H.

Life's Little I[ronies] will be pub[lishe]d as soon as the Harpers can get the American edition ready – End of Jan., I expect.[123]

P.S. You must overlook the liberty I took in suggesting alteration of the tale. I am vexed with myself for it.

119. Harper and Brothers were Hardy's publishers in the States at this time. He probably had in mind discussing the serial publication of *Jude the Obscure* in *Harper's Magazine* (New York and London). By the following April, the novel had so changed that Hardy wished to cancel his agreement (*Life*, p. 263).

120. Charles Moule, later President of Corpus College, Cambridge, who had known Hardy since they were boys. They had visited medieval buildings together and dived on summer mornings from a boat in Weymouth Bay (*Life*, p. 387). Charles was a brother of Horace Moule, Hardy's greatly loved friend and mentor who took his life at an early age. Another brother became Bishop of Durham. Their father was Vicar of Fordington on the outskirts of Dorchester; in some ways he was the original of Angel Clare's father; his magnificent work during the cholera plague provides the background climax for Hardy's story 'A Changed Man'.

121. Hardy's London engagements in December included the final revision with Mrs Henniker of 'The Spectre of the Real' (*Life*, p. 261).

122. See the note on Shelley's 'Epipsychidion', p. xxxvi.

123. It was published by Osgood, McIlvaine and Co. (London) in February, and by Harper and Brothers (New York) in March, 1894.

25.   Max Gate,
                                             Dorchester.
                                             Jan. 15, 1894

I have just received your yesterday's note, and am glad to
hear that you are taking more rest, for I fear you have been
feeling less well than in your kindness you let me know of. I
hope not?

My neuralgia has quite gone – it is not what I often get.
Thank you for telling me of the remedy.

I think more cruelties are perpetrated on animals by butchers, drovers, and cab-people, than by vivisectors. I wish you
and I could work together some day for the prevention
of such barbarities.

I have met Henry Harland at the Savile Club,[124] I think, but
I may be mistaken. I have found out no more about Mrs
Clairmont, but if I go to stay with the Jeunes, as they want me
to do soon, I may possibly hear something of her, though I am
not greatly curious.

I hope the bequest of your uncle will not cause you to
desert literature and break up our comradeship in that pur-
suit, just now when you are getting so nicely into notice? But
perhaps it will.[125]

I am creeping on a little with the long story, and am
beginning to get interested in my heroine as she takes shape
and reality: though she is very nebulous at present. *Life's
Little Ironies* comes out at the end of the month. Don't order
it, of course.

I have been thinking that the sort of friend one wants most
is a friend with whom mutual confessions can be made of
weaknesses without fear of reproach or contempt. What an
indescribable luxury! Do you want such an one for yourself?
– I wonder if I shall ever find one.

                                    Ever sincerely yours,
                                    Tom H.

124. Hardy had been a member of this club since 1878. Henry Harland (1861–1905), novelist and writer of short stories (of which the best
known is 'The Cardinal's Snuff-Box') was born of American parents in
St Petersburg. He became editor of *The Yellow Book*.

125. Lord Hungerford Crewe had just died, leaving Crewe Hall and
the Crewe estates to Lord Houghton, Mrs Henniker's brother, who left
Ireland and became Earl of Crewe in 1895.

26. Max Gate,
Dorchester.
Sunday night, Aug. 4. '95[126]

My dear friend: I hope I have not seemed unkind in not sending a letter to meet you, as I did last year, and as I meant to do this. But I have been so ill since I saw you that I c[oul]d not write a line, and have got up for the first time to-day. It was a sudden attack of English cholera, and for four days I have been confined to bed and dosed with medicine and iced brandy. It stopped last night, and I have now only to regain strength, for I feel, as you may suppose, very shaky, though curiously enough I have been in good spirits throughout.

I imagine you are at Eltville[127] by this time. I hope you had a good passage. Did you cross Wedn[esda]y night? (You gave me no dates) – And by what route? And when do you go on?

I am impatient to restore and revise the serial story for the volume, and this has been a vexing hindrance.

I am overwhelmed with requests from Editors for short stories, but I cannot write them. Why didn't you go on being my pupil, so that I c[oul]d have recommended you as a substitute!

126. The gap of a year and a half in the correspondence does not imply a breakdown in friendly relations or the destruction of letters to conceal evidence. There is nothing to indicate that the friendship did not continue harmoniously. That the correspondence continued is clear from p. 47. It may have been on a diminished scale; the 'Max Gate' letters as a whole for this period show a considerable reduction, and this is hardly surprising if one remembers that at this time Hardy not only completed *Jude the Obscure* but revised six of his novels and their prefaces for the uniform edition of 1895–7. His social engagements in London and outside did not decrease noticeably in 1894 and 1895; his *Life* (p. 264) mentions his visit to the Women Writers' Club (probably with Mrs Henniker, who became President of the Society of Women Journalists in 1896) and dining with Major Henniker at the Guards' Mess, St James's (p. 266).

By the end of August 1895, Hardy found the 'labour' of altering *Jude* (not to offend the readers of the magazine in which it appeared serially) and of restoring the MS. to its original state had completely destroyed his will to improve the text as he had intended. He sent it off unrevised to the publishers (*Life*, pp. 268–9; compare the third paragraph of this letter).

127. On the Rhine, west of Mainz.

I have made myself a present of Wharton's *Sappho*[128] – a
delightful book. How I love her – how many men have loved
her! – more than they have Christ I fear. Tell me if you are
well, and in good spirits.

Ever sincerely and aff[ectionate]ly,
Tom H.

Monday morn. Am much better – shall work to-day. I enclose a par[agraph] from this morning's *D[aily]Chronicle*.

27.   Max Gate,
Dorchester.
Monday. Aug. 12. 1895
My dear friend : You will have reached Marienbad about the
time this letter gets there, I am thinking, though I don't like
to reckon much upon your movements since I found myself
wrong in supposing you on the Rhine when you were still in
London. I am recovered of my attack, though I feel a little
weak still. Perhaps, however, that is no great disadvantage, for
I have no wish to go out much, and so have more time for my
clerical drudgery – for what I am doing is hardly literary
work. In addition to the proofs of the monthly volumes[129] I
am restoring the MS. of the Harper story[130] to its original state.

128. Hardy's interest in Sappho may be seen in an early novel, *The
Hand of Ethelberta*, and *Jude the Obscure* (the epigraph to part III is
taken from H. T. Wharton's book); more particularly in *The Well-
Beloved* (Aphrodite, 'the Weaver of Wiles'). It is in connection with
the last novel that Hardy wrote to Swinburne on imitations of a
Sapphic fragment (*Life*, p. 287). His own 'Sapphic Fragment' is included
in *Poems of the Past and the Present*.
129. Preparation for the Wessex Novels, the uniform edition published by Osgood, McIlvaine and Co., had probably begun before 1895.
In January of that year Hardy had completed the revision of the text
and preface of *Tess of the d'Urbervilles*; by July he had finished six
novels (Purdy, p. 279).
130. *Jude the Obscure* appeared in instalments in *Harper's New
Monthly Magazine* from December 1894 to November 1895.

Fortunately I wrote the alterations and abridgments in blue ink – which makes it easy to recover the first form. Curiously enough, I am more interested in the Sue story than in any I have written.

I am so glad to hear that you meant to stop at Nuremberg. If you adhere to your programme you are there at this moment probably. How I sh[oul]d like to explain the quaint architecture to you! But that's all over, I suppose.

We had a man staying here one night last week – Mr F. Wedmore,[131] the critic, who remembered you as a girl when he visited your father at Fryston. It was pleasant to hear him recall his recollections of the 'bright lively girl'.

I have only promised to go to two places this autumn – the Jeunes, and the Pitt-Rivers's.[132] I don't mean to stay anywhere long – till next year, when I hope to have plenty of leisure.

I seem to see nothing in many modern writers but *form* – good form, certainly. I am led to say this by having tried to discover a great poet in Robert Bridges.[133] But he hands the torch on no further than the rest of them do.

When am I to hear that zither?[134]

Tell me how you find Marienbad. Numbers of people seem to be drifting to German baths this year. You have set the fashion perhaps.

A good book for carrying on a long journey is the G[olden] Treasury[135] as it contains so much in a small compass.

131. Frederick Wedmore (1844–1921) wrote mainly on art (including Whistler's etchings). See pp. 96 and 171.

132. General Pitt-Rivers was the first Inspector of Ancient Monuments; his collections in Oxford and Dorset are well known. His home was Rushmore near Shaftesbury, Dorset. A description of the illuminated grounds and the dancing (led off by 'the beautiful Mrs Grove', daughter of the General) at the time of the Hardys' visit is found in Hardy's *Life* (p. 269). See letter 29.

133. Robert Bridges (1844–1930) became Poet Laureate in 1913. He is best known for his *Testament of Beauty* (1929) and the first edition of Gerard Manley Hopkins's poetry in 1918.

134. Mrs Henniker had played the 'zithern' in Dublin during the Hardys' visit.

135. Hardy's copy had been given him by Horace Moule. It remained a favourite book throughout his life.

I have been looking for a motto for the title page of *The
Woodl[ande]rs*[136] and not being able to find one, composed it.

Believe me, always,

Y[ou]r affect[iona]te friend,

Tom H.

P.S. *The Way they Loved at Grimpat*[137] was sent me by the
author. I will look it up.

28.   Max Gate,
                                              Dorchester.

                                              3.9.'95

My dear friend: I have just returned here from Athelhampton Hall[138] – and we are leaving this morning for Rushmore
(the Pitt-Rivers's) and had hoped and intended to write to you
at Marienbad at least once a week (as I conscientiously began
to do). But I have not! (to my loss). I had not, for one thing,
foreseen the difficulty of getting replies from you in time. Your
last letter reached me on the *Monday week* following the Sunday I posted mine.

No: you had not told me Mrs Moulton[139] was there – or
anybody. Did you take the journey with Anna[140] only – and

136. The lines are:

Not boskiest bow'r,

When hearts are ill-affin'd,

Hath tree of pow'r

To shelter from the wind!

They apply not only to *The Woodlanders* (the revision of which for
the Wessex Novels edition Hardy had just completed) but also to
Hardy's domestic affairs, aggravated by *Jude the Obscure*, which Mrs
Hardy strenuously opposed. See Evelyn Hardy, *Thomas Hardy*, 'The
Division'.

137. This novel, published in 1894, was written by Erminda Rentoul
Esler.

138. Dating from Edward III's reign, it was extended in Henry VII's,
and is generally Tudor in design. For eight generations it belonged to
the Martyns whose medieval tombs may be seen in Puddletown Church.
In 1895 Athelhampton Hall ('Athelhall' in 'The Waiting Supper' and
two of Hardy's poems) was the residence of Alfred de la Fontaine, with
whom Hardy often dined. See p. 88.

139. See p. 9.

140. Mrs Henniker's German servant.

are you staying in a hotel, or do you occupy a house by yourself, (*sic*) I wonder if you see many of the English who are also
there. I fear I have not this time gathered any very clear
notion of your life there.

We return from Rushmore Friday – and I shall mostly be
at Max Gate, where two or three people are coming from
London to stay with us. Though I shall if possible be taking
little day-journeys to Oxford, Reading, etc – and other scenes
of the Jude story. (What a pity that you never visited any of
them with me after all.)

I have been sleeping much better (thank you for inquiring).
The sleeplessness was owing I think to my staying too long
over my writing table, and not going out.

Yes – I am rather surprised at your reading any book by
J. S. Mill[141] – and still more that you agree with him on anything. I hope the baths are strengthening you – and that you
will come back hale and ruddy.

Ever sincerely
Tom H.

29.   Max Gate,
                                             Dorchester.
                                          Sept. 11, 1895

My dear friend: This time your letter travelled to me at a
decent pace – arriving by the Monday afternoon post – a two
days' transit. I do not think Marienbad would suit me just
now – heat, and particularly hot baths, pulling me down
terribly. Where I was last week, on the top of the high Wilts
downs, suited me eminently, and I felt quite languid on coming
back here nearer the coast. (Rushmore is very high up – near
Shaftesbury, described as 'Shaston' in *Jude*) It was a pleasant
visit, (notwithstanding the trying temper of the hostess) – the
most romantic time I have had since I visited you at Dublin.

How we waste our labours in reading without system – or
even with system. I have been led to think again of this by

141. Hardy and Sue Bridehead, the heroine of *Jude the Obscure*,
admired the works of J. S. Mill. (See *Life*, p. 330 and *Jude the Obscure*,
IV iii, where Sue quotes Mill. For other references, and Mill's influence
on Hardy, see Pinion, pp. 207–8.)

looking over some notes of reading that I took years ago, and finding I had forgotten them entirely. To stick to a few books and read them over and over again is the only way – introducing some really valuable new book as a sauce now and then.

I am going to get Mill's *Subjection of Women* – which I do not remember ever reading.

I fear that after the Vicar I cannot be of much service in saying anything that will commend your stories to an editor or publisher. But I do remember thinking that 'In The Infirmary'[142] was a strong little sketch, which had in it much of the actuality of life itself.

The God in the Car[143] has been lent me – I am not so struck with it as I expected to be – My taste inclines less and less towards smart writing.

I am gradually working my way through the proofs.[144] Do you go to Kiedrich this time? How restored you will be when you come back! By the way, Miss Dowie (Mrs Norman) author of *Gallia, The Girl in the Carpathians*,[145] etc. – has come to Shaftesbury on my recommendation of the bracing air.[146] I think it will become a health resort some day.

Ever yours
T.H.

30.   Max Gate,
                                             Dorchester.
                                             10 Nov. 1895
My dear friend: I think I am pretty sure to be in Town by Thursday: so that I could lunch on that day, or Friday or

142. Mrs Henniker's short story (included in *In Scarlet and Grey*, 1896). See p. 211 for 'the Vicar'.

143. Anthony Hope's novel *The God in the Car* was published in 1894. He is best remembered for his 'Ruritanian' romances, *The Prisoner of Zenda* (1894) and *Rupert of Hentzau* (1898).

144. For the Wessex Novels series. At this time he was working on *The Woodlanders*.

145. These novels by Ménie Muriel Dowie were published in 1895 and 1891 respectively.

146. Hardy describes the air as 'medicinal' in *Jude the Obscure* IV i, where Shaftesbury is 'Shaston'.

Saturday – just as may suit you. Perhaps, too, I might call and have a little talk with you some afternoon before I return?

My hesitating to send *Jude*[147] was not because I thought you narrow – but because I had rather bored you with him during the writing of some of the story, or thought I had.

I am rather indifferent about his reception by the public: and you may, *of course,* criticize quite freely without offending me. Though not a novel with a purpose, I think it turns out to be a novel which 'makes for' humanity[148] – more than any other I have written: an opinion that will probably surprise you. I suppose I have missed the mark in the pig-killing scene the papers are making such a fuss about: I fully expected that, though described in that particular place for the purely artistic reason of bringing out A[rabella]'s character, it might serve a humane end in showing people the cruelty that goes on unheeded under the barbarous *régime* we call civilization.

It is curious that some papers consider the story a sort of manifesto on the marriage question, though it is really one about two persons who, by a hereditary curse of temperament, peculiar to their family, are rendered unfit for marriage, or think they are. The tragedy is really addressed to those into whose souls the iron of adversity has deeply entered at some time of their lives, and can hardly be congenial to self-indulgent persons of ease and affluence.[149] Indeed, there is something *bizarre* in the tragedy of *Jude* coming out as the last fashionable novel. But one cannot choose one's readers. I think you will admit that, if the story had to be told, it c[oul]d not be told with more reticence.

147. The novel appeared on 1 November 1895, the eighth in the Wessex Novels edition.

148. The word 'morality' has been crossed out. Some of the arguments stated here are repeated in three letters to Edmund Gosse (*Life,* pp. 271–3). In the third, written on 4 January 1896, Hardy says that he is certain of only one thing about the novel, that it 'makes for morality'. In the second he is much more explicit about the marital relationship of Sue and Jude than he dared to be in the novel. The following July, he wrote that *Jude* 'makes for morality' more than any other book he had written (*Life,* p. 280).

149. The reader interested in Hardy's style may wish to note how he improved on this sentence by adopting a second biblical expression in the preface which he wrote for *A Laodicean* in January 1896.

It is a gale of rain here today, and I am staying indoors as head-nurse to Em who, I am sorry to say, has a bad swollen face, neuralgia, etc.

Let me know when you go back to London. I send some of the names[150] you ask for.

Ever yours sincerely
T.H.

p. 95.

'Eulogist of Shakespeare'	Ben Jonson
'passed into silence'	R. Browning.
'musical one'	Swinburne
'enthusiast, poet, and formularist'	Newman, Keble and Pusey
'rake, reasoner, and sceptic'	Bolingbroke
'civil to Christianity, etc'	Gibbon

p. 96.

'apologized for Church in Latin'	can't remember!
'Evening Hymn'	Bishop Ken
'itinerant preacher'	Wesley

p. 97.

'Home of lost causes'	M. Arnold.
'corn law convert'	Peel
'Chap[ter] on Xty'	Gibbon
'last of optimists'	Browning
'Apologia'	Newman
'no polemic'	Keble
'Spectator'	Addison
'prelate'	Ken.

31.

Max Gate,
Dorchester.
Nov. 30, 1895

My dear friend:

I will keep next Friday (2 o'clock?) for lunching with you, with the greatest pleasure. How pleasant it will be to see you in

150. The key provided explains the allusions in II i of *Jude the Obscure* to the scholars, saints, and statesmen Jude associated with Christminster (Oxford).

your own house[151] – which I have never been inside, though I know exactly where it stands. You, too, have never been inside mine: I hope that will not continue to be the case. I think I am sure to be in Town Thursday also: – will you be at home at any time of the afternoon if I call? If not then, perhaps you will be accessible at some other hour or day.

I feel I want to look at some pictures. Sir G. Douglas, who was staying here a day or two, earlier in the month, wants me to go to the N[ational] Gallery to see one that has been cleaned and re-hung, which has much impressed him.[152]

Letters about *Jude* continue to flow in – among them a long one from L[ad]y Londonderry[153] this morning, and one from Mrs Craigie.[154] The latter had a fearfully rough crossing: she expects to be back in England by New Year's Day. A young German lady whom I know also writes this week – with, of course, a foreigner's complete unconsciousness of any impropriety in the book: indeed the only people who faint and blush over it are fast men at clubs, so far as I can see.

I am not reading anything new just now. Please keep well. I have a most original place to recommend you to go and stay at when unwell: but I shall not tell its name till I see you.

Ever yours sinc[erel]y
T.H.

151. The Hennikers had moved to Sloane Gardens (cf. p. 51).

152. Hardy's interest in painting was such that during the period in London when he was working for the architect Arthur Blomfield he spent twenty minutes each day the National Gallery was open, for several months, studying a single master only on each visit. For the influence of painting, general and specific, on Hardy's works, see Pinion, pp. 193–200.

153. Lady Londonderry is first mentioned in Hardy's *Life* with reference to London visits in 1893. He says that she is a beautiful woman still, and that she remained his friend 'through the ensuing years'. He last saw her in 1918 (*Life*, pp. 257, 386). She was the mother of Lady Ilchester, to whom there are several references in later letters to Mrs Henniker.

154. For Mrs Craigie, see p. 1. She had been divorced, and admired the way Hardy had dealt with the marriage question in *Jude the Obscure* (which she ranked with Michelangelo's 'Last Judgment').

155. The reviewer declared that there was probably no novel dealing with 'the closer relations of men and women that was quite so free from lasciviousness as this'.

32.   Max Gate,
                                                    Dorchester.
                                                      11.2.96
My dear friend: I am sending a copy of *The Saturday
Rev[ie]w*[155] – though I don't suppose you will care to read a
word in favour of poor *Jude*. It was thoughtful of you to send
me that nice little letter. I suppose that from today forward
you will be frequenting the gallery of the House?[156] If all is
well I go to London again next Monday morning the 17th to
stay at Harley Street as before. Em was going there with me –
but she is unwell, I am sorry to say, so perhaps I shall go
alone. I shall have nothing to do, so far as I know, Monday
afternoon, and could call on you.[157]

Today I had a cablegram (illegitimate word!) from Harpers
of New York, asking me to send off the play[158] to them immediately. Said play is in possession of Sir F. Jeune at the
present moment, who keeps it locked in his dispatch box.
T.H. wires to Osgood, McIlvaine and Co to go to Lady J[eune]
and get her to get the key of dispatch box, deliver up play,
wh[ich] they are to mail to N[ew] Y[ork] instantly. Query – has
all this been done in time?

I don't myself believe that anything will come of it; although I tell you all this, and though a popular Mrs Fiske, a
lovely American (I am told) is wild to play the title part.

I forgot to tell you that I did not ask Mrs B. to give me that
particular seat at the lecture – I did not know where I was to
be. I thought you –

                         Yours ever sincerely
                              Tom H.

156. It can be assumed that her brother, now Earl of Crewe, was not
absent from the House of Lords, although he did not enter seriously
into politics until 1899. He was leader of the Liberals in the House
from 1908, and later Leader of the House.

157. It was on Sunday, 2 February 1896, that Hardy called on the
Hennikers, and Mrs Henniker's husband, now a major, told the story
against himself which is quoted in Preface 1 (p. xvi).

158. Hardy's dramatization of *Tess of the d'Urbervilles*, prepared
some time in 1894–5, was sent to Harper and Brothers, his New York
publishers, who acted as agents for its production. The play was considerably modified by Lorimer Stoddard and eventually produced
with Mrs Fiske as Tess at the Fifth Avenue Theatre, New York. Meanwhile Mrs Patrick Campbell had been disappointed at its not being
produced in London. There was a reading of the text at St James's
Theatre, London, to protect Hardy's copyright (see later, p. 62).

33.   16, Pelham Crescent,
                                             South Kensington.
                                             June 1, 1896

My dear friend: I am glad to get your little note. I was just
thinking of sending out one on a voyage of discovery, not
knowing where you were.

I returned from Dorset last Wedn[esda]y, and before leaving packed up and sent off a few books for the Crewe bazaar,
which you will find awaiting you at Sloane G[ar]d[e]ns. You
will say they are the sweepings of my study. – I much wish I
could have sent some copies of the new edition.[159]

I think I may say I am now quite well – the two or three days
at Max Gate, where the air is extraordinarily dry, effected a
cure which Brighton failed in.[160] It would set you up when
you are languid, I am sure, and we hope you will try it some
day – though there w[oul]d be not a soul for you to speak to
except ourselves.

I fancy it was the same malignant quality in the air of London that pulled down both Major Henniker and myself. I am
very sorry that his illness sh[oul]d have been so serious as it
evidently was.

We are going out this week, for the first time in the evening
for nearly two months, to one or two places. I met Lady
Fitzg[eral]d at a little party at Lady Queensberry's one afternoon.

I congratulate you on getting 'A Brand of Discord' accepted.
The title is rather good. Shorter, Clodd, G. Douglas,[161] and 2
or 3 other Bohemians are coming here to tea to-morrow. I wish
you could also. Can you come on the afternoon of the 11th –
next Thursday week? – try to if you can. Lionel Johnson,[162]
Douglas, a great American authoress who is a total stranger to
us, etc., are coming then. You will perceive how very small are
the functions we attempt this season.

159. Hardy had completed the revision of the first thirteen volumes
of the Wessex Novels.

160. The spring had been damp, and Hardy suffered from 'a rheu-
matic attack' for several days, with a relapse in May. On his doctor's
advice, he had gone to Brighton with Mrs Hardy (*Life*, p. 276).

161. For Douglas, Clodd and Shorter, respectively, see pp. 10, 23, 36.

162. Lionel Johnson (1867–1902), poet and critic, had written *The
Art of Thomas Hardy* (1894), a series of essays which contain some fine
assessments of Hardy's fiction.

The unexpected result of *Jude* is that I am overwhelmed with requests for stories to an extent that I have never before experienced – though I imagined before publishing it that it w[oul]d considerably lower my commercial value. By the way, I have been offended with you for some time, though I have forgotten to say so, for what you said – that I was an advocate for 'free love'. I hold no theory whatever on the subject, – except by way of experimental remarks at tea parties, and seriously I don't see any possible scheme for the union of the sexes that w[oul]d be satisfactory.

I have been asked to stand as Liberal Candidate for the Lord Rectorship of Glasgow University: they have asked me twice, but I have declined.[163] I will come to see you Sunday. But perhaps you will let me know that you have really returned, or are returning.

Ever sincerely yours

Tho. H.

Remembrances to Miss Thornhills.[164]

P.S.   I don't think much of Platt,[165] from what I have seen of his writing: mere sexuality without any counterpoise. I am now reading the *Life of J. A. Symonds*[166] – There is a feeble attack on *Jude* in this month's *Fortnightly*.[167] How much better I c[oul]d cut it up myself!

T.H.

34.   Hôtel Mohren,

Liège,

Belgium.

Sept. 24, 1896

My dear little friend: I have been wandering about over here since I last wrote, and have not stayed at any one place long

---

163. Hardy's reply is given in his *Life*, pp. 276–7.

164. This should be read 'the Miss Thornhills' (see letter 48). In a letter from the Savile Club, written 5 February 1896, Hardy told his wife that the Miss Thornhills were returning to Brighton in two or three weeks (Weber, p. 38).

165. Possibly William Platt, author of *Women, Love and Life* (1895), *Youth's Love-Lore* (1896), and *De we Live, do we Love?* (1896).

166. By H. R. F. Brown (1895).   167. By Robert Yelverton Tyrrell.

enough to give it as an address. After crossing to Ostend, where we stayed observing its frivolities a few days, we went on to Bruges – a bygone, melancholy interesting town, as you probably know from experience – and thence to Brussels and to Dinant, on the Meuse. There I made the acquaintance of a veritable gambler – who was staying at our hotel – and for the first time really perceived what it is to be possessed of the gaming fever. He won largely at the tables yesterday, before dinner, and at dinner time I persuaded him to leave off; but he would not, and returned to the rooms in the evening. I saw him this morning looking wild, and he said he had lost everything, except enough to pay his fare to England. The curious thing is that he fully believes in his ultimate success by means of a system, and is going to Monte Carlo in November to retrieve all his losses! [168]

The 'Grasshopper' (bicycle), which has accompanied us, has been the source of extraordinary alarms, (and expenses!) It disappears unexpectedly on the railway journeys, and turns up again just as unexpectedly – its discoverer exclaiming 'V'la le *veloze* de Madame! '[169]

I should so much have liked to go through with you some of the churches etc., that I have seen. I have mostly kept away from the fashionable hotels – life is so much easier among the natives than where the English and Americans are.

Much admiration has been expressed for the mediaeval brick architecture of Belgium, but after Bruges I craved the sight of a *stone* building again.[170]

This city is a sort of Belgian Sheffield, and, though pictur-esque, is entirely given over to manufacture. In a day or two I shall reach Brussels again, where my address (till about a week hence, or more) will be

Hôtel de la Poste
Rue Fossé aux Loups 28.

(If you should write put *M*^r)

168. Hardy had clearly been interested in the subject of gambling before he wrote *A Laodicean*. His interest in this particular gambler is shown in the detailed notes which he made (*Life*, pp. 282–3.

169. This happened at Liège (*Life*, p. 283).

170. His preference for stone was vigorously expressed: 'the ashlar back-yards of Bath had more dignity than any brick front in Europe' (*Life*, p. 282).

E's shoulder, where the bicyclist ran into her, is practically well, though she occasionally feels twinges. There is a man staying at this hotel just like L[or]d Salisbury. I hope the sea has made you strong and well – and that you are not killing yourself with literary labours. It is 20 years since I was last in this part of Europe, and the reflection is rather saddening. I ask myself, why am I here again, and not underground.[171] The chimes are playing 10 o'c[lock].

Ever y[ou]rs
Tom H.

35.   Max Gate,
                                             Dorchester.
                                             Oct. 12. 1896

You see I am here again at last, having arrived from Dover Thursday night, after crossing from Ostend Wednesday between two gales; though there was quite enough wind in the interim to be pleasant. I received your card at Brussels as you hoped, and was glad to find your nice letter awaiting me here. The eight weeks of nearly continual movement has been upon the whole an agreeable and instructive time – the English half[172] of it perhaps more so than the foreign one.

---

171. Hardy was preparing to write *The Dynasts*. At the beginning of October he was in Brussels searching for the scene of the eve of battle ball and visiting the field of Waterloo, as his *Life* and *A Laodicean* show he had done over twenty years previously. He and Mrs Hardy had travelled much in 1896, both in England and abroad; but the disparity between Hardy's inner and outer life was great. In September he had written opposite the lines in Arnold's 'Dover Beach', 'Ah, love, let us be true/To one another ...', 'Sept. 1896 – T.H./E.L.H.'. Some time during the year he had written in the thinly disguised autobiography of 'The Dead Man Walking'

And when my Love's heart kindled
In hate of me.

It was the year he wrote the third of the poems 'In Tenebris', in which he wishes he had died in childhood.

172. Before travelling to Belgium, the Hardys had been to Malvern, Worcester, Warwick and Kenilworth, Stratford-on-Avon, Reading, and Dover, where they stayed about a fortnight and Hardy read *King Lear* (*Life*, pp. 281–2).

I agree with you in your liking for Holland. It was by the
merest chance that it was not included in our itinerary. The
Hague pictures I well remember years ago,[173] but I have never
seen the Amsterdam ones. What strikes me in foreign galleries is that (excepting such as the Louvre and the Florence
galleries) they seldom contain such a proportion of the *finest*
works of the best masters as our National Gallery does, and
they always make me feel what slight excuse there is for
neglecting such an incomparable selection. The names of
foreign painters that have scarcely reached England – for no
unworthiness in the works – strike one curiously, and are, as
you say, too numerous.

My own attention has been this time given mostly to Mem-
ling, Pourbus, and Rubens.

I have lost sight of nearly all the periodicals lately, and have
not yet seen the new *Saturday*. I am delighted that your
recent reviews have been good. 1,000 copies' sale makes, I
believe, what publishers consider a success; so you have
achieved it.[174]

Merriman's *Sowers*[175] I dipped into last summer, and saw
that there was something in it. *Flotsam* I read only the end of,
in *Longman's*: so if I do not quite reach your level of enthusiasm for the writer as yet, it may be from want of knowledge.

Before leaving Brussels I strolled quite alone over the Field
of Waterloo.[176] Only shepherds and ploughmen were there.[177]
I liked Spa, and found Brussels amazingly bustling and noisy
for its size. E. could not bike there at all. The machine has
reached home undamaged.

You will have heard of the deaths of Du Maurier[178] and the

173. From his visit in 1876 (*Life*, p. 110).

174. *In Scarlet and Grey* (tales) was published in 1896.

175. Hugh Stowell Scott (1862–1903) wrote under the pseudonym of
Hugh Seton Merriman. His novel *The Sowers* was published in 1896.
Another of his novels, *Flotsam*, concluded its serial appearance in
Longman's Magazine in 1896.

176. This was Hardy's third visit. The first took place on his honeymoon in 1874; see Evelyn Hardy, 'Emma Hardy's Diaries, Some Fore-
shadowings of *The Dynasts*', *English*, XIV, Spring 1962.

177. See *Life*, p. 284.

178. George du Maurier, author and illustrator of *Trilby* (1894), had
done the illustrations for Hardy's *The Hand of Ethelberta* and *A
Laodicean*, both serial and volume issues.

D

A[rch]b[isho]p of Canterbury, and of L[or]d Rosebery's resignation.[179] I think he may feel as I do, that on the American question[180] a theological policy must not be allowed to assume the disguise of a humanitarian one. I must run up to see you when you return, and shall be glad to have one or two of the photos.

Ever your sincere friend
Tho. H.

36.   Max Gate,
                                           Dorchester.
                                           Nov. 8. 1896

I have received your note this morning. But don't you know that I called on you last week when I was in London? – last Tuesday the 3rd, the day of my arrival, at a little past 5, to know if you had returned from Eltville, and, if you had, to give you a pleasant surprise. But your servant said you were not at home, and I left two cards with my London address on them.

I am glad to hear that your stories are selling well. The Jeunes are surprised at the unfounded attacks on me that the volume is made the vehicle of. She read 'The Spectre', and Sir F. read it, and neither could discover the impropriety reiterated by the pure-minded reviewers – bless their prurient hearts! But you must keep better literary company in future[181] than is

Your sincere friend
T.H.

37.   Max Gate,
                                           Dorchester.
                                           Nov. 29. 1896

My dear friend: I am busy too, but not in such an attractive way as you seem to be, with 'many letters and interests'. But

179. From the leadership of the Liberal Party.
180. As a result of frontier differences between Venezuela and British Guiana, the Monroe Doctrine had been invoked.
181. See the note on p. 33.

London, as I know, necessitates endless notes and engagements, which one escapes down here, with a loss of pleasure, and a gain of melancholy repose.

It did not occur to me that my story – or sketch[182] – was a sad one. The marriage w[oul]d have resulted in unhappiness for certain, don't you think?

I have not yet seen y[ou]r Xmas story.[183]

With respect to 'Hymns that have helped' I *did* say I liked, or had liked formerly, those I mentioned. Only I had never found any help from them in the sense intended. Stead[184] ought to have drawn a distinction between those people who had merely liked particular hymns, and those who had really been assisted in life by them – if anybody ever was. I think the word 'soothed' should have been used instead of 'helped'.

I am glad you have seen the T.P.s.[185] I got to like Mrs T.P. very much last summer. I had never known her so well before.

This January weather makes writing irksome: one wants to be continually moving about. I wonder if you went to, or are going to, the Ibsen play?[186] It is a page of real life, undoubtedly, and you sh[oul]d see it. But you have changed, I remember, from what you were 3 years and more ago, when you went with me!

I shall look for y[ou]r sketch in the *Speaker,* which I see, though I have left off taking it in. I find the *Saturday Review* brighter in its literary criticisms, and more amusing in its dramatic ones, than any other weekly that I come across just

182. 'A Committee Man of "The Terror" ', which appeared in *The Illustrated London News,* 22 November 1896.

183. 'At the Crossing' appeared in *The Speaker,* 19 December 1896.

184. Hardy's reply to W. T. Stead, editor of *The Review of Reviews* (*Life,* pp. 274–5) was not printed with other replies. His choices –

'Thou turnest man, O Lord, to dust',
'Awake, my soul, and with the sun,'
'Lead, kindly light'

– were merely listed in Stead's *Hymns That Have Helped,* 1896 (Purdy, p. 269).

185. The Rev. T. Perkins and his wife, of Turnworth. Dorset. The rector's 'staunch support of the principle of justice for animals' (*Life,* p. 333) endeared him to the Hardys and Mrs Henniker.

186. *Little Eyolf,* at the Avenue Theatre, London.

now. I have a 'tradition'[187] in its Christmas supplement – quite short. Something like it occurred in my mother's family, who, from time immemorial down to 100–150 years ago, were yeomen in this county farming their own land[188] – which now belongs to L[or]d Ilchester.

Aff[ectionate]ly y[ou]r friend
Tom H.

38.   Dec. 6. 96[189]

Many thanks for your little 'Brand of Discord' which I have read; and like everything about it except the title. It is as good as anything you have done, and resembles rather the work of an experienced writer than of a novice.

T.H.

39.   Max Gate,
Dorchester.
Dec. 30. 1896

My dear friend: I ought to have acknowledged receiving your Xmas card and kind letters before this – (which, considering how busy you always are, I don't deserve) but I too have been hard pressed in sending off the copy of *The Well-Beloved* to the printers[190] – which owing to the necessity of setting up the

187. The tradition relates to the Duke of Monmouth after the battle of Sedgemoor and the Swetman family, from whom Hardy's mother was descended. They lived at Melbury Osmund, north of Melbury Park and House, the home of the Earl of Ilchester. See *Life*, p. 6, and 'The Duke's Reappearance' in *A Changed Man*.

188. The decline of the Hardy family and other local families is associated with one aspect of the *Tess of the d'Urbervilles* story. See the end of chapter XIX of the novel, *Life*, pp. 214–15, and letter 99.

189. A postcard. See p. 51 for another view on the title.

190. Hardy revised the serial edition of *The Well-Beloved*, which appeared in 1892, improving the conclusion very considerably. The preface and the next letter indicate that he did not send the revised text to the publishers until the end of January 1897. It formed the seventeenth volume of the Wessex Novels.

type in America also, has, as you know, to be dispatched early from England.

I am so sorry to hear that you have felt overstrained. I have been all right in health, and have had a Christmas of the dull kind which contents so-called 'pessimists' like me – in its freedom from positive sorrows. An old choir of waits, however, came from a village a few nights ago, and sang to us the same carols that used to be sung by the 'Mellstock' Choir – (the characters that I like best in my own novels.)[191]

It must be a pleasant change for you to get to Crewe, but I suppose you will soon return to the social distractions of London. I have lately grown to feel that I should not much care if I never set eyes on London again.

Mrs Sheridan,[192] whom I have seen two or three times lately, agrees with me in being thankful for negative Christmases. I also have seen Sophy – now Mrs Walker. Agnes Grove[193] has another article about to appear – did she tell you?

It rains in torrents this afternoon. Anything, however, is better than a snowy Christmas. I wonder if you are interested as much as I am in the Peterborough Cath[edra]l restorations? Nobody but those who have had to carry them out knows the difficulties of such problems – whether to preserve the venerable *lines*, or the venerable *substance*, when you cannot do both. I am glad that I saw the west front intact when returning from the north about 4 years ago.[194]

Forgive an uninteresting letter, and, wishing you a happy New Year, I am,

Ever sincerely yours,
Tho. H.

191. See not only *Under the Greenwood Tree* but the poems 'The Dead Quire', 'The Paphian Ball', 'The Rash Bride'.
192. Mrs Brinsley Sheridan of Frampton Court near Dorchester. When she died in 1918, Hardy wrote that she had remained a staunch friend for thirty-two years; he thought she was the first neighbour to call at Max Gate (*Life*, p. 383).
193. Lady Grove (1864–1926), the daughter of General Pitt-Rivers (p. 43). She married Sir Walter J. Grove, Baronet, in 1882, and was the writer of many articles.
194. In the autumn of 1891, Hardy visited Durham, York and Peterborough. Here he was interested in the verger's story of two bodies, one of a maid of honour to Catherine of Aragon and the other of 'a woman of various ages' (*Life*, p. 239).

40.   Max Gate,
                                              Dorchester.
                                       Sunday, Jan 24, '97

My dear friend:

I have to-day finished the correction of the little sketch or
story of *The Well-Beloved* (which is to come out I believe next
month, and might come out now but for America): [195] and I
must now answer your nice last letter. I am so sorry the weather
has given you the toothache. I *wish* I could suggest some remedy: but I am such a hopeless doctor. During this very cold
time I have been free from aches (our air is so dry and fogless –
you ought to live down this way 6 months out of the 12). I hate
the frost nevertheless – it makes my fingers slippery as glass, so
that I can hardly hold a pen firmly. I believe you have had
much snow; we have had only the merest sprinkle which soon
disappeared.

I am glad that you enjoyed your visit to L[or]d Winchester's.[196] I don't know the present Digbys, though I knew the
late Lady D. and know her daughter Lady Ashburton. She
was a nice neighbour while living near here a short while. But
the ordinary Dorset landowners only tolerate an author; they
do not associate with him (especially when he is such a fearful
wild fowl[197] as this misunderstood man is supposed to be).
Writing this recalls to my mind Lady Waldegrave's[198] answer
to Browning, when he proposed to her. 'We dine our poets, Mr
Browning, but we do not marry them.' *Mutatis mutandis,*
that's the spirit down here – much intensified of course.

I do remember taking in Lady Evelyn Ewart to dinner

195. It was published (after a delay caused by an unexpected demand
for it) on 16 March 1897. The American edition appeared at the end of
March.

196. His residence was near Andover, Hants.

197. Hardy discovered after the publication of *Jude the Obscure* that
the local gentry had 'a pathetic reverence for press opinions' (*Life*,
p. 276). The phrase here used from *A Midsummer Night's Dream* is a
reminder of Hardy's numerous Shakespearian quotations and allusions.
The Digby family resided at Minterne House, Dorset.

198. Lady Waldegrave (1821–79) married her fourth husband,
Chichester Fortescue, Chief Secretary for Ireland, in 1863, after inheriting the Waldegrave estates. She transformed Strawberry Hill,
which had belonged to Horace Walpole, into a social centre for guests
belonging to the Liberal Party.

somewhere – possibly at Lady Wimborne's[199] house in London.

I am going to read Mrs Steel's novel,[200] and, in fact, lots of books soon. The Byrons seem to object to the publication of more of Lord Byron's letters: just as if any possible revelation could affect his character at this time of day!

I have been thinking that of all men dead whom I should like to meet in the Elysian fields I would choose Shelley,[201] not only for his unearthly, weird, wild appearance and genius, but for his genuineness, earnestness, and enthusiasms on behalf of the oppressed.

Ever y[ou]rs aff[ectionate]ly,

Tho. H.

41.   Max Gate,
                                                         Dorchester.
                                                     Feb. 19, 1897

My dear friend:

I am much obliged for the *Author's year book*, which is interesting: though the addresses of authors are of no use to anybody, I sh[oul]d think, but publishers and begging letter writers. The sketches in pen and pencil, including that of yourself, are a more agreeable feature than the addresses of so many poor wretches. I don't know how the editor got mine.

I have thought over your request about Zola. I would not mind asking him, even though I don't know him, if I did not feel certain that the person to do so must not be another novelist. I am trying to think of somebody. If Henry James were not a novelist also he w[oul]d be the man; but he is likely to know some personal friend of Zola, and you might therefore sound him on the matter.[202]

---

199. The Hardy's attended a ball at Lady Wimborne's, Canford Manor, at the end of 1881, when they were living at Wimborne.

200. *On the Face of the Waters* (1896) by Flora Annie Steel.

201. See note 44, p. 14.

202. Emma Hardy did not want her husband's name to be associated with Zola's even on the subject of vivisection. It looks as if she had made her views clear, for on the day Hardy wrote the above she wrote to Rebekah Owen, saying that she did not wish him to be 'hand in glove' with Zola.

I shall try some day to be on the Committee of some Animals' Society: but I have not enough money yet.

You disappointed us by not coming: but of course you could not.

I am bothered by having to get up a 'copyright' perform-ance of *Tess*[203] – a business I hate: but it must be done, to secure the rights of a play based on the novel which they are bringing out in America.

I hope you will get on with your 1 vol. story[204] now, and that the Bournemouth week invigorated you.

Ever sincerely y[ou]rs,
Tho. H.

42.   Max Gate,
                                      Dorchester.

4. 3. 97

My dear friend:

I left London before your little note reached me, which I have therefore only received to-day. Many thanks for sending it. I might have stayed a day or two longer, but I had got rather tired, and the weather was bad.

I am so grieved that you have been bearing pain. I did not once think you were unwell till just before I left Harley St. They[205] told me you might possibly have come to lunch if you had not had a cold. It was too late for me then to write a line.

Driving up Regent St[reet] in the rain one day, and looking at the tyranny of the strong over the weak I met an electric omnibus, and it seemed a joyful presage of the future. Believe me

Ever y[ou]r affec[tiona]te friend
Tho H.

203. See note 158, p. 50.   204. *Sowing the Sand* (1898).
205. The Jeunes.

43.   Max Gate,
                                                  Dorchester.
                                              March 31. 1897

My dear friend:

I send some amusing paragraphs anent the personation of *Tess* in New York by Mrs Fiske, of which perhaps you have heard.

I should have replied to your last nice note sooner than this if I had not been so worried. Among other things my poor little innocent book *The Well-Beloved* has had a horrid stab delivered it in one quarter, *The World,* which is as unaccountable as it is base.[206] You will imagine how it amazed me when one of my reasons for letting the story be reprinted was that it c[oul]d not by any possibility offend Mrs or Mr Grundy, or their Young Persons, even though it c[oul]d be called unreal and impossible for a man to have such an artistic craze for the Ideal in woman as the hero has. It is truly the unexpected that happens.

I have read *Hellas*[207] many times. What an embroglio we shall get into about Greece. We – or rather Em – had an anti-vivisection meeting in our drawing-room last week. You mistake in supposing I admire Zola. It is just what I don't do. I think him no artist, and too material. I feel that the animal side of human nature should never be dwelt on except as a contrast or foil to its spiritual side.[208]

                                              Ever your friend
                                                  Tom H.

I have just had a nice letter from Pearl Craigie. Tell me if you are quite well now.

206. Hardy was 'surprised' and 'grieved' by this 'ferocious review'. For an exposure of critical misinterpretation, Hardy's *Life* (pp. 285–7) deserves close reading.

207. Shelley's poetic drama was published in 1822. Hardy quoted from it in his preface to *The Dynasts* ('Riddles of death ...') and in his *Life* (p. 383).

208. Hardy could not have written this without thinking of *Jude the Obscure.*

44.   Max Gate,
                                           Dorchester.
                                           April 27, 1897
My dear friend:

I was in London last week, and I meant to find out if you
had returned or were about to return from Brighton, but some
things intervened, and I did not get to Sloane Gardens. You
would probably have let me know if you had, however.

We are in doubt about taking a house in London this
season, the one we have had in former years having been let,
though I have seen another which might do.[209]

The Well-Beloved is selling remarkably well for a book
written so many years ago (except the three or four last chapters). I wonder if you are getting on with your novel? What
is it about, though perhaps that is a secret. I have not read
anything lately except old books. I hear from America that the
Tess play is a great success, but I really know very little about
it, and dread having to go into the question of its coming to
England, my interest in the theatre, which was never very
strong, having nearly died out.

                          Ever your affec[tiona]te friend
                                  Tom H.

This is only a note to find out where you are.

                                  T.

45.   Savile Club,
                                           107, Piccadilly. W.
                                           Tuesday. 1 o'c[210]
My dear friend: I am much disappointed at y[ou]r not having
a spare moment till Thursday evening, as it again prevents my
seeing you, for though I have been keeping all to-day and to-
morrow for you I have to leave Thursday morning. But I
ought to have considered the demands there must be upon
y[ou]r time during the London season, and have given you
longer notice of my request. Hoping I may be more fortunate
next time I am
                          Ever y[ou]r affect[ionat]e friend
                                  Tom H.

209. They stayed in London for two or three weeks, and then decided
to travel in from Basingstoke (*Life*, p. 292).
210. The year of this note is uncertain.

46.   Gd. Hôtel de la Paix,
                                                    Genève.
                                              3 June 1897[211]

My dear friend: I have received your nice letter, and am
inclined to think you *rather* good, for very few women so
busy, and unwell to (*sic*), w[oul]d have so promptly replied
to my dull note. We have gone hither and thither, to the top
of the Wengen Alp facing the Jungfrau, among other
places, also to Interlaken, Zermatt, Thun, etc. etc., and have
not felt inconvenienced greatly by the heat till within the
last 2 or 3 days. Here it is like a melon-frame, and we shall
soon clear out to move homeward.

At Zermatt I saw the exact place where the tragedy
occurred on the Matterhorn in wh[ich] Whymper[212] was the
only Englishman saved. Yet it is only myself who am pulled
down a little, Em being in excellent health and vigour. I
think you, too, w[oul]d be well here now, since you, like her,
enjoy warmth by the water side.

It is ten years since we were in Switzerland last, and,
strange reverse of what is customary, I have been much
more impressed this time than I was then. The windows
here command a full view of the Lake, and the haunts of
the poets; also of the 'arrowy Rhone' (Byron is literally
true in what he says of 'Lake Leman' (Geneva) in *Childe
Harold*. Yet what is the use of coming to such places for
association's sake? Those who write rapturously about them
from Rousseau onwards care nothing about them *now*.[213]

I am so sorry to hear that Lady Grove has been so ill. I have
not seen her since you and she were at our house last year,

211. The date should be July. The Hardys did not leave for Switzerland until the middle of June, and they reached Geneva after being
in Lausanne (where Hardy sat in Gibbon's garden from 11 to 12 p.m.
on 27 June, exactly 110 years after the historian had completed his
Autobiography there) and staying at Zermatt (*Life*, pp. 293–4).

212. It was while staying with Edward Clodd at Aldeburgh that
Hardy met Edward Whymper, and heard the story of this climbing
tragedy. See *Life*, pp. 264, 294, and 'Zermatt: To the Matterhorn'
(*Poems of the Past and the Present*).

213. The sentiment is found in a note Hardy made at the time:
'These haunts of the illustrious! Ah, but *they* are gone now, and care
for their chosen nooks no more!' (*Life*, p. 295).

and thought she had only had a slight illness, some time ago.

I have no book ready or in hand: of course I should have told *you* if I had.

We think of getting home by the middle of next week, I shall be delighted to read the Chapman's and Cassell's stories you have written. Not only is it untrue that I have a novel ready, but also that I have changed my style, am in doubt about a title, etc. etc. Indeed I have not given a single thought to novels of my own or other peoples (*sic*) since I finished the corrections of *The W[ell-]B[eloved]*.

I wonder if I ever told you that the plot of that story was suggested to me by the remark of a sculptor that he had often pursued a beautiful ear, nose, chin, etc. about London in omnibuses and on foot?

I don't think it can be true that Lady J.[214] writes Belles Lettres in that horrid *World*. She told me some time ago that the woman who then wrote them came to her party one evening, and pointed out her description of it. She told me also the lady's name, but I have forgotten it. She also wrote to me expressing her indignation at the libel of my last book in the *World*:[215] as did also Lady Londonderry – the latter expressing her contempt for the paper.

Please let me hear from you soon after I get home, and tell me where you are.

I thought of going this afternoon to try to find the cottage in which Shelley and Mary lived, a little way below Byron's 'Campagne Diodate' (*vide* Dowden's *Shelley*)[216] but I doubt if I shall.

Ever yours sincerely
Tom H.

E. is actually thinking of hiring a bicycle: I don't feel up to it!

214. It is assumed that this is Lady Jeune.
215. See pp. 29 (note 92) and 63.
216. Edward Dowden, *The Life of Shelley*, London, 1886. The cottage where Shelley and Mary lived in the summer of 1816 was separated by a vineyard from the Villa Diodati, where Byron lived.

47.   Max Gate,
                                             Dorchester.
                                         July 22. 1898[217]

My dear friend:

I had been thinking of you, and curiously enough, looking at a map of Torquay, when your letter came (nicer than
some of them) – though I had not the least suspicion that
you had left London. I have just come back from a bicycle
journey to Bristol, Gloucester, and Cheltenham,[218] so that
we have crossed each other's path lately. It was blazing hot
crossing the Mendips, where we had to push our bicycles 2
miles uphill. This was on Sunday morning, and when we
entered Bristol we were white as millers, and formed a
contrast to the churchgoers, the backs of my hands being
blistered through my having put on no gloves that day. I
went to the afternoon service at Bristol Cath[edra]l – and
next day to the same service at Gloucester – a most interesting building for it was there that the Perpendicular
style was *invented*: you can see how it grew in the old
masons' minds.[219]

Mr John Lane[220] has been here to see me, with a friend.
He came unexpectedly, but we talked of your forthcoming
stories, *he* beginning the subject (a good omen for you!).
He caught the last evening train to London to meet the
lady he is to marry, who was just arriving. I trembled at
the consequences of his missing it, and it was by the merest
chance that he did not.

The name of the American magazine is *The Independent*[221] – 251 Broadway, New York. I will forward the story,

217. There is no reason to think that the correspondence between
Hardy and Mrs Henniker had not been maintained during the past
year.
218. 'Bicycling was ... in full spirit with the Hardys' in the summer
of 1897; in 1898 he cycled 'more vigorously than ever ... sometimes
with Mrs Hardy, sometimes with his brother' (*Life*, p. 298).
219. See note 60, p. 19.
220. The publisher, who accompanied Hardy on several West
Country tours.
221. Hardy had published two stories in this magazine. The first
(1884) was a version of 'The Duchess of Hamptonshire' (*A Group of
Noble Dames*); the second was 'The Doctor's Legend' (1891. See Pinion,
pp. 81–3).

with a letter, if you send it to me.

My thumb is all right now, except that the nail is rather distorted, and the joint a little stiff. I do not take kindly to publishing my stray short stories. They don't seem to me to be worth reprinting: I must get something else ready – not the 'long novel' which the papers persist in announcing. I have two more wheel expeditions in my mind – one to the Jeunes when they come down to Arlington, and another to Exeter Cath[edra]l. But I doubt if I shall feel justified in sparing the time for them.

Your affec[tiona]te friend
Tho. H.

What a pleasant dinner party yours was![222]

48.   Max Gate,
                                 Dorchester.
                              August 12, 1898
My dear friend: I have just written a line to Major Hen-niker[223] to tell him from Em that we have a spare room at his service during the manoeuvres, if it w[oul]d be of any use to him. This is a more airy spot than any hotel in the town, and he could come and go as the duties demanded, just as if he were at a lodging. We are not swell at dinners, but probably that would not affect him. It would be very pleasant if he should come.

I return Mr Lane's letter, which must be provoking enough. Yet he only tells the same story that the publishers all tell – that they cannot make any money out of a 3/6 vol. of short stories, however good they may be, the sale required for a profit of any account being so large. I know you will be angry at what I am going to say; but if I were you I should wait awhile.

I am so sorry to hear about Miss Thornhill's illness: I thought she seemed fairly strong: her sister will I hope be revived by her visit to you. Turgeneff is a true artist, certainly, though it is some years since I read anything of his.

<hr>

222. The Hardys had been in London from April to July.
223. Hardy expected Dorchester to be the centre for Southern Army training.

Stevenson's[224] essays far surpass his stories in my opinion.

What can have been the cause of your suffering so in the head? Poor thing: I quite ached for you when I read of your pains. *Possibly* rheumatism from a draught may have had something to do with it. I get that sometimes. I write this rather in haste, so it is not much.

Ever y[ou]rs sincerely
Tho. H.

49.   Max Gate,
                                                             Dorchester.
                                                             30. Aug. 1898

My dear friend:

I should not have seen the paragraphs you send but for your kindness. The country is very beautiful out there just now, and seems to surprise people who did not know that Dorset had any claim to landscape.

I was going to write yesterday evening, on my return from the camp, to which I had bicycled. But the rain came down in sheets, and I was sodden below the waterproof cape: a head-wind all the way back, and a total ride of 35 miles, left me too tired to do anything.

Lady Audrey Buller[225] has been here: she called Friday, and thinks Max Gate very pretty – She thinks your novels are very literary and finished – quite different from the run of women's novels. She has gone on to the Portman's (*sic*) – close to Blandford[226] – where the Southern Army now is, and as soon as she has seen Sir R[edvers] again is going to send us word where we are to go to see the march

224. Robert Louis Stevenson (1850–94) had been a friend of Hardy's. He was one of the early visitors to Max Gate, and a great admirer of *The Mayor of Casterbridge* (which he thought of dramatizing: *Life*, pp. 179–80). Hardy was hurt to find that Stevenson and Henry James had derived deep satisfaction from privately condemning *Tess of the d'Urbervilles*; to him they were the Osric and Polonius of novelists. (See *Life*, p. 246, and Orel, pp. 149–51, 273–4.)

225. Wife of Sir Redvers Buller (1839–1908). He was made Lieutenant-General in 1894 and Commander-in-Chief at the opening of the Boer War. He was a cousin of Hardy's friend, Lord Carnarvon. In the year of this letter he was in command at Aldershot.

226. Bryanston House near Blandford, the seat of Lord Portman, was completed in Elizabethan style in 1895.

past. I don't know if I shall feel up to it.

I wish you would come down to Salisbury for a day or two, which is the centre of the occupied country[227] for the ensuing week. I would then run up and meet you, and we could go to the Cathedral. If Major Henniker could come too he could witness some of the movements. I am sorry the first intention of making Dorchester the Southern Centre was abandoned; and that he did not put up here, wh[ich] I had been looking forward to for a long time.

I hope you still keep your appetite: as long as one can eat one can do anything: I lost mine about a fortnight ago, and felt quite run down, so that I could not get across to the camp when it was at its best. (I find I have written on two sheets of paper.)

Mr Perkins and Mr Trist came one day. They have started an anti-vivisection van. Miss Beatrice Harraden[228] has also called – (*Ships that pass in the Night*). She is lodging in a farm house near here, finishing a novel. (Everybody seems achieving novels except me.)

You don't say how long you are going to be at Eton.[229] As you are not keeping at home you ought to give Wessex a trial. I will then tell and show you a mysterious occupation I have been amusing myself with lately.

I have not yet been to Exeter, though I had hoped to get there this summer.

Your affect[iona]te friend
Tho. H.

50.   Max Gate,
Dorchester.
Sept 22, 1898

My dear friend:

I wonder if you are still at the address you gave: if not, my letter will no doubt be sent on. I read the reviews of *Sowing the Sand*,[230] and return them herewith. They are

227. For Army manoeuvres.

228. Her novel *Ships that Pass in the Night* was published in 1893.

229. For a few weeks during the summer of 1898, the Hennikers exchanged houses with the Vice-Provost of Eton.

230. Mrs Henniker's latest novel, published in 1898.

not a bit too good for the story, in which there is much (as there always is) which the critics apparently did not see. However, they are highly favourable and encouraging so far as they go.

You have not yet sent me the MS. you spoke of. I am ready to read it at any time with pleasure, though I may be away from home from Saturday next the 24th for 3 days or so, on a visit to Exeter – I mean a wheel trip for the sake of the journey mainly, a cathedral being a pleasant goal for such an outing. Since planning it our neighbour at Athelhampton Hall has asked us to meet Lady Dorothy Nevill[231] at his house where she is about to stay. I shall be sorry to miss her, but fear the weather will change if I postpone the excursion.

The 'mysterious occupation' (which I have now finished) is one you will not have guessed I think. It has been the making of some sketches in possible illustration of some verses of mine which I think now of publishing.[232] I told nobody I was doing the sketches, as I was by no means sure that the attempt w[oul]d come to anything; and my injured thumb (still a little painful at times) made the work still more precarious. At last I decided – a few days ago – to send them up to the publishers. You may have heard me speak of the verses. Some of them have been lying about for many many years – with no thought on my part of publishing them.

I think I told you Mr Perkins and Mr Trist came one

231. Lady Dorothy, daughter of Horatio Walpole, third Earl of Orford, was born in Horace Walpole's house, 11 Berkeley Square. She recollected staying in her youth at Islington House, Puddletown, which belonged to her father; the church with its 'orchestra' of one trombone, a cracked fiddle and an ancient flute, and its melancholy services; and lively rides over heath and gorse commons, often to a delightful old inn, 'The Traveller's Rest' ('The Quiet Woman' of *The Return of the Native*). Such recollections and their interest in Horace Walpole gave her and Hardy much to talk about. He had met her more than once at Lady Jeune's, and enjoyed her quick wit and down-to-earth utterances (cf. p. 99). See the pen portrait of her in Edmund Gosse, *Some Diversions of a Man of Letters*, London, 1919, and *The Reminiscences of Lady Nevill*, edited by her son, Ralph Nevill, London, 1906.

232. *Wessex Poems*, published with Hardy's own illustrations in December 1898. The MS. and original sketches are in the Birmingham City Museum and Art Gallery.

day. Those Americans who used to come here[233] think of taking a house, and 700 acres of shooting (near Coniston, Lancs.) not to shoot over, but *to keep the birds from being shot* – a truly charming intention. I am in up and down spirits: *down* as a rule. Stratf[or]d Place is one of the healthiest spots in London, and will certainly suit you better than the Chelsea district.

Ever y[ou]rs,
Tho. H.

51.   Max Gate,
                                    Dorchester.
                                    Monday. 17.10.98

My dear friend:

You thought your last letter dull, but I am afraid this will be worse, for I am just in the middle of the tedious business of discovering printer's (*sic*) and other blunders in the proofs of these *Wessex Poems*. I am afraid that the paragraphs in the papers have raised expectations which the volume will sadly disappoint. I would readily have told you about the sketches if I had attached any importance to them, or thought they would interest you. I had mentioned them to nobody (except here) before I did to you, and how the paragraph alluding to them got into the papers is a mystery. They are small pen-and-ink drawings – much the

233. Rebekah Owen and her sister Catherine had visited the Hardys and toured various parts of Hardy's country in 1892 and 1893. They were over again exploring in 1895–6. In New York they visited the first dramatic performance of *Tess of the d'Urbervilles*, with Mrs Fiske in the leading role, and Rebekah promptly reported its success to Hardy. By the end of 1897 they had decided to settle in England. They arrived in 1898, hoping to settle near Dorchester. The summer passed, and no suitable house was found. By the end of the year they had decided to live in the Lake District, at Belmount Hall between Ambleside and Hawkshead. As the years passed, Rebekah discovered that Hardy's interest in their friendship had gradually been eroded. The remarkable story of these two admirers of Hardy's work, their efforts to become better acquainted with him, and the bitter eventual disappointment of Rebekah, is told in Weber, *Hardy and the Lady from Madison Square*, Colby College, 1952.

worse from my years of unpractice. You please me by your
caring about them.

The date of the book's appearance will be dictated largely
by the rate at which they get it printed in New York. We
must wait for them so as to publish simultaneously, for
copyright reasons.

All that about myself – I read the *Speaker* story[234] of yours
immediately: and liked it because you ventured on a
strongly tragic situation. The man in the cottage with his
two wives (as they were essentially) made a vivid scene,
which it seemed almost a pity to create for such a short tale:
it would have carried one three times as long.

I wonder if you are settled into your house by this time.
Moving house is (to me) a dreadful experience. No wonder
you feel tired. You will, I think, be stronger up there[235] than
you were in Chelsea. I wish I could afford to have a flat in
that neighbourhood: we tried for one last season, but were
compelled to go to Kensington. I have not been off the
premises to-day; and intend to walk in the dark after
dinner, if it does not rain.

Ever aff[ectionate]ly
Tho. H.

52.   Max Gate,
                                             Dorchester.
                                             13.11.98

My dear friend:

I am living such an uneventful life down here that a
letter from me is not worth your receiving. Beyond some
pleasant bicycle rides – which I keep up to make believe
winter is not hovering round – I have no activities just now.

Certainly I did not despise the story I sent on to the
N[ew] Y[ork] *Independent*. There have been some of yours
which I liked better perhaps; but, as I told the editor, this
one had a moral which was as sound as it was unobtrusive.
Whether he will take it or not will depend upon his supply

234. 'The Lonely House on the Moor', in the October 1st number.
235. In the West End (13 Stratford Place) after Sloane Gardens,
Chelsea.

of short stories at present. No doubt he will write to you direct, as I gave him your address, in case he would prefer doing so.

Do the Jeunes[236] know you have gone so near them? Dorothy Allhusen[237] wants me to come and see her at Stoke Poges in Dec[ember]. If I am in town I shall run down: not otherwise.

I hope you have not lost the MS. of 'The Three Corporals' (it sounds an interesting title) – I sh[oul]d try another magazine with it if you can get it back.

I find there was an article about my books in yesterday's *Academy*. I have no copy, or I would send it on. The *Wessex Poems* are out of my hands, and are waiting for the American issue. I suppose the book will appear the beginning of Dec[ember]. The sketches are *quite* unimportant – as, indeed, are the poems.

I shall pounce down upon you if I run up to town between this time and Christmas. Let me hear if you get a reply from the *Independent*.

Ever yours
Tho H.

53.   Max Gate,
                                  Dorchester.
                                  Jan 1. 1899

My dear friend:

I meant this to reach you as a New Year's greeting, but I am a day late. It will not matter much, for immersed as you probably are in the festivities of the season you will hardly find time to read letters. Nevertheless I wish you a happy New Year, and that all good things may be yours throughout it.

I was pleased to hear that you liked the poems. Your discrimination is real and keen in preferring those you name. I am rather disconcerted by the number of newspaper pens

236. At 79 Harley Street.

237. See p. 31. She lived at Stoke Court, Stoke Poges, Bucks, and had been Hardy's friend from her girlhood (*Life*, pp. 281, 418). (For Hardy's visit to Gray's grave, see *Life*, 303–4.)

the verses have set going when I consider how very long ago some of them were written.[238] You may like to know that Swinburne writes warmly about them, those he names as his special favourites being

> In a Wood
> Friends Beyond
> Her Death and after (*sic*)
> Tranter Sweatley
> The Slow Nature
> The Dance at the Phoenix

I was asked to spend Christmas at Cambridge, and I am told I missed a good time there by not going. But my pleasures are all past, I fear!

Yours ever sincerely
Tho H.

54.

Max Gate,
Dorchester.
30.1.99

My dear friend:

I hope you have got through your visit to Lord Winchester's without being caught by the cold that came last week. I fear it is not over yet, though here we have no frost at present. Frost has always a curious effect upon my mind, for which I can never account fully – that something is imminent of a tragic nature.[239] This week, however, the cheerful sense of coming long days has begun, and of the outdoor possibilities of summer, and I already think of excursions to Cathedrals and Abbeys, with a fine disregard of railway time tables. Having used up all the cathedrals within 80

238. About one-third of the poems are early poems, most of them being written in 1866 when Hardy was in London.

239. The recurrence of frost imagery in Hardy, in association with adversity or tragedy, is remarkable. It occurs in one of his earliest poems, 'Discouragement', in the first 'In Tenebris', and in the tragic scene and outlook of 'The Darkling Thrush', for example. It reinforces tragedy in *Desperate Remedies*, and reaches its fictional climax with the Arctic birds at Flintcomb-Ash in *Tess of the d'Urbervilles*. For Hardy 'the Frost's decree' was synonymous with Shelley's 'sightless tyrants of our fate' (p. 17).

miles or so last year, it becomes difficult to decide on future ones.

The reviews have now pretty nearly had their say about the poems – a very poor say, with a few noteworthy exceptions. I am much obliged to you for telling me what the people thought of them. I did not expect that they w[oul]d provoke any animosity from any journal, but they did,[240] and though I now see the reason why, I did not *fore*see it. Whatever England may not be great in, she is the greatest nation in cant that the world has ever seen.

Your story will I suppose be out in a day or two in the *Idler*. 'Three Corporals' is an excellent title. I have had a most amusing application from a magazine – for photographs of self and *parents,* for reproduction. What will they think of next to do with authors except reading their books! I hardly see how you are to be quiet in London for writing – knowing so many people as you do. Now here one can be quiet in reality – and even here we had the excitement the other day of the gale blowing our ivy down. Why don't you get a sea-side home near here, to come to for some months yearly; then I c[oul]d come and express opinions on your literary doings.

Ever y[ou]rs,
Tho H.

55.   Max Gate,
                                            Dorchester.
My dear friend: 15.2.99

I did not hurry to tell you what I thought of the 'Corporals' – which I read *immediately* – being under the impression that you were busy with social affairs, to the displacement of literary. Had you been a 'woman-writer' struggling with a pen in a Grub street garret, it might have quickened me.

Well: I am glad to say, sincerely, that this tale is the best thing you have done, in my opinion. Strikingly pic-

240. *Wessex Poems* did not excite the critics unduly. Among the adverse comments, it was stated that Hardy's verse was 'immature' and that he was 'unfit for this medium of expression'.

turesque, it seizes hold of one immediately, and I never felt more disappointment in the reading of a tale than when I turned over the leaf and found there was no more. The pity of it lies in that: you have cut it off ruthlessly, when you might have raised a large design on your foundation. To speak of it as a story to *sell* – if you were to carry it on, without letting the gipsy die, and reintroduce that girl of the shooting gallery (who arrests the attention from the first moment of her appearance) it w[oul]d make a good one-vol[ume] story.

But, as a transcript from life the case is different. The sense that you have recklessly thrown away a fine opening upon a mere sketch is absent now you tell me it is mostly true: or even if it is a study of human nature with no aim at story, but at the inconsequence of life. And this leads me to suggest that you write a series of *true* stories of soldier-life – announcing them as such. You are in a position to come across a great many. I do not recollect that anything of the kind has been done of late years. I sh[oul]d limit the chief actors to privates and N.C. officers.

I must have given a wrong impression of the criticisms on the *W[essex] Poems*. I sh[oul]d have said that the reviews were all that c[oul]d be wished (except a few spiteful ones, quite minor,) as friendliness, but that the complaints of pessimism were absurdly conventional, and of the nature of cant. – Did I tell you that I have had an application for leave to set 'At an Inn' to music?[241] You have never noticed that one, by the way. You know I sh[oul]d *not* be sarcastic if I were to drop in and criticize y[ou]r work! Will you go to see the Rembrandts with me if I come to London?

Again congratulating you on 'The 3 C's'.

I am, ever y[our]s,
Tho H.

P.S. I have never met L[or]d Rosebery's daughters,[242] so far

241. No tune for this poem has been discovered, nor can we be absolutely certain that it is to be associated with Mrs Henniker; see note 47, p. xxxv and the note on p. 20.

242. The engagement of Mrs Henniker's brother, Lord Crewe, to Lady Margaret Primrose, second daughter of Lord Rosebery, was announced in February, and they were married in Westminster Abbey in April 1899.

as I recollect, though I know him. What a nice time you
must have had at Crewe.[243]

56.   Max Gate,
                                                 Dorchester.
                                                 13.4.99

My dear friend:

I was going out on a short cycle ride this afternoon, but of
course it rained, and the only thing that happened to
cheer the gloom was the arrival of your letter, which has
just come. I am delighted at the prospect of your getting
one of your stories on the stage, and I should think Mr
McCarthy[244] would be just the person to help you prepare a
dramatic version: he has the skill, and he is likely to deal
fairly in the matter. So close with him at once. The novels
of women authors seem to make good plays. Mrs Burnett's
Woman of Quality[245] for instance, which is running successfully I believe.

I see that Pinero's successful play[246] has been denounced
by the B[isho]p of Wakefield as the most immoral play of
the century. As the late B[isho]p burnt my *Jude* because
he thought it the most immoral book of the century (or
something to that effect) it would seem that the air of
Wakefield must have a sort of maddening effect on the
ecclesiastical mind, or why should its bishops run amuck
in this intolerant way?

I did not know that your attack of influenza had been
so severe, and am very sorry it has hung about you so. The

243. The engagement was announced just after the coming-out ball
of Mrs Henniker's niece at Crewe Hall.

244. Justin McCarthy, Irish politician, historian, and novelist (1830–
1912).

245. *A Lady of Quality* (1896) by Mrs Frances Hodgson Burnett
(1849–1924), novelist and dramatist, whose juvenile story *Little Lord
Fauntleroy* has probably outlived its author's name.

246. *The Gay Lord Quex,* a comedy by Sir Arthur Pinero (1899), was
greeted with enthusiasm by Edmund Gosse. He urged Pinero to continue providing comedy as a change from melodrama and farce and
Ibsen (Charteris, p. 260).

sea air is a certain remedy. I had a visitation of the same complaint about a fortnight ago, which has taken away all my energy, and left a slight cough, which I suppose will go. I do not know when we shall go to London: for myself I would rather go into a monastery.

I was going to send y[ou]r brother *Wessex Poems* – but I felt they were so inappropriate for a wedding present that decided I would not. I, too, was surprised that 'At an Inn' was asked for to set to music. I almost rejected it when scraping together the pieces.

Ever yours
Tho H.

57·   Max Gate,
                                             Dorchester.
                                             July 25. 99

My dear friend:

I have been here ever since leaving London, not having felt vigour enough to do anything or go anywhere. But the eye is practically well, though a little weaker than the other as yet. Thank you for remembering about the lotion.[247]

I wonder if you have gone or are going to Westgate[-on-Sea]. We fortunately left London before the great heat set in; but you like a high temperature I know.

I am starting tomorrow if all goes well for a 2 or 3 days bicycle tour in the New Forest – just to make a beginning, for I want to go further later on.[248] I miss the music one can get in London,[249] and the chief objection to a country life is that difficulty of hearing good music when one wishes to – though to be sure at this time of the year there is little enough anywhere.

247. Hardy records (*Life*, p. 304) that this weakness, which never entirely left him, was due to 'influenza', from which he suffered in London this summer.

248. He cycled a great deal with his wife and other companions in the late summer. No details are given in his *Life* except that he never exceeded forty or fifty miles a day.

249. See his notes for concerts at the Imperial Institute (*Life*, pp. 281, 292).

I have just read Tolstoi's *What is Art?*[250] – a suggestive book, in which are a good many true things, and many more that hover round the truth but just miss it – at least as I judge. Two short stories of mine have been appearing in Paris in the *Journal des Débats* – translated by Mlle Rolland.[251] Which of your stories is the play to be based on? And are you filling your inkbottle to set about adapting it? There is room for a good play anywhere just now – the specimens of dramatic art that we see upon the English stage being mediocre to a degree. I find far more interesting forms of art at the music halls. May your name soon appear on the omnibuses beside that of Mrs Allen the Hair-restorer and the Little Liver Pill genius!

Tell me if the galvanism does good: I think the seaside would do more.

Ever yours
Tho. H.

58.   Max Gate,
                                       Dorchester.
                                       13.8.99

I wonder if you have got out of town yet, my dear friend, or if you have stayed on till you go to Westgate. Also what the medical man has been able to do for you. I am as weak as a cat again, and the cause of it I cannot tell, for I have really been doing nothing. I am now going to try some tonics. I think I told you I was going on a short bicycle tour in the New Forest etc.? (*sic*) last month? It only lasted two days, the weather being almost too warm. However I got to Southampton, and went thence to Romsey, Salisbury, and home, ignominiously performing a few miles by train. At South[ampto]n there was an evening concert in the Pavilion on the Pier, and having nothing else to do I went – in

250. Published in 1898, and admired by Bernard Shaw.
251. Mlle. Rolland had already translated *Tess of the d'Urbervilles* into French. In May of this year she sent Hardy a fly-sheet of her translation of 'A Tragedy of Two Ambitions'. She visited Max Gate. and was a devoted friend of Hardy for many years.

knickerbockers – and admired the people in front in evening clothes.

An acquaintance of ours, who used to keep the Grammar
School here, has started a preparatory school at Westgate.
He is an able classic, and if you know anybody who wants
preparing, I think he would do it well. He has not asked me
to recommend him, but I enclose prospectus.

Of course you ought to see Canterbury when you are near
it, if you have never done so. I have been dipping into
Justin McCarthy's *Reminiscences*.[252] The early part of the
book is almost history, and very readable: the latter interesting, but not very substantial. His amiable view of
people might be read as satire, but of course he did not
mean it as such: I mean when he states that he has never
observed certain weaknesses and vices in public men that
have been imputed to them, and then recounts them.

You will remember my saying I had never had any necessity for a dentist? As a judgment, about a fortnight ago a
front tooth came out – absolutely without a flaw in it. – I
have done nothing to remedy it, and do not intend to, but I
begin to fear my dentist-tenant will find a means of taking
out the rest some day. I congratulate Major Henniker on
the cups – what a number![253]

Always yours
Tho H.

59.

Max Gate,
Dorchester.
Aug. 23, 1899

My dear friend:

The little book has come, and I have been reading it in
the garden this morning. Many thanks to you for taking the
trouble to get it and send it to me. I am quite unacquainted
with the name of the compiler, but a certain gentleness of
quality which characterizes the selections leads me to think

252. His *Reminiscences* were published in 1899.
253. Major Henniker excelled in sport: rifle-shooting, fencing,
rackets and tennis, rowing, punting and sculling.

she must be a woman. Anyhow I shall carry the volume in
my pocket as you suggest. It was only the day before yesterday that I carried with me in that way another little book
you gave me long ago – *Ballades & Rondeaux*.[254] This was
on a visit to Mr Perkins at Turnworth Rectory – which is
just a good bicycling distance from here. E. also went, and
we came back the whole way by moonlight reaching home at
12.[255] Mr P. had a thanksgiving evening festival (is that
what they call it?) with potatoes and pumpkins all over the
church – and he asked us to stay to it, which made us late.
There is no railway within miles and miles of the village, so
that one is always tempted to go there.[256]

I had not got so far as to *you* in Mr McCarthy's book
when I last wrote. Yes: he writes very nicely about you; but
then could not help it, you see.[257]

I am grieved to hear about the pain in your eye. To my
disappointment, also, the weakness in my own comes back
at intervals of a few days – a rheum – left by the influenza
I had in London. The sight however, is unaffected. I hope,
most sincerely, that the play will bring profit to you: for
unless you get money by it, it will hardly have been worth
doing. The worst of theatrical labour is that things move so
slowly in connection with them.

Yesterday a representative of the *D[aily] Chronicle* came
here to ask me about Stonehenge. He was on our lawn at
3 p.m. and this morning about $\frac{1}{2}$ past 10 the paper containing the interview was here.[258] The letter announcing his
visit did not reach me till he had gone – altogether a very
quick business – I forgot to say that I have taken one bottle

254. See p. 15.
255. Both the Hardys would enjoy this. Before his cycling days, in
September 1877, Hardy had noted: 'Rapid riding by night – the moon
and the stars racing after, and the trees and fields slipping behind'
(Evelyn Hardy, *Hardy's Notebooks*, p. 51).
256. For Turnworth and Mr Perkins, see the note on p. 57.
257. See the quotation in Preface 1, p. xviii.
258. The article (beginning 'Yesterday I went down to Wessex to
ask Mr. Thomas Hardy what he thought about Stonehenge') was printed
in *The Daily Chronicle*, 24 August 1899, and this seems to indicate an
inaccuracy in the date of Hardy's letter. Stonehenge was for sale, and it
had been rumoured that a wealthy American had made an offer for it.
Hardy supported the view that it should become national property.
The interview is included in Orel, pp. 196–201.

of St Raphael wine – and it has picked me up – or at any rate
I am free from that dreadful langour.

Ever y[our]s sincerely
Tho H.

60.

Max Gate,
Dorchester.
Saturday

My dear friend: as I directed my letter 2 days ago to you at
Lowestoft Villa, I send this line in case the other has mis-
carried. I am glad to know from your note received this morning that you are settling down to practical stagery – I refer to
your getting notes on racing from L[or]d Crewe,[259] which is the
right way, only you must not sink your play in your knowledge.

The D[aily] C[hronicle] asked permission to print that chapter from *Tess*[260] and of course I did not object. It is odd that *I*
sh[oul]d be looked upon as an authority on Stonehenge, when
there are others who know so much more about it – e.g. Lady
Grove's father, Gen[eral] Pitt-Rivers,[261] who has devotedly
crawled among the stones on his hands and knees inspecting
rabbit-holes, etc. You ought to visit the spot, if you never have
done so. Yes, they say that Antrobus[262] is hard up. I told the
D[aily] C[hronicle] reporter that it was rather a misfortune for
a man to inherit a place of that national importance, but he
omitted the remark. I like the little book much.

Ever yours
Tho H.

P.S. I was interested on looking into the list of old books
wanted to purchase, in this morning's publishers Circular, to
find among first ed[itio]ns of Dickens, Fielding, etc., 'Henniker's *Foiled*'.

259. Lord Crewe became a Steward of the Jockey Club in 1899.
260. A 'word picture' of Tess at Stonehenge (from Hardy's novel) was
printed on 25 August 1899.
261. See p. 43.
262. The successor to Sir Edmund Antrobus, who died in April 1899,
and owner of Stonehenge and its neighbourhood.

61.   Arlington Manor,[263]
                                              Newbury.
                                         Sept, 17. 1899

I have just remembered, my dear friend, that on a previous
occasion when I have been staying here, on a Sunday morning
like the present, I wrote to you: and that thought prompts me
to do so now. I hope you reached Glen Dye[264] safely, and are
having good weather. Possibly, however, you are in a Scotch
mist, there being frequent showers here.

I came across the country from Stonehenge on Friday, at
which spot Sir F[rancis] and Lady J[eune] met me by appointment, with their motor-car. We rushed up and down hill –
particularly the latter – at tremendous speed for turnpike-road
travelling, and reached here about 8 – the car having done
about 70 miles that day.

I suppose this unfortunate war with the Boers will come – at
least that is the opinion of Sir Coleridge Grove,[265] who is staying
here, amongst others. Will it affect you at all? – as I see some of
the Coldstr[eam]s are to go.[266] It seems a justification of the
extremest pessimism that at the end of the 19th cent[ur]y we
settle an argument by the sword, just as they w[oul]d have
done in the 19th cent[ur]y B.C.

The *Daily Chronicle* asked me to sign an address of sympathy with M[me] Dreyfus, but I did not, on the ground that
English interference might do harm to her husband's[267] cause,
and w[oul]d do her no good.

M[ary] J[eune] has enquired of me if I know how you are,
and Madeleine[268] wants to call on you when you are at home.
You won't mind my bringing her some day? I return to-

263. The home of Sir Francis and Lady Jeune.
264. A beautiful wooded valley in the Grampians north of Fasque
(p. 30).
265. Major-General Sir Coleridge Grove (1839–1920).
266. Major Henniker commanded the Second Battalion of the Coldstream Guards during the Boer War (1899–1902), won several distinc-
tions, and was made a C.B. for his services.
267. Alfred Dreyfus, a Jew and artillery captain in the French army,
was falsely charged with handing defence secrets to a foreign power,
found guilty at the end of the trial of 1893–4, and imprisoned. The
efforts of his wife and friends to prove him innocent provoked such an
outburst of anti-semitism that Zola attacked the Government in his
famous *"J'accuse"* of 1898. Not until 1906 was the verdict reversed.
268. Lady Jeune's daughter, Madeleine Stanley; see note 101, p. 31.

morrow, and hope to take a few little journeys near home on
the bicycle before the weather breaks up.

Ever sincerely
Tho H.

62.   Max Gate,
                                          Dorchester.
                                          Oct. 11. 1899

I imagine you to be back in town by this time, dear friend, in
all the excitement and interest, and, I should add, regret,
which the sense of war in the near future always awakens, even
amongst people less closely connected with the army than you
are. I constantly deplore the fact that 'civilized' nations have
not learnt some more excellent and apostolic way of settling
disputes than the old and barbarous one, after all these centuries; but when I feel that it must be, few persons are more
martial than I, or like better to write of war in prose and
rhyme.[269]

Such a position appears to have been now reached; and the
sooner we get at it, and get it done, the better, I think. You
refer to the suffering of the horses in war, and unfortunately
the Boer horses seem to be already undergoing much hardship
from exposure.

Since returning from Arlington I have been using the fine
weather in taking little day excursions to places in this neighbourhood. Are you any better for your visit to the North? I
hope you have nothing that you want to publish just now, for I
fancy books will be neglected for newspapers awhile.

Is it the opinion in military circles that the S. Africa business
will soon be over?

Swinburne's sonnet in to-day's *Times* disappoints me, but
probably it was dashed off in a hurry.[270] I was about to send a

269. A remarkable statement from one who felt the tragedy of war
as deeply as anyone. To see *The Dynasts* in perspective one must recognize the survival of the boy in Hardy, the romance which battle cam-
paigns had held for him from his early years, and his adult, almost
despairing, sense of the futility of war and the irrationality of man.

270. 'The Transvaal' (9 October 1899). Swinburne's outburst, ending
'Strike, England, and strike home', appeared on the 11th, it should be
noticed.

few rhymed lines to some paper, on Game Birds,[271] but shall probably keep them by me now, for other slaughter will fill people's minds for some time to come.

Ever sincerely yours

Tho H.

63.   Max Gate,
                                                       Dorchester,
                                                       9. Nov. 1899

My dear friend:

We felt so sorry to-day to see in the papers that L[or]d Crewe was ill that I have written a line to him, though I fear that letters are often an additional infliction at such times. I do hope his illness has been much exaggerated.

How have you been getting on in your loneliness? I hope we shall hear of the arrival of 'The Gascon'[272] in a day or two. I fancy you thought my sonnet on the departure too tragic?[273] But I was not at Southampton on the Saturday when you were there. I went Friday, and saw off 5000 altogether: Em's nephew, who is staying here, bicycled up to South[ampto]n on Saturday; he saw the Gascon (sic) go, though he did not observe you anywhere he says. (You may remember meeting him at our flat one day last summer).[274]

Before I forget I want to ask if you will be so kind as to let us have a photograph of Major Henniker. I can't possibly get it signed, of course, now; but unsigned will do. He is going to be framed with the other celebrities; you see I reckon on getting it. In uniform preferred; and the *latest*.

Two other scraps of verse of mine on war subjects are coming out in a day or two I believe – one in *The Graphic*.[275] If you

---

271. 'The Puzzled Game-Birds', eventually published in *Poems of the Past and the Present* (1901).   272. Major Henniker's troopship.

273. 'Embarcation' (sic) appeared in *The Daily Chronicle*, 25 October, under the title 'The Departure'.

274. Emma Hardy's youngest brother had died, and the Hardys had his son and daughter, Gordon and Lilian Gifford, staying with them at Max Gate for long periods, Lilian off and on to the time of Hardy's second marriage.

275. 'The Going of the Battery' (*Poems of the Past and the Present*) appeared in *The Graphic*, 11 November 1899.

don't see it, and w[oul]d like me to send you a copy I will get one. The fact is, the incidents of departure have rather come in my way by accident. The latest was the going of our Battery of Artillery (stationed in this town) and as they left at 10 at night, and some at 4 in the morning, amid rain and wind,[276] the scene was a pathetic one.

If Miss Thornhill is with you please remember us to her. I am not sure if I may not be running up to town for a day or so before Christmas.

How is your head? It was very good of you to go all the way to Southampton.

Ever y[ou]rs sincerely
Tho. H.

64.   Max Gate,
                                         Dorchester.
                                         24. Nov. 1899

My dear friend:

It was with the keenest interest and anxiety, as you will readily imagine, that I opened the *Times* this morning and read that the Coldstreams had been engaged with the Boers at Belmont. They are pushing on more rapidly than the Natal force, don't you think? Did you know any of the wounded?

I am hoping to receive to-morrow in time to post to you before Sunday this week's *Literature* in which are published my few lines entitled 'The Dead Drummer'.[277] The thought it embodies is a mere passing one of no profundity, but it happens to be curiously apposite to the moment.

I am trying to write a little story long promised to *Harper's Magazine*:[278] but I have not been able to get on with it much

276. On 2 November. The departure here described is the subject of the above poem.

277. The title was later changed to 'Drummer Hodge'. A note added to the title in *Literature* indicated that the drummer was a native of a village near 'Casterbridge' (Dorchester); he may have come from Bockhampton, Puddletown, or West Stafford, the villages Hardy knew best.

278. 'Enter a Dragoon', the last prose story Hardy wrote, did not appear in *Harper's Monthly Magazine* (New York) until December 1900.

E

owing to a distressing nausea and headache which lasted nearly all last week – what they call a chill on the liver I think – but I had no doctor. I was better by Monday, and went and stayed a night at Athelhampton Hall[279] – an old Tudor manor house 6 miles from here – owned by a friend – Mr de la Fontaine: and staying there at the same time was Sir Hubert Miller.[280] We all walked to 'Weatherbury'[281] church the next morning.

I am sending with this the sonnet on the departure of the troops which I wrote for *The Daily Chronicle*. You show your sympathetic nature by being touched by 'The departure (*sic*) of the Battery'. It was almost an exact report of the scene and expressions I overheard. There are two more verses in the original: but I omitted them in sending the lines off, not to burden the *Graphic* too heavily. The *Academy* of last Saturday reprinted them.

I thanked you by a mere P. Card only for the beautiful photograph of the Major. It was really good of you to give us such a nice one – so exactly like him. – Mr Pike is a friend of ours – rather an interesting man being a vegetarian, and one who has renounced shooting after being convinced by the arguments of his wife that it was wrong. The animals are so tame round their house that the squirrels run up their shoulders when they go outside.

I am so sorry that you have felt pulled down. I wish you could run down to the sea for a while. It is the London *East* Wind that does you the harm, I am convinced. We are still under the tepid influence of the Gulf Stream here.[282]

Ever yours sincerely
Tho H.

W[oul]d you mind returning 'The Departure' – as it is my only copy.

279. See p. 44.
280. Of Alton, Hants. He had retired from the Coldstream Guards in 1892, and thought Arthur Henniker 'the very best type of Guardsman'.
281. 'Weatherbury', the village of *Far from the Madding Crowd*, is based on Puddletown, less than a mile from Athelhampton Hall.
282. Hardy had written similarly in his letter to Lord Crewe (see p. 86).

65.   Max Gate,
                                               Dorchester.
                                             Dec. 19. 1899

My dear friend:

'The hand of Midian prevails against Israel'. I wonder how
you have been bearing the tension of the last week or two? As I
do not see that you were present at the memorial service to
L[or]d Winchester[283] yesterday it has occurred to me that you
may be ailing, and unable to go out? What a Christmas for us
this will be: I do not remember such another. I have not run
up to London after all, this month: but I have written a little
poem, of 2 stanzas only, on the scene at the War Office after a
battle,[284] which, though I have not witnessed it, I can imagine
with painful realism. Our Dorset regiment has gone out, as
perhaps you saw, and of the Artillery and Infantry in our two
barracks here as a rule we have only 2 *men* left at present. Col.
Long of the Horse Artillery, who has lost the guns at the
Tugela, and is dangerously wounded, is well known here,
where he was lying with his battery down to 2 or 3 years ago.
But of course you know an immense number of the names we
get sent home. I am so sorry for Buller, as possibly the reverse
he has met with might have occurred to a Napoleon in the
circumstances.[285] Speaking generally however, I think our generals are deficient in strategic instincts, though they have a
superabundance of courage. This Imperial idea is, I fear,
leading us into strange waters. Personally I was not so sanguine
of success at the beginning as most people were, and I am not

283. He was killed at the age of forty-one at the battle of Magersfontein, 11 December 1899. Mrs Henniker had recently been his guest
(p. 75). Her husband had been engaged in this battle (see note p. 92);
since 29 November, when he succeeded Lieutenant-Colonel Stopford,
who was killed at Modder River, he had been in command of the
Second Battalion of the Coldstream Guards.

284. 'At the War Office, London (Affixing the Lists of Killed and
Wounded: December 1899)'. The poem was first published in a facsimile
of Hardy's MS. with the title 'At the War Office After a Bloody Battle'
(Purdy, p. 108).

285. Napoleon was never far from Hardy's thoughts at this time, when
he was making preparations for *The Dynasts*.

The Boers had surrounded Ladysmith, Kimberley, and Mafeking, and
Buller on his way to the relief of Ladysmith had been checked at the
Tugela River, losing over a thousand men in killed and wounded. See
note 225, p. 69.

now so disconcerted at the want of it as they. I always imagined the business w[oul]d take us 3 years, rather than 3 months, and I still adhere to my opinion. Write soon, and do send my remembrances and hopes and wishes when you are writing to Africa.

                    Ever yours sincerely, with sympathy
                                Tho H.

I can send you the W.O. poem, if you w[oul]d like.

66.   Max Gate,
                                        Dorchester.
                                       Jan. 26, 1900

My dear friend:
    The only pleasant intention which has graced this wet and dreary day has been the cheerful one of writing to you. How have you been since you last wrote, and is the influenza clean gone? It has got even down here into the villages.
    I read your 'Lady Gilian' with the greatest interest. All thanks for sending it. Like nearly all your stories, it makes one wish there were more of it. The opening scene is beautiful, and tender, and I don't know any woman but yourself who could have written it. It is this which makes me wish the latter part had been worked out at greater length. But as it stands it is charming, and too good for the cursory reading it is likely to get in a periodical.
    My little poem 'At the War Office' comes out in the new paper, The Sphere, today. I will get a copy for you if you don't meet with it; it is the scene I told you of. I have also finished the two short stories[286] – one for Harpers Magazine, and the other for the aforesaid paper.
    There seems soon a likelihood of a turn in affairs in S. Africa. Have you heard lately from Major H[ennike]r? Is his health good? What a stress it must have been to stand fire for 12 hours and more! We are sending off volunteers soon from here, and even though it will be some time before they get out

    286. 'Enter a Dragoon' (see p. 87) and 'A Changed Man', published in The Sphere, April 1900.

I fancy there will be quite enough left for them to do. I am just interested in — of all authors in the world — Otway the poet.[287] Really his *Venice Preserved* is a strong play, though nobody reads it now. S. Phillips's play[288] seems to have been a great success, but I have not read it as yet.

I heard from Anthony Hope[289] a few days ago, and earlier from W. Besant;[290] but with these exceptions I have not been much in touch with the literary world, except those silent members who greet me from my book-shelves. Did you know, by the way, that my publishers are in difficulties? Fortunately they do not owe me much.

With best wishes believe me, ever yours sincerely

Tho. H.

67.   Max Gate,
                                                     Dorchester.
                                                     Feb. 25. 1900

My dear friend:

I was glad to get your letter, and to hear that you are fairly well. But I fear that London is not a likely place to make you strong, even though it may be the headquarters of good advice. Probably Bournemouth for a fortnight would give you a good start for the spring? If you do think of it, remember you are to come on here.

Possibly you know by this time the result of the attack on

287. Thomas Otway is remembered for his great tragedy, *Venice Preserved* (1682). In her correspondence of 1915, Florence Hardy stated that her husband did not care for Otway.

288. Stephen Phillips (1864–1915), poet and dramatist, enjoyed a short-lived success with his verse plays, the best being *Paolo and Francesca* (1899), to which Hardy here refers.

289. Novelist; see note, p. 46.

290. Sir Walter Besant (1836–1901) was knighted in 1895. As a novelist he won his reputation mainly from his collaboration with James Rice. His most important work is a historical survey of London in ten volumes. He was the founder of the Rabelais Club; Hardy attended the inaugural dinner in December 1879, and was pressed to join as 'the most virile writer of works of imagination' then in London (*Life*, p. 132).

Cronje,[291] which I do not. How horrible it all is: they say that his wife and other women are in that river-bed with his unfortunate army: and the mangled animals too, who must have terror superadded to their physical sufferings. I take a keen pleasure in war strategy and tactics, following it as if it were a game of chess; but all the while I am obliged to blind myself to the human side of the matter: directly I think of that, the romance looks somewhat tawdry, and worse. I do not, of course, refer to this particular war, and the precise shade of blame or otherwise which attaches to us.

I met a religious man[292] on Friday (by the way, he is son of the old parson whose portrait I partially drew in Angel Clare's father), and I said, We (the civilized world) have given Christianity a fair trial for nearly 2000 years, and it has not yet taught countries the rudimentary virtue of keeping peace: so why not throw it over, and try, say, Buddhism? (I may have said the same thing to you). It shocked him, for he could only see the unchristianity of Kruger.[293]

I wonder if you have had a cablegram from Major Henniker lately? He must be in Kimberley[294] by this time, must he not? I wonder if he suffers much from the heat. But I think he likes hot weather. Lady Grove was in Dorchester a week or two ago, and she came out to see us – bringing a friend in khaki (young Ivor Guest, Lady Wimborne's son) who is leaving next week for S. Africa. She has just heard from Lady Wynford, who is at Cimiez:[295] but is coming back soon.

I have read no recent books: when I get to London I am going to read them up. I should like to be in town for a day or two just now; but a miserable sick headache, with pain at the back of the head, has been almost chronic with me for the

291. The Boer general Piet Cronje defended Modder River, and had defeated the British attempt to surprise him at Magersfontein. New forces under Lord Roberts forced his army to surrender at Paardeberg two days after this letter was written, and Buller relieved Ladysmith the following day.

292. Henry J. Moule (1825–1904), Curator of the Dorset County Museum, and son of the Rev. Henry Moule. See note 120, p. 39.

293. Paulus Kruger (1825–1904), at this time President of the South African Republic.

294. Kimberley was relieved by General French shortly after the battle of Paardeberg.

295. A residential suburb of Nice.

last month, though I eat scarcely anything in endeavours to prevent it. I fear I must see a doctor.

Always yours

Tho. H.

Poor Mr Bunbury: I met him at your house I think. It must be grievous to you knowing so many.[296]

68.   Max Gate,
                                                Dorchester.
                                                3.4.1900

My dear friend:

Your little – too little – story has been lying on my table ever since I read it on the day of its arrival: and now I have taken it up and read it over again. (I mean the one in the *Universal Magazine*).[297] I feel quite a Philistine's vexation that it all ended as it did – or as you say it did. I shall assume that the gentleman in the railway carriage was *another man*, who had happened to write to Mrs Agnew! See how childish we are, or somebody is!

I was gratified to hear that my visionary verses[298] pleased you. I sent them off all on a sudden, having put them away when I wrote them, early in the winter, thinking that the fancy might be too peculiar to myself to interest other people.

I was going to London this week, but am now inclined to wait till after Easter. I dare say you are seeing numbers of people. I am seeing few or none, but I make little journeys about the country on the invaluable but now vulgar bicycle. You said you had been in the country. Whereabouts? And have you heard lately from Major H[ennike]r? I cannot quite understand from the papers where he is.

The clouds have closed in suddenly on this very wet afternoon, so that I can scarcely see.

Ever yours
Tho H.

296. i.e. who have been killed or wounded.
297. 'Past Mending', February 1900.
298. 'The Souls of the Slain', a fantasy on those killed in the war, was published in *The Cornhill Magazine*, April 1900.

69.   Max Gate,
                                             Dorchester.
                                             1.6.1900

My dear friend:

I am back here again after my circular tour, as it may be
called; but go to London next Tuesday to finish out my time
there of another 2 or 3 weeks with Em, who is there now, having gone up a few days ago. Your letter to me at Harley St.
was a particularly nice one, following too that pleasant lunch
and afternoon. What a time I stayed! But you were responsible for that, remember!

When I got to Stoke Court[299] I found a whole housefull –
including Mrs Craigie, Anthony Hawkins, L[or]d and Lady
Londonderry and Birdie,[300] the Chancellor of the Exch[eque]r
and Lady Lucy Hicks Beach[301] and their girl, Mr Brodrick,[302]
Lady Hilda, and their girl (just out, L[ad]y H. says), the new
Sol[icito]r Gen[era]l and some nondescript young people who
made evening hideous by raving out music-hall war songs and
whacking at the piano till we others c[oul]d not hear ourselves
speak. As I knew most of the people there the visit was not unpleasant, though when members of the Gov[ernmen]t get
together they talk shop rather drearily. I duly delivered your
messages, wh[ich] all were pleased to have.

I ought to mention that Sir Evelyn Wood[303] came Sunday
aft[ernoo]n for half an hour, and assured me that the war
w[oul]d be over soon and the soldiers returning. Events since
seem to be bearing out this. Also that one young man at Stoke
(I forget his name for the moment) who came home wounded,
and is now all right, told me that he received his wound in
the battle of Belmont, and that he was quite near Col. Henniker in that engagement.

299. The home of the Allhusens at Stoke Poges. Mrs Allhusen was
Lady Jeune's daughter.
300. Anthony Hope Hawkins was the novelist 'Anthony Hope';
'Birdie' was Lady Ilchester, daughter of Lord and Lady Londonderry
(p. 49).
301. Wife of the Chancellor of the Exchequer.
302. Mr Brodrick later married Mrs Allhusen's sister (see p. 108).
303. Sir Henry Evelyn Wood (1838–1919) had served in the Crimean
and Zulu wars, and in Egypt in 1882. From 1886 he held home appoint-
ments. In 1897 he was made Adjutant-General of the Army; in 1903,
Field-Marshal. He was the brother of Kitty O'Shea (see p. 207).

I have just been reading Arthur Symons' book of poetry *Images of Good and Evil*. Also his essays on *Symbolism*:[304] the latter are disappointing; the verse I like – some pieces particularly. Where will you stow away your loot? How interesting that I should have been there when it came.

Y[ou]rs ever sincerely
Tho H.

70.   Max Gate,
                                        Dorchester.
                                        July 29, 1900

My dear friend:

I was on the point of dispatching a letter to you last night, but it was too late: and this morning yours arrived. As I should have written and sent mine off earlier in the day if some people had not arrived and hindered me, it seems that we may have been influencing each other's minds. It was so kind of you to send the *P[all] M[all] Magazine*[305] containing 'A Faithful Failure', over which I was puzzled to recall how I could have read it before. I did not see the proof, did I? However, it interested me to read it again, and to find that, as usual, I regretted its shortness. That suggestive style of writing is one that you have quite made your own. For once the illustrations suit the story. It is grievous to think how many a faithful failure gets slighted and snuffed out thus, for some superficial defects that offend our cruel fastidiousness.

I have had no energy of late to write anything. You have the advantage over me in being at the seaside. I can always soon get to it, but don't often, though last Sunday I bicycled to Weymouth in company with Thorneycroft[306] the sculptor,

304. Arthur Symons (1865–1945). *The Symbolist Movement in Literature* was published in 1899.
305. Mrs Henniker's story appeared in the August number.
306. William Hamo Thornycroft (1850–1925), a sculptor like each of his parents, earned fame for his public statues. Gladstone died in 1898. King Alfred was buried at Winchester; the statue marked the millenary of his death. Thornycroft's bronze head of Thomas Hardy is in the National Gallery. Hardy regarded Mrs Thornycroft as the most beautiful of women; she was in some ways his model for Tess.

and Mrs Thorneycroft, who have been staying with us – nice people both of them. He is doing a statue of Gladstone for the Strand – the open space that will be left after the widening: also another of King Alfred for Winchester.

I read Wedmore's story[307] and will return it. It is artistic and up to date: quite like him. But I have been bothered by a weak watery eye, which began in London, and seems to have something to do with summer dryness and heat, as I had it this time last year. I am sorry that Col. Henniker met with a slight mishap: I wonder if he has any idea when he is coming home. He ought to be proud of himself as well as of his men! It must be getting tedious over there: the winding up of a war is always so. I hope you will tackle the play you are trying your hand on: it is a difficult change from novel-writing. I am about to read D'Annunzio's *Virgin of the Rocks*,[308] by W[illia]m Archer's[309] recommendation, when I met him in town, but I prefer dipping into old books mostly.

The Sixpenny *Tess* has had a great commercial success, the publishers tell me – they printed a hundred thousand for England only. I am so glad to know that you are getting stronger.

Always yours sincerely
Tho. H.

71.   Max Gate,
                                                      Dorchester.
                                                   Oct. 22. 1900
My dear friend:

I remember that it is a year ago that we were in the excitement of sending off the army to the Cape. I spoke to some of the men at Southampton, who expected that they would be home in three months. Well, twelve have passed, and they have not yet returned. Have you heard from Col. Henniker lately,

307. For Wedmore, see p. 43. His tale *The Collapse of a Penitent* was published in 1900.

308. Gabriele d'Annunzio (1863–1938), Italian poet, novelist, and dramatist. A translation by A. Hughes of his recent novel was published in 1899, entitled *The Virgins of the Rocks*.

309. William Archer (1856–1924), dramatic critic and translator of Ibsen.

and are you expecting him soon? I should imagine that he must be nearly tired of the campaign by this time, and all of them. It is sad, or not, as you look at it, to think that 40,000 will have found their rest there. Could we ask them if they wish to wake up again, would they say Yes, do you think?

However, I was not meaning to write like that, and you must forgive me. What have you yourself been doing? Things theatrical, or more exclusively literary? Mrs Pat [Campbell][310] has written to ask me for a play: but though I try I cannot kindle enough interest in myself in the British stage to care to write for it. By the way, the Stage Society is going to give (in Nov[ember]) two performances of that casual little thing of mine 'The Three Wayfarers',[311] which you once wanted to see.

I am puzzled what to do with some poems,[312] written at various dates, a few lately, some long ago. If I print them I know exactly what will be said about them: 'You hold opinions which we don't hold: therefore shut up.' Not that there are any opinions in the verses; but English reviewers go behind the book and review the man. I am of opinion that the present condition of the English novel is due to the paralysing effect of English criticism upon those who would have developed it – possibly in a wrong direction in many cases, but ultimately towards excellence.

I read Lord Crewe's letter in Saturday's *Times*, and thought it well argued, and, of course, of a far higher literary quality than most letters to *The Times*. Still, the external policy of the Tories is mostly *smarter*, (Heaven forbid that I should say *better*, in a moral sense,) I think, than that of the Liberals.[313] That seems to me to be the *crux* in politics; external or foreign policy. You must play that game as other nations play it, and they will not play it humanely. At home you may give your humanity free play. To educate Europe is such a big thing!

---

310. See note 158, p. 50. She still wanted the part of Tess.
311. See p. 2.
312. *Poems of the Past and the Present*, published in November 1901, contained a large number of poems charged with unorthodox opinions, chiefly on God and the Immanent Will, which he was contemplating in preparation for *The Dynasts*.
313. See note 156, p. 50.

6.30. Since writing the above I have been out on a little cycle tour with our niece,[314] who is staying here – to Upwey, where there is a wishing-well. We duly wished, and what will result remains to be seen. I sometimes go, too, to Cerne Abbas, where there are the ruins of the old abbey (on land belonging to Lady Grove's brother): and I have been endeavouring to make out where the buildings stood. It is an interesting and difficult problem, to waste time upon, owing to the meagreness of the remains.

If I come to London this autumn I shall let you know.

Always yours
. Tho H.

I have just been correcting (at the request of the author) the life of William Barnes, in the *Dic[tionary] of Nat[iona]l Biography*.[315] Have you read T.E.B's poems?[316] It is a pity he was a parson, as it compels him to write parsonically – as it did Barnes also.

T.H.

72. Max Gate,
Dorchester.
Christmas Eve: 1900

This is my Christmas card, my dear friend; all written by my-self. I wonder whether you are in London, or have run down to

314. See note 274, p. 86.
315. Hardy first knew Barnes (1800–1886) when the latter was a schoolmaster in Dorchester. He was an admirer of Barnes's Dorset poetry, and reviewed his *Poems of Rural Life in the Dorset Dialect* in *The New Quarterly Magazine*, October 1879. At Max Gate, towards the end of Barnes's life, Hardy was his close neighbour. Hardy wrote his obituary in *The Athenaeum*, and in 1908 edited a selection of his poems for the Oxford University Press. The author of the life of Barnes in the *Dictionary of National Biography* was Thomas Seccombe. For Hardy's writings on Barnes and his poetry, see Orel.
316. Thomas Edward Brown (1830–97) was a Fellow of Oriel, and, after teaching thirty years at Clifton College, returned to the Isle of Man, where he was born and had begun his teaching career. (At the Crypt School, Gloucester, where he was headmaster, he taught W. E. Henley.) He is remembered by a few lyrics, but he wrote some notable narrative poems in Manx English.

Crewe Hall or elsewhere? If in town, it is, I fear, rather de-
pressing to you to think that this is the second winter you have
spent there alone, in spite of our expectation and hope that
the war would be over long before now. I said, if you recollect,
that it would be three years before all was settled and quiet,
and I don't think I shall be far wrong. War resembles a snow
storm in one respect: it is grand and romantic at the first, but
dreary and tedious in its disappearance.

I am sorry indeed to hear that you have been feeling tired
again. I always think Bournemouth would be a good place
for you to winter in. You mention Lady D[orothy] Nevill.[317]
She was down here in the summer, and amused me much as
usual. It was just at the time that 'harvesters' are so troublesome if one gets among the grass, etc., and we were all suggesting remedies for their sting: one used ammonia, another vine-
gar, etc.; she said 'Well, for my part, I scratch.'

I was induced by a review to buy Q[uiller-]Couch's *Oxford
Book of Verse*[318] the other day; and was much disappointed:
the selected names are a good and fairly exhaustive list, but the
specimens chosen show a narrow judgment and a bias in favour
of particular views of life which make the book second-rate of
its class. An *Englishwoman's Loveletters*[319] turns out to be a
novel: it was suggested, I suppose, by the Browning Loveletters (*sic*), which made such an excellent novel, and a true
one.

My 'Soldiers' Wives' Song'[320] finishes up my war effusions, of
which I am happy to say that not a single one is Jingo or
Imperial – a fatal defect according to the judgment of the
British majority at present, I dare say. The *Cornhill* editor
has asked me for another, but I cannot rise to war any more.
With best wishes from

Your affec[tiona]te friend
Tho H.

317. See the note on p. 71. 'Harvesters' are commonly known as
'harvest bugs'.
318. Arthur Quiller-Couch (1863–1944), Cornish poet and novelist
('Q'). Hardy's judgement anticipates much later critical views.
319. By Laurence Housman (1900). A second edition of the Browning letters appeared in 1899.
320. 'Song of the Soldiers' Wives and Sweethearts' was published in
The Morning Post, 30 November 1900. A copy of it may have formed
Hardy's Christmas card to Mrs Henniker.

73.   Max Gate,
                                                          Dorchester.
                                                        Feb. 15. 1901
My dear friend:

We seem to have entered on a new tract of time since we last communicated (as a lawyer down here used to say) with each other – Here we are in a new reign,[321] and with a general sense of the unknown lying round us, which in itself is a novelty. Not that such changes affect me greatly, if at all. But what French editors call 'Le God save' has to be sung somewhat differently by me when I feel musical,[322] and my money all looks old-fashioned pending the new coinage: so that I feel there *is* a change.

But I ought not to begin with 'frivol'[323] – (the Right Reverend inventor of that dignified word has also passed away), since you may be unwell, or depressed on account of the tedious dreary length of the war: in which case I ask you to forgive me. That I should for one moment write anyhow but gravely is a marvel, for I have been unwell and sad enough myself in the interval – feeling that I could not write a letter or do anything. I have felt much better – indeed quite well – during the last week.

I wonder if you saw some lines I wrote about the Queen,[324] that were printed in the *Times*? I did not send them to you (or anybody) for they were really not worth calling your attention to. I wrote them during a bad headache, and posted them immediately and they came out the next day – so that they have all the crudeness of an unrevised performance.

W[illia]m Archer – whom you know – came here about a week ago. He experimented on me in a new kind of interviewing: knowing him well I did not mind it at the time, but I have felt some misgivings since, and suppose I shall be thought to have prompted the production when it is printed.[325] It is,

321. Queen Victoria, in whose reign Hardy, now aged 60, was born, died on 22 January, and was succeeded by Edward VII.

322. Hardy mentions relatively small changes to which he must become accustomed, the first relating to alterations in the National Anthem.

323. See p. 5.

324. 'V. R. 1819–1901' appeared in *The Times* on 29 January.

325. See William Archer, *Real Conversations*, London, 1904, pp. 29–50. He and Hardy talked on many things: local, literary, philosophical, and spiritual.

however, only a discussion of abstract subjects: and the second person might have been anybody for that matter.

Please let me know what news you have had from S. Africa, and if anything to cause you anxiety. As to your hope that the horses and mules will receive compensation somewhere for their sufferings, I, too, hope the same, though according to modern philosophies they, like ourselves, will pass into nothing, and have to be *re-willed*[326] into existence as other horses and mules before they have a chance of such compensation.

Have you seen many people lately? — many more than I have, of course. I had thought of taking a little flat in London this year again; but Emma seems averse to the trouble of doing it: so that I cannot say what our plans are. My being unwell prevented my going to see William Watson.[327] I hope he is well by this time. Believe me

Ever y[ou]rs sincerely
Tho. H.

74.   Max Gate,
                                      Dorchester.
                                      April 4. 1901

My dear friend:

We shall be much pleased to ask Miss Beele to call here some day, if she does not mind the distance. I am just now in the middle of a cold — having been without one all the winter; I hope to escape altogether this season. But that was not to be; so I stay in for a day or two.

A gloom has been thrown over the house by the tragic death of a favourite cat — *my* cat — the first I have ever had 'for my very own'. He was run over by the train on Monday night; and I blame myself for letting him stay out, after taking the trouble to shut him up myself every night all this winter.[328] We have had railway accidents to three cats — although the line is $\frac{1}{4}$

326. Hardy alludes half-seriously to the philosophy of the Immanent Will, which was to play a critical part in the design of *The Dynasts*.

327. The poet William Watson (1858–1935) was at Bournemouth, recovering from an accident.

328. Possibly the cat commemorated in one of Hardy's best poems, 'Last Words to a Dumb Friend' (*Late Lyrics and Earlier*).

mile off: and we cannot think what fascination it can have
for cats, that they should be caught thus.

You will think I am telling you rather small news, but
everything in my life has been small lately, in the ordinary
sense. – March was enough to make you, or anybody, unwell! I
hope now the wind has changed you will recover. I do not
mind the east wind here, but in London it chills me through.

I often see the *Daily Mail*, and I have read about Col. Henniker in it. I suppose there is an excitement in the chase
of enemies, but he must be getting weary of it by this time.
What a campaign he will have to tell of when he comes back!

I will be sure to let you know when I reach town. As I get
older I find that my interests in London move further and
further away from the West End (barring the residences of a
few friends) and centre in the older parts where dead people
have lived. Did you know either Sir Arthur Sullivan or Sir J.
Stainer?[329] The history of music, and in a lesser degree, of
musicians, attracts me much always, and I am sorry I never met
either of those. The history of the theatre is to my mind nothing to the history of the concert room.

Hoping that you will speedily be quite well believe me
always

Y[ou]r affec[tiona]te friend
Tho H.

75.   27 Oxford Terrace,
                                         Hyde Park. W.
                                           16.5.1901

My dear friend:

I have just received your kind letter of invitation to your
farm.[330] But for a whole week since coming here (some tempor-

329. Hardy had loved hymn music since his boyhood, and his interest
in these two composers was almost certainly enhanced by his enjoyment
of some of their well-known hymn tunes. Sir Arthur Sullivan (1842–
1900) is famous for his collaboration with W. S. Gilbert in a long series
of comic operas. Sir John Stainer, who wrote *The Crucifixion*, was Professor of Music at Oxford from 1889 to 1899. His death on 30 March
1901 prompted Hardy's reflections.

330. Hardy's letter to his wife on 27 April 1901 (Weber, p. 49) suggests
that this could have been at Clewer (*not* Clewes) near Windsor.

ary rooms we have taken for a month only) I have had a violent cold; first influenza, now a cough and remnants of a general kind, and though I am mending I am not yet sure about accepting or fixing any engagements, and have cancelled all – except one for the end of next week to go down to Aldeburgh,[331] by the sea, where I have been before, which may set me right again. I return here on Whit Tuesday. Anthony Hope and Sir G. Robertson[332] are also going I believe. However I cannot go unless I am a little better.

I am sorry to hear of your touch of rheumatism – which I have been free from for a long while. Yes; as I said, I wrote to the Colonel, and should have had much pleasure in doing so long ago if I had not felt that he might have more serious matters to think of than letters.

We have been saying how foolish it seems to have come away from where we were well, and, as you are now, surrounded by birds' songs and young leaves, to make ourselves ill in a city!

I hope to be screwed up to a higher note when I have been to Suffolk. Meanwhile believe me always

Your aff[ectiona]te friend
Tho. H.

76.   27, Oxford Terrace
                                       Hyde Park W.
                                       June 2. 1901

My dear friend:

How very kind and thoughtful of you to remember my poor old birthday! It has been rather a heavy day for me – not for mental reasons, for I do not recollect a year in which I met it with more equanimity: but for purely physical ones, the visit to Aldeburgh not having pulled me together after the general debility due (I suppose) to that attack of influenza. This will explain to you my backwardness in availing myself of the

331. At the invitation of Edward Clodd (p. 23).
332. Sir George Robertson (1852–1916) had served long in India, first in the Medical Service, then in the Foreign Office. He was continually employed on the Kashmir frontier, and besieged in Chitral in 1895.

pleasure of going down to see you where you are, which I
should otherwise have proposed to do the moment I came back
here from Suffolk. This moment of writing is the first in which
I have done anything today, all the time having been spent
lying down, in sheer languor. But I am hoping it will go off in
another day or two, and I will ask you to tell me an afternoon
on which I shall find you at home if I *can* come. My impression
is that I walked too far down there – though the result otherwise was very pleasant.

We (Hawkins, Sir G. Robertson, Dr Frazer, author of *The
Golden Bough*, and one or two others) went down the Alde
in Clodd's boat on the Saturday, and on Monday went to
Boulge, to the grave of Fitzgerald (translator, or re-writer, of
Omar Kayyham [*sic*]) walking all the way from Woodbridge and back in intense heat.[333] However we found the
rosebush thriving that was planted at his head: you will
remember that it was raised from a hip brought from the rose-
trees round Omar's grave at Naishpur (*sic*). I spoke of you to
Sir G.R. who was glad to be remembered by you. Altogether
we had a cheerful time. A man home on sick leave from S.
Africa came in to dine one evening, and he told us dreadful
experiences of being *compelled* to drive his horse to death on
the forced march, and of having to abandon others not quite
dead.

We are here till the 15th. Em is also very languid, and goes
practically nowhere, though on Wedn[esda]y afternoon we
did go to hear Kubelik the violinist.[334] I hope the air of your
farm has made you robust.

Always yours
Tho H.

333. Edward FitzGerald (1809–83) spent many years in and around
Woodbridge, near which he was born. He lived with his father at Boulge
Hall from 1835 to 1838, and it was at Boulge, some three or four miles
from Woodbridge, that he was buried. In 1893 members of the Omar
Club planted on his grave a rose-tree grown at Kew Gardens from the
seed of a rose on Omar's tomb at Naishápúr.

334. See *Life*, p. 308. The Hardys seem to have heard several concerts at the end of May. They heard Ysaye and Kubelik, and Hardy
describes 'a feat of execution' by the latter.

77.   Max Gatc,
                                             Dorchester.
                                             July 25. 1901

My dear friend:

Your pleasant letter finds me hunting up the poems[335] I told you about, and trying to decide which to print and which destroy. To tell the truth I want to pack them off, for I am tired of them. Only think – I have found some I wrote so long ago as in 1866; two or three seem worth saving, though I am hardly a good judge.

Just after that pleasant afternoon I spent with you I received a letter from the Colonel: an excellent letter, giving in brief positive style a most vivid impression of how things are going on over there. I was very glad to have it. I sincerely hope that the war will soon be over, and that we shall welcome him home at no distant date.

I was amused to learn from you that, feeling so well, you are going off to Schwalbach to get better still – rather greedy of you that is, I think. Since I have been back here I have had a weak eye, but it seems to be almost well now. Our visitors the members and guests of the Whitefriars Club[336] seemed to like our reception of them much. There were 100 in all, and of course we did not know a quarter of them. We put up a marquee, opening from the drawing room, and they had tea in it.

Browning is excellent to fall back upon in hot weather: how slowly and surely he is overtopping Tennyson. And yet Browning has his weaknesses.[337] An article – quite a long one – appeared in *Literature* about my books the other day: I can let you see it if you w[oul]d care to and have not done so: the writer is a stranger to me.[338]

335. For *Poems of the Past and the Present*. Three poems written in the 1866 period were included.

336. A group of writers and journalists who visited Max Gate at the end of May 1901. Hardy's mother (aged eighty-eight) was pushed in her wheelchair by her daughters to the foot of Yellowham Hill to see the dusty visitors from London pass in their open carriages (*Life*, pp. 308–9).

337. Hardy had learned much about versification from the poetry of William Barnes and Robert Browning. The 'weaknesses' probably allude to Browning's optimistic philosophy, which Hardy rated no more highly than the smug Christianity of a Dissenting grocer.

338. In this article, which appeared in the July 1901 number, Stephen Gwynn compared Hardy's prose to that of Maupassant and Mérimée.

Let me know when you depart for Germany. I have been no nearer to the place than Coblenz and Mainz; but think I must go that way again some day. Will you be in London in Nov[ember]? I am thinking of being there.

Ever sincerely yours
Tho H.

78.   Max Gate,
                                          Dorchester.
                                          Sept. 25. 1902

My dear friend:

I saw in the papers a few days ago that Col. Henniker had sailed for home, and was so glad to think that he had at last reached that stage of his long campaign of three years, without being, as I suppose and hope, much the worse for it. It will be a great pleasure to see him again when I come to London; and also to see you, for I have thought of you since the death of dear Lady Fitzgerald[339] more than you may suppose from my silence. I hope you are as well as we can be in this sorry world.

I have done very little during this wet summer we have had. Some of my work has been that of correcting a few bad misprints and other errors in my books for the new edition which Macmillans are about to bring out. You must not suppose it to be caprice on my part that has led me to change my publishers. Osgoods having merged in Harpers, and Harpers having passed into a receiver's hands, I had virtually no English publisher, but only a branch of an American firm, and it seemed forced upon me to readjust things. Macmillans have been my Colonial publ[ishe]rs for many years.

I have taken some bicycle rides; one into the Vale of Blackmoor. I want to take one to Bath and Bristol, if weather permits. The motor-cars are rather a nuisance to humble roadsters like me, one never knowing whether the comers are Hooligan-motorists or responsible drivers.

Ever yours
Tho H.

I had a caller the other day who was an interesting man: Hugh

339. Mrs Henniker's sister died suddenly in 1902.

Clifford, Gov[erno]r of North Borneo, now at home on leave. I
wonder if you know him.

T.H.

79.   Max Gate,
                                       Dorchester.
                                    Nov. 28. 1902

My dear friend:

I have read with great interest the account of the reception
of Col. Henniker down in Suffolk,[340] and of your share in the
proceedings. What a proper thing it was for the parishioners
to accord such a welcome – not more than he deserved, seeing
what a long service over there his has been. Much ceremony
has been bestowed on the return of some who have only been
away a few months. It must feel very odd to sit in a carriage
pulled by human beings and to have to make a speech at the
end. It is a blessed thing that authors have never to undergo
such an ordeal.

A friend of ours has lately died at Florence, the daughter of
Poet Barnes.[341] Having known her in early life I wrote a little
obituary notice of her, which was in yesterday's *Times*[342] – She
was a gentle and charming woman, and had lived in Florence
between 30 and 40 years.

I don't think I have written to you since my visit to Bath. I
had a pleasant time there – as pleasant as could be in a place
last visited to see those who are now dead. That unhappily is
my case nearly everywhere now: those I used to find in homes
I find in the churchyard.[343]

However, I carried[344] my bicycle and cycled to Bristol, etc.
I could not help thinking that Bath would be an excellent
place for you to stay at for a week or two in the winter: and

340. Colonel Henniker's parents lived at Thornham Hall near Eye,
Suffolk.
341. Lucy Baxter had lived in Florence for many years and written
on Italian art. Her biography of her father was published in 1887.
342. 'Recollections of "Leader Scott"' (her pen-name).
343. Compare 'Paying Calls' (*Moments of Vision*).
344. This suggests that Hardy travelled by train to Bath, taking his
bicycle with him.

there are concerts every day. I found in a shop there a first
edition of Hobbes's *Leviathan* for – 6d. I did not know it was
a 1st ed[ition] when I bought it, or I sh[oul]d hardly have had
the conscience to take it.[345]

I am sorry to say that I am writing under the throb of a
neuralgia about my face, which makes this a poor sort of letter.

Believe me
Ever yours
Tho H.

Let me hear soon from you.

80.

Max Gate
Dorchester.
Sunday, Dec. 7. '02

My dear friend:

I am pleased to send you the few lines I wrote on the death
of Mrs Baxter as you wish to see them, and also a MS. copy of
the verses which appeared in the *Sphere*[346] a week or two ago. I
am unable to send the paper itself.

My face ache has practically gone off, though I feel it lurking
in the background. Strangely enough going out in this frosty
weather does not seem to aggravate it, though damp does.

Yes: Madeleine's[347] coming marriage does interest me, knowing her sentiments on such matters so well as I do, and that she
has always kept an open mind on matrimony. The event is a
triumph of the obvious, the Brodrick and Jeune households
having been so intimate for so many years and such near neighbours. I tell her the least she can do for me in the circumstances will be to keep down the war expenses of the country so
that I and other poor authors may not be oppressed by income
tax, and she says that S[t] J[ohn] promises to be duly influenced
in that direction.

345. For a more interesting account of how Hardy acquired this
bargain, see his *Life*, p. 317.

346. 'The Man he Killed' (*Time's Laughingstocks*) appeared in *The
Sphere*, 22 November 1902.

347. Madeleine Stanley married St John Brodrick, later Lord Midle-
ton, on 5 January 1903. He was Secretary of State for War (1900–3), and
for India (1903–5).

I hear that the weather in London is even colder than we have it here. Sir G[eorge] Douglas has been up there during the last few days, but he says the discomforts are so great that he means to clear out and depart sooner than he had intended.

What a pleasure it will be to see another book of stories from your hand. Why not write some extra ones this winter to put into the volume. People think so much of quantity.

Ever yours
Tho. H.

81.   Max Gate: Sunday
4.1. '03

My dear friend:

We are thinking of going up to town to-morrow morning, unless the weather should be very unpleasant. Emma thinks she would like to see M.S. married, and I have a few little matters to attend to besides. As we shall probably return Wednesday I will take my chance of finding you indoors Monday or Tuesday afternoon.

I hope Brighton has done you a world of good.

I have to thank you for that pretty little edition of *A Shropshire Lad*,[348] which I did not know of. It is in my pocket at this moment.

We shall be at the Langham Hotel if we come – the J[eune]s being unavailable with this affair going on.

Ever y[ou]rs sincerely
Tho H.

P.S. I had no idea you c[oul]d muster so many as 16 stories:[349] when did you write them. Best wishes for the new year.

348. *A Shropshire Lad* was published in 1896, and Hardy had met the author, A. E. Housman (1859–1936), probably for the first time, in 1899, and entertained him at Max Gate in 1900 (*Life*, pp. 304, 306). The edition Mrs Henniker gave Hardy must have been the 1900 reprint in 'The Smaller Classics' series.

349. See p. 111.

82.   Max Gate,
                                       Dorchester.
                                       March 17. 1903

My dear friend:

Your last letter found me disabled by rheumatism, which stuck about me a long while, and left a lassitude that I have only now got over. I think I caught the complaint by standing out of doors in the rain superintending the lopping of some trees. I had been thinking about a week before that I had not for years had an attack, and possibly never might again. We were going to stay for a day or two with Lady Grove at Sedge-hill,[350] but had to put her off on two occasions on account of it. In fact I have been scarcely out of the house (except just to Dorchester, etc.) since I was in London.

I hope Brighton did you some permanent good, but the London season seems to be so early this year that doubtless you have had some trying functions from which humble people are sheltered.

R. L. Stevenson's letters,[351] which you say you have been reading, are very attractive, particularly to those who knew him. The very fact of his not being quite 'thorough' as a man and as an author (i.e. critic of life), makes the letters, perhaps, all the more pleasant reading. In my enforced idleness I have been reading H[enry] James's *Wings of the Dove*[352] – the first of his that I have looked into for years and years. I read it with a fair amount of care – as much as one would wish to expend on any novel, certainly, seeing what there is to read besides novels – and so did Em; but we have been arguing ever since about what happened to the people, and find we have wholly conflicting opinions thereon. At the same time James is almost the only living novelist I can read, and taken in small doses I like him exceedingly, being as he is a real man of letters.

If we come to London this year we shall probably go into

350. Sedgehill Manor, Lady Grove's house north of Shaftesbury.
351. *The Letters of Robert Louis Stevenson to his Family and Friends*, edited by Sidney Colvin, 1899.
352. *The Wings of the Dove* was published in 1902. Hardy's comments on Henry James are rather ambivalent: he has a ponderous way of saying nothing at infinite length; his subjects hold interest only as long as one has nothing larger to think of; he is the Polonius of novelists, and yet 'a good novelist'. See *Life*, pp. 181, 211, 246, 370 and the note to p. 69 (*supra*).

quite miniature lodgings of a Dickensian cast, finding the smallest house or flat a burden, and of course saving something – though not much, because the servants have to be kept on here, and may therefore just as well be taken up to town and made use of. But why sh[oul]d I bore you with this! Did you go to the Winter Exhibition at the Academy? I liked it much. I saw that Col. H[ennike]r was at the Levée the other day.[353]

> Believe me
> Ever ~~aff~~(!)
> sincerely yours,
> Tho H.

83.   Max Gate,
                                               29: 3: 03

My dear friend:

I would not write to thank you for your kind gift of *Contrasts*[354] – a quite unexpected pleasure – till I had read it, and digested it. I was not aware that you meant to publish it so soon. Several of the stories I was familiar with, having read them when they were printed in periodicals.

The tale I like best, and the one I think the best in point of art, is 'In a Rhineland Valley'. This is a charming story, in which just enough is told, and just enough happens, to create an abiding impression. It develops, too, on lines of character entirely, owing nothing to the 'deus ex machina' that helps out lower forms of narrative art. 'Lady Coppinger' I also like, though I ought to have put 'After Thirty Years' next to the 'Rhineland Valley', as having the above mentioned characteristic also, though it is slighter. The soldier sketches I like for their detail, which makes one feel that you can speak with authority about them. 'The Homecoming of Job' is excellent, up to his death, which I take leave to doubt. But I won't particularize any more, for I like them all.

353. Colonel Henniker was presented to the King at Buckingham Palace on 9 March in recognition of his appointment to command the Second Battalion, Coldstream Guards, and of his active service throughout the Boer War.

354. Mrs Henniker's third volume of short stories (1903).

This is only a postscript to my other note – I suppose you are in London still. I just have seen in a paper that somebody has given Henley[355] a motor-car – for which he is grateful in rhyme, or rather in non-rhyme. What an appropriate gift for poor W.E.H. and what a thoughtful friend he must have. I fear I shall have to stick to the old bicycle: for one reason (apart from expense) I get exercise on it, while on (*sic*) a motor one gets chills and toothache.

Ever y[ou]r friend
Tho H.

84.   Max Gate,
                                                                 Dorchester.
                                                                 Sept. 13. 1903

My dear friend:

I had a sort of spiritual intimation that you were wandering about, and not at Stratford Place. I cannot imagine you taking part in an agricultural Exhibition this year without also imagining you wet through. Our yearly one took place in deluges of rain, and I did not go near it.

I have not yet really read the *Shambles of Science*,[356] but everybody who comes into this room, where it lies on my table, dips into it, and, I hope, profits something. For my part, the world is so greatly out of joint that the question of vivisection looms rather small beside the *general* cruelty of man to the 'lower' animals. I hear them complaining in the railway trucks sometimes, and think what an unfortunate result it was that *our* race acquired the upper hand, and not a more kindly one, in the development of species. If, say, lions had, they w[oul]d have been less cruel by this time.[357]

I do recollect that story you speak of, and can conceive

355. W. E. Henley (1849–1903), poet, critic, and playwright, was a cripple from boyhood. His poems *In Hospital*, written in 1873–5, were published with other verses in 1888. He collaborated with R. L. Stevenson in a series of plays. Several volumes of verse followed.

356. By Lizzy Lind and L. K. Schartau, London, 1903.

357. For another of Hardy's statements on vivisection, see *Life*, pp. 346–7.

that it would make the *beginning* of a play. Walter Besant[358] used to say that his method of dramatizing was (you knew that he wrote plays with *some* success) to take a story, up to a certain point; then strike out with no regard to the story at all. This is an excellent plan when the story is not well known.

I am sorry about the manoeuvres – and hope your Colonel won't catch cold. As you are a military lady (one of our cats has jumped up here)[359] I vent the following small grievance to you, in the hope that you will hand it on 'to the proper quarter' as they say. Our Dorset regiment has been known from time immemorial as the 'Green Linnets' – the facings having always been green. Of late the facings have been white, for no known reason, since some other regiments of the line still retain their green facings. As we fought under Clive at Plassy, and all through the Peninsular War in green (I suppose), this change is a petty annoyance which I resent, though I am not aware that the reg[imen]t itself does.

The usual rank and file of summer tourists have called here, and I have given mortal offence to some by not seeing them in the morning at any hour. I send down a message that they must come after 4 o'clock, and they seem to go off in dudgeon. I was a tourist myself last week, and as such was shown over Montacute House, Somerset (a show mansion of great interest). The amusing thing was that the residents sat like statues, reading in their library, and without speaking a word, whilst I was inspecting it, as if they, too, were part of the architecture. They are a very ancient family,[360] I admit.

Let me hear again soon please.

Ever y[ou]r affec[tiona]te friend
Tho H.

358. See note 290, p. 91.
359. There is a slight smudge on the page.
360. Montacute House, a splendid example of Elizabethan architecture, was built for the Phelips family, which held it to the present century. One of the family is the 'Richard Phelipson' of 'Montislope', who is mentioned in Hardy's 'Master John Horseleigh, Knight' (*A Changed Man*).

85.   Max Gate,
                                                 23 : 12 : 03
My dear friend:

I must make a prosy letter do duty for a Xmas card, for I cannot match in this latitude the pretty one you have sent me.

I had hoped to be able by this time to send you an early copy of the drama[361] I mentioned to you in the summer (I think) as having in my head to publish, though I have said very little about it owing to my doubts on the question, the play being, in fact, only one-third the proposed whole, and until the last moment before sending up the MS. to the publishers I did not decide to print now, but thought of keeping the MS. till the thing was complete, which would have meant a year or two's delay. However it will be out at the beginning of Jan[uary], and you will know what to think of it, though whether it will interest you at all, or anybody, I am in heathen ignorance, never having attempted the kind of performance before.

I was in London for a few days at the end of last month, but I did not stay over Sunday, as the rainy days gave me a cold in the head. You were, I believe, at Aldershot at the time. Em spent a week partly at Dover, partly at Calais, the air there having an invigorating effect upon her, but I did not go on to her as I had intended. You must miss the battalion very much. I suppose colonels when they retire frequent the Service Clubs, and look at maps, and fight their battles over again? at least I think I should if I were one. I have been dipping into an amusing book, *The Creevy Papers,*[362] which I think you will like if you have not already met with it. The Waterloo part reads like additional chapters of *Vanity Fair,* the Creevys being people quite of the Thackeray pattern.

If I should run up to town again this winter I shall try to see you. I find that after three days a cold develops, so that I must see London in snatches in winter, or not at all. It seems to have the same effect on most people who rush there out of

361. Part 1 of *The Dynasts* was ready for publication in December 1903, but for copyright reasons was not released until January 1904 when the American edition was ready.

362. Thomas Creevey (1768–1838) kept a journal, which is full of interest and entertainment for the social historian. He was a Whig M.P., and treasurer first of Ordnance and then of Greenwich Hospital.

fresh air, but not on the Londoners themselves. We shall have a lively political time next year, I fancy – do not you? A Tory lately calmly admits to me that they have no statesmanship on their side to speak of (omitting J.). I wonder if the Liberals have, outside the few whom we can all readily think off (*sic*).

A Happy Christmas and new year,
Ever y[ou]r friend
Tho H.

86.   Max Gate,
                                                   Dorchester.
                                                   March 14. 1904

My dear friend:

I wonder whether you are back again from Brighton and living on in London as usual. I have had a good deal of correspondence in one way and another about *The Dynasts,* which seems to have puzzled most readers as much almost as if it had been written in Hebrew. I daresay you saw the discussion I had with the *Times* dramatic critic[363] about it: no good was done, I imagine, by my answering him, but I was in the mood to do so just for once, and when you begin a newspaper correspondence there is no telling when you will end. To judge by the letters I got, however, I convinced most people that he was wrong.

Yours is an excellent, independent criticism, and I like what you say about the H[ouse] of Commons debate.[364] The almost universal cry is that it – the debate – is a *tour de force,* and not poetry. The answer is, of course, why should it not be? In such a quantity of scenes, one scene presenting a satirical picture of our legislators was justifiable – that is, if irony and political smartness may ever be versified. However the reviews have been a curious experience for me – particularly the American ones. As time goes on and the better class of critics get hold of the book (there were a few competent early ones certainly),

363. A. B. Walkley. Hardy's replies, 'A Rejoinder' and 'A Postscript', are reproduced from *The Times Literary Supplement,* 5 and 19 February 1904, in Orel, pp. 141–6.
364. The third scene of the first act of *The Dynasts.*

it seems to rise in public opinion: which, with other things, rather puzzles me to decide whether to carry it on to the end or not. When printing it I doubted if I should do more than the first part.

I have just lost my oldest friend in Dorchester – Henry Moule[365] (brother of the present B[isho]p of Durham). He was very old fashioned, and, of course, quite differed from me in opinion on many things; yet we always avoided those, and found plenty of others in matters of local history, antiquities, and water-colour painting, to which he has been devoted all his life.

I am hoping that the treacherous weather, which killed him, did not injure you, as it did so many. I have had face-ache, ear-ache, and aches of other sorts, but am getting rid of them. I nearly went up to the Jeunes in Feb[ruary] as they are very lonely now that the girls are gone, and Francis[366] in India. I suppose we shall be in London some time in the Spring, but we shall not take a house – nor even flat, so far as I know.

Always yours

Tho H.

P.S. Swinburne says that the broaching the Admiral scene[367] has been told him of *another* adm[ira]l. I always heard it of Nelson. He also tells me that his father was a great friend of Collingwood's. I quite understand your distaste for the scene – men like it: women don't.

T.H.

365. See note 292, p. 92. He was an able painter (some of his pictures of scenes in the Hardy country are in the Dorset County Museum) whom Hardy had in mind at the beginning of 'Old Mrs Chundle', a story which Moule told Hardy and which has never been published in England. (For an account of it, see Pinion, pp. 83–5.) Hardy refers to his loss in his *Life* (p. 321).

366. See p. 118. He died of typhoid fever in India.

367. An inn scene, the seventh in the fifth act of *The Dynasts*, in which it is said that the sailors 'broached the Adm'l' because they had run short of grog. Nelson's body was preserved in spirits on its way from Trafalgar to London.

87.   Max Gate,
                                       Dorchester.
                                  April 18: 1904

My dear friend:

I write a line to thank you for your words on the death of
my dear mother. Owing to her deafness, and, of late years,
inability to go out except in a Bath Chair, she has been for
some time out of sight of the world, but to myself and my
sisters she did not seem old. I often talked to her about you,
and I think she had seen your portrait. She also read one or
two of your books,[368] though for the moment I cannot remember which; and of Col. H[enniker] when his portrait appeared
in the papers during the war, she said that she 'liked his look'.
There is a small, though good, likeness of her in last Sat-
[urda]y's *Graphic*, from an oil painting by my sister.[369]

I suppose I shall be in Town in a week or two, when I have
attended to a few quite small matters that have now to be
settled under my father's will.

                        Your affect[iona]te friend
                           Tho H.

88.   Max Gate.
                                       25:9:04

My dear friend:

I am glad to get your brief note (also the enclosure of this
morning), for my uncertainty as to your exact whereabouts
was enough to make me put off from day to day writing a letter
at a venture. My fancy was that you had got to Ireland. Let
me know when you go. Your being over there will remind me
of old times – very romantic ones – when I was younger than
I am now, though you seem the same as you were then.[370]

I have not been abroad, though I cannot say that I have
done much as yet to the second part of *The Dynasts* (It is, of
course, in outline already). I am doing the battle of Jena just

368. Hardy's love of tales and literature undoubtedly came from his
mother. When he was little more than eight, she gave him Dryden's
Virgil, Johnson's *Rasselas,* and *Paul and Virginia.* Her 'good taste in
literature' came from her mother (*Life,* pp. 7, 16, 321).

369. The portrait by Mary Hardy is in the Dorset County Museum.

370. In May 1893.

now – a massacre rather than a battle – in which the combatants were *close* together; so different from modern war, in which distance and cold precision destroy those features which made the old wars throb with enthusiasm and romance. Not that the present war[371] lacks those features, though somehow it seems an anachronism, and to belong to a hundred years ago. I do not read any books about it – only the telegrams in the papers.

I really think it time that you got on with those short stories: many are written, but few worth reading. The last thing I printed was a romantic poem in verse, in the August *Fortnightly*,[372] which was liked, though (they say who know) not so 'strong' as the '*Trampwoman's Tragedy*'[373] – my best performance I am told. I have absolutely no opinion about them. You will be able to form your own when I republish them in a volume.

I had known young F[rancis] Jeune[374] from childhood, and shall miss him: his father, I think, particularly feels his loss. I am sorry they have no other boy. To my mind he was not quite strong enough physically for soldiering, which requires rude health for success.

I have been going about this and the next county – to Yeovil, Wells, Glastonbury, Shaftesbury, etc., but not elsewhere. I met W[illia]m Watson, Money Coutts,[375] and Mr and Mrs John Lane at Glastonbury by chance – and had a pleasant evening with them. I think Weymouth would suit you in the winter – the part called Rodwell, not the Esplanade.

Ever y[ou]rs

Tho H.

371. The Russo-Japanese War, 1904–5.

372. 'The Revisitation' appeared in *The Fortnightly Review*, and is the opening poem of *Time's Laughingstocks*.

373. 'A Trampwoman's Tragedy', declined by *The Cornhill Magazine* as unsuitable for 'a family periodical' and published in *The North American View* in November 1903, was admired by many writers, including Gosse. Hardy seemed to think it his best poem (*Life*, pp. 311–12), though at other times, as we shall see, he favoured 'The Darkling Thrush' and 'When I set out for Lyonnesse'.

374. The son of Sir Francis and Lady Jeune, who died in August 1904. Sir Francis never seemed to recover from the shock.

375. Francis Burdett Money-Coutts, a forgotten poet; see W. Archer, *Poets of the Younger Generation*, London, 1902, pp. 105–17.

Mary Jeune, wife of Sir Francis Jeune, *c.* 1900

24 : 5 : 1909

My dear friend: How strange —
I was thinking of either writing or
calling to see if you were in London
(where I was last week) when your
nice letter came. It was purely
by accident that I was up there
when Meredith died: I turned the
corner at the top of St James's Street
that morning, & saw the announcement
on a placard before me. It was a
sad shock, for he sent to ask if I
would run down & see him some time
ago, & I was intending to this summer.

First page of Hardy's letter on the death of George Meredith

89.   Max Gate,
                                                 Dorchester.
                                               Dec. 22. 1904

My dear friend across the water – as I must call you now –
this is a letter by way of Christmas card – (my spirits having
of late years ceased to rise to the height signified by one of
those festive productions). I duly received your pretty one,
and am glad to know the sort of house you are in: a warm-
looking one for the winter in appearance, though its character
may not bear out its look.

I am sorry to hear that you have suffered from chicken-pox.
How *did* you get it? You must have gone into some place
where the germs were – among somebody's chickens I
suppose.[376] I don't think I have ever had it. But our house here
is so isolated, and we see so few people, that even the few
maladies which visit the town do not come out to us. In
counterpoise I *always* get influenza if I stay any time in
London.

I will not forget your governess, if we ever can have anybody to lunch again. But that appears problematical at present, for a sort of hymeneal catastrophe has befallen this
establishment, *three* of our servants having got married last
Saturday, only the page remaining, and an unexpected difficulty arises from the fact that no new servant will come till after
Christmas day, so that we have to get on by calling in temporary help. Our girls often go off with husbands thus, and
I think it must be that the fresh air here gives them a colour
and makes them attractive.

I think you are right in preferring 'Fellow Townsmen' to
'The Three Strangers': there is more human nature in it.
'The Withered Arm' is largely based on fact.[377] I wonder if
you saw my 'Time's Laughingstocks' in the August *Fortnightly.*[378]

376. This sounds like a feeble joke, until it is realized that the
ailment was commonly thought to derive from poultry 'at some distant
date' (O E D).

377. All three stories have been included in *Wessex Tales* since
1888, 'The Three Strangers' being the story which was successfully
dramatized as 'The Three Wayfarers'. For a further note on 'The
Withered Arm', see the preface to *Wessex Tales*.

378. In which 'The Revisitation' was entitled 'Time's Laughingstocks, A Summer Romance' (Purdy, p. 138).

F

Why of course I must come to your play[379] if I am in Town.
But as to my being able to tell you by wire how it is going,
that will be beyond my power I fear, for if I take any personal
interest in the author of a play my judgment becomes para-
lyzed: though a stranger's play I can judge well enough. I
shall have to nudge my next neighbour – who perhaps may be
Walkley! – and ask him what I am to tell you. – It is true, as
you say, that all the money nowadays goes to the dramatists
and not to the novelists (except Hall Caine and Miss Corelli).
Barrie, I am told, is wealthy to oppression, and money still
insists on rolling in to him.

A man named Harper, a stranger to me, has written a book
called *The Hardy Country*,[380] with a manner of authority,
though I knew nothing about it till I saw the book, and it has
numerous errors. It is rather hard upon the landowners of this
part of England that their property should be so called by
these tourist-writers.

When are you going to London? I have to run up for a day
or two between now and February.

Ever yours
Tho H.

90.   Max Gate,
                                              Dorchester.
                                           Sunday 26: 2: 05

My dear friend

I am quite sorry to be unable to be in London this coming
week. Several things prevent it – among others I have been
feeling a little out of sorts – (as used to be said before you
were born), and on this account it is fortunate that I declined
an invitation from my fellow-*county* man Treves (Sir F. T.)[381]

---

379. *The Courage of Silence,* a four-act comedy (1905).
380. C. G. Harper, *The Hardy Country*, London, 1904.
381. Sir Frederick Treves (1853–1923), a native of Dorchester (where
he attended the school kept by William Barnes), Surgeon to the Royal
Family, and author of *The Country of 'The Ring and the Book'*, was
the first President of the Society of Dorset Men. He held this office
from 1904 to 1907, when he was succeeded by Hardy.

to be his guest at the Dorset Society's dinner to-morrow, though I should much have liked to talk over old Dorchester days with him. But as I cannot meet you this time at the Empress (what lofty titles we see! To go one better than that, the next Ladies' Club will have to be called the – well – Virgin Mary's[382] I suppose?) I shall hope to do so later on.

The Cornhill Magazine for March (just out) contains the romance in verse[383] that I told you of – about an actor and his wife – a woman of rank: as it is sure to be on your club table I do not send my copy, but if you do not come across it I will forward it with pleasure as you know. Please give my kind regards to Lady Grove if you meet her: she may know the family of my romance.[384]

You have become such a will of the wisp lately – or rather jill of the wisp[385] – that I hardly know how to address this – but I will send it to the club.

I hope the tooth-ache has gone? – You never told me if it passed off. Don't fatigue yourself overmuch about that play. I shall remember the date.

This is a frivolous letter to write with a headache in progress,

Ever yours sincerely
Tho. H.

I should much have liked the meeting at your club if I could have been there. I hope you are to be in Town a long while.

382. Hardy's humour was tactless; see p. 15.

383. 'The Noble Lady's Tale' concerns Lady Susan and her actor husband, the romantic couple who lived at Stinsford House and are buried at Stinsford Church. Hardy had heard his father talk of seeing her in a red cloak in the garden as he sat in the old church gallery when he was a choir-boy, and had learned much about her and her elopement in Horace Walpole's letters (*Life*, pp. 9, 163–4, 250).

384. The Ilchesters. Lady Susan was the daughter of the first Earl and Countess of Ilchester, who are the subject of the first story in *A Group of Noble Dames*. See p. 125.

385. A term Hardy introduced in *The Well-Beloved*.

91.   Max Gate: 12:9: '05
My dear friend:

I am sorry to find that I shall not be in London, either in
passing through outwards or homewards, at an hour which
will be very convenient for you (I fear) to see me. I am going
to the Crabbe[386] celebration at Aldeburgh on Saturday next,
and I arrive at Waterloo St[atio]n Friday at 2. o'clock, leaving
Liverpool St[ation] at 3.25. I return Monday or Tuesday –
possibly (if I go to see Norwich Cath[edra]l) Wednesday –
when I should have an hour or so about 3. o'clock, to spare,
before leaving Waterloo by the 4.55 train.

If, however, you do not mind my coming *if I can,* I will wire
to you which day, from Aldburgh (*sic*).

I could leave here by an earlier train Friday, and call about
½ past 11, if that would not be preternaturally early, and you
are engaged the following week.

If any of these hours are quite awkward do not trouble to
answer this, and I will hope for another opportunity.

As you do not feel nervous about the operation I feel
assured, and assume that it is an ordinary one. Surgeons are
so skilled now that they can do almost anything. At the same
time I regret its necessity.

With regard to the play,[387] the truth is that I did not tell you
how much I liked it, in my wish to be critical, under the impression that criticism was what you required. Your idea that
anything I could say would influence a manager was, I felt, unfounded in fact; a manager thinks all outside opinion rubbish.
George Douglas liked it *very* much, did I tell you? And as for
myself, when I saw the people marshalled on the stage in the 1st
and 2nd acts I felt as if I were looking at a play by Sardou.[388]

                                   In haste, ever yours
                                   Tho H.

I will in no event call without letting you know an hour or
two beforehand. Sh[oul]d like to see you.

386. Hardy had accepted Edward Clodd's invitation to stay at Aldeburgh, where the poet Crabbe had been born 150 years previously.
Hardy attended the celebration because he honoured Crabbe as 'an
apostle of realism' who wrote three-quarters of a century before 'the
French realistic school had been heard of' (*Life,* p. 327).

387. Mrs Henniker's *The Courage of Silence.*

388. Victorien Sardou (1831–1908), the most successful playwright
of his day in France.

92.   Max Gate,
                                              Dorchester.
                                            Sat. even[in]g.
                                            Oct. 21, 1905
                                  (Centenary of Trafalgar Day)

My dear friend:

I have just received your little letter, which it was so good
of you to write. I am, as you know well enough, really glad
that you are getting through this ordeal so successfully. Having
heard from General Henniker that you were getting on by
degrees I thought I would not write till I could know that a
possible wish to answer would do you no harm, lest you should
be worried by the sense of having to do so.

I may tell you now without fear of doing mischief that I
was much more anxious about the result of what you were to
endure than I admitted when I saw you, and when I wrote last.
I trust that it will have been worth while to risk it? Does the
surgeon feel that results will justify it? As the winter is coming on there will be no inducement for you to get about too
soon, and my opinion is that the longer, in reason, you can
rest the better.

My porings over military history to which you allude have
resulted at last in my finishing the second Part of *The Dynasts*.
It is a great weight off my shoulders as I do not feel such a huge
bulk of work before me as when I was further back. (Gen.
H[enniker] sent me a military term I was doubtful about, for
wh[ich] I am much obliged to him). I do not quite know
when this 2nd part will be published: all depends on
America.[389]

Dorchester has been celebrating Trafalgar to-day. You may
like me to tell you that my relations are the only people we
can discover in this part of the county who are still living
in the same house they occupied on the day of the battle 100
years ago (in the direct line of descent).[390] Lord Ilchester's

389. Hardy remembered the delay in the publication of Part I.
Copies of the English edition of Part II, which appeared in February
1906, were sent to America to be bound, and were published in March.

390. Hardy's birthplace at Higher Bockhampton was built by his
great-grandfather for Hardy's grandfather in 1801. In 1905 it was the
home of his brother Henry and his two sisters, Mary and Katharine
(the name of the younger being consistently spelt 'Katherine' by
Hardy).

people are in the same house,[391] but the present L[or]d is not descended directly: and so with most others. But this is a rather small and local item to send all the way to Ireland!

Ever most sincerely
Tho H.

(Write when you can.)

93.   Max Gate,
Dorchester.
Dec. 21. 1905

My dear friend:

As this is meant to be a Christmas-cardy letter (in answer to yours last sent, and the card a day or two ago) it ought to beam with a 'seasonable' spirit, which it is sure not to do. Though here, it may be, old fashioned sentiment lives on as long as anywhere – at any rate on such questions as killing a host of harmless animals to eat gluttonously of, and drinking quarts of liquor, by way of upholding the truths of Christianity. I have just had calling here, on his way to Cornwall, Mr Lewis Hind[392] – who says I once met him at your house, though I had forgotten it – and he says that all he can see in the town (Dorchester) is beef. I take care not to go there just at these times, on that account. I had an interesting talk with him. He seems bent on art-criticism now, and goes about the world looking at pictures.

Somebody has sent me a volume of poems called *Poems of the Real* which reminds me of our title (do you remember?) 'The Spectre of the Real'. Another volume of verse has also come to-day, *Devices & Desires*,[393] which seems, from a hasty glance within, to be of my tone rather. But I may be wrong, and one is apt to be full of self-conceit on such matters.

391. Melbury House in Melbury Park, in *The Woodlanders* country and adjacent to the village where Hardy's maternal grandmother lived before her marriage. (The MS. of the novel provides ample evidence that Hardy ostensibly transferred the setting to a region a few miles further east.)

392. Lewis Hind (1862–1927) wrote on painting and poetry, and was editor of *The Academy*, 1896–1903.

393. *Poems of the Real* has not been traced, and may have been published privately. The third edition of E. P. H. Lulham's *Devices and Desires* was published in November 1905 by R. Brimley Johnson.

Now I must make a confession. I did not send that Magazine with the Wessex article.[394] I did not see it for some time, but was induced to buy a copy by hearing of it accidentally. There was no harm in it, I suppose, except that it seemed as if I had assented to its publication, which I had not done.

You must be getting on if you can read the *Political History of England*.[395] I hope you really are? – stronger and stronger? When will you be in London again? I was there the first day or two of this month – and met some scientific people at the Royal Society's Dinner. How strange that Wedmore sh[oul]d just have read *The Well-Beloved*. It seems to have come to life again, as L. Hind says he has just read it. It was called, I remember, when it was published, the worst novel of the year, which perhaps it was.

Are you going to turn your attention to the stage, or to fiction, or to politics, when you get vigorous again? Now you are to answer this inquiry, and not skip it. Politics have played me the shabby trick of coming to a crisis just at the moment when I meant to bring out *Dynasts II*. I suppose it must wait. I want to get on with the third part, but I feel rather gloomy about it, as indeed about most things; and do little.

I shall be glad to see the story in the *Pall Mall Mag[azine]*.[396] I read your little one in the *Court Journal*, and as usual, wished it had been longer. I have now lent it to my sister – the one who painted the portrait of my mother that appeared in *The Sphere* and other illustrated papers. If you were here she would like to paint you: she does women best.

Best wishes for Christmas and the New Year. (You know I mean it.)

Ever sincerely y[ou]rs
Tho H.

Our county has lately lost a noble lord – its L[or]d Lieutenant[397] – the one who was angry with me for putting a legend of his family into 'The First Countess of Wessex'.

394. Probably 'Thomas Hardy and the Land of Wessex' by Clive Holland in *The Pall Mall Gazette*, November 1905.

395. Of this monumental work in twelve volumes, only one volume had appeared – Volume x by William Hunt, who collaborated with Reginald Poole in editing this series.

396. Mrs Henniker's 'His Best Novel' appeared the following July, and 'A Bunch of Cowslips' in *The Court Journal*, 2 December 1905.

397. The fifth Earl of Ilchester. See note 602, p. 189.

94.   Max Gate,
                                           Dorchester.
                                           Feb. 11. 1906

My dear friend:

   This is just a line to ask you where you are (and, of course,
how you are), as I want to send you part II of *The Dynasts* –
if you would like to have it – and it may as well be sent direct.
It is not exactly a woman's book, as you know, but as you
are in the army, and may be naturally supposed to take an
interest in the wars and rumours of wars, there may be an
exception in your case.

   Well: what do you think of the Elections? Frederic Harrison,[398] in writing to me, calls it 'a revolution'. I tell him it is
a revolution in which the weapons are criss-crosses and black-
lead pencils instead of bayonets and barricades.[399]

   As you know, the husbands of both Madeleine B[roderick]
and Dorothy A[llhusen] are out – I am sorry for them rather –
I mean the wives. I had a poem in *The Spectator* a week or
two ago on a typical Ejected Member's wife[400] – perhaps you
saw it.

   Why you have never heard that my sister paints portraits
is that she is only an amateur, is almost a hermit, and does it
only for her own amusement. It was she who did that striking
likeness of my mother which appeared in the illustrated
papers.

                                    Ever y[ou]rs
                                       Tho H.

Probably you know that Lady Grove is at Adelboden, Switz-
[erlan]d on account of a lung complaint? I am so sorry, but she
says it is getting well.   T.

   398. Frederic Harrison (1831–1923), Fellow of Wadham College,
Professor of Law, Positivist, and Liberal, was a remarkable man, and
wrote many books. His scientific positivism probably influenced Hardy
– for example, in his ideas on immortality as seen in *Wessex Poems*,
though Hardy was less a rationalist and evolutionary optimist. The
'Apology' to *Late Lyrics and Earlier* supplies a valuable hint of their
difference in outlook.

   399. The 'revolution' alludes to the sweeping Liberal gains in the
January elections in support of Campbell-Bannerman and against the
Unionists and Conservatives.

   400. 'The Rejected Member's Wife' was published in *The Spectator*,
27 January 1906, as 'The Ejected Member's Wife'.

95.   The Athenaeum,
                                         Pall Mall, S.W.
                                              16:5:06
My dear friend:

   We are staying on in Town (did I tell you?) till July 15, and
I send this on a voyage of discovery, to learn when you are
likely to be back. I have had influenza as usual, though not
severely; but the weather here is still productive of such
calamities.

   I have been doing very little. At my publisher's a few days
ago I met a young man – Mr Owen Wister, author of *The
Virginians, Lady Baltimore*, etc., whose novels of his native
country (America) are just now in vogue, and are readable.
Last night, at a Scotch University Club dinner (to which I
went as the guest of Gosse[401]) I heard a Scotchman sing 'Annie
Laurie'[402] beautifully, but unfortunately the audience were
youngish men who liked comic songs, and I had to endure
those melancholy productions for the most part.

   If you have come, or are coming, you will, of course, let me
know. Many thanks for your letter of appreciation of *The
Dynasts II*. It was very good of you to work through it – for it
does not, as a rule, appeal to women, I think.

                                         Ever yours
                                         Tho. H.

96.   The Athenaeum,
                                         Pall Mall. S.W.
                                              12:6:06
My dear friend:

   I have seen in the papers that you have been getting on
very well, and I therefore would not write to trouble you or

---

401. Edmund Gosse, who had been a friend of Hardy and admirer
of his work for more than thirty years, was now Librarian of the House
of Lords, and lived at 17 Hanover Terrace, overlooking Regent's Park.
He addressed Hardy as 'Dearest and most admired of friends', and the
friendship remained unbroken until Hardy's death.

402. Hardy was interested in the origin of this song, and there are
several letters on the subject in the Max Gate correspondence.

Gen[eral] Henniker unnecessarily with inquiries.[403] But at the same time I shall, as I need not tell you, be very glad to know exactly how you are progressing, when you really can write or send a message.

London is carrying on its old games of the season as usual, though I have nothing to do with them. We are in Town till about July 17. I want to do a little work at the British Museum,[404] but cannot get on with it very rapidly.

Believe me

Ever yours sincerely

Tho. H.

97.   1 Hyde Park Mansions

London. W.

29:6:1906

My dear friend:

The Magazine with your little story in it has arrived, and I read the tale which much interest last night. I don't know when you wrote it, but fancy it is the same you mentioned to me in a letter some time ago.

I notice the same delicate touches as of old, and also, as usual, the characteristic which you share with Sir Walter Scott — that which makes you suddenly finish up your narrative with a run, as if you feared you had bored the reader in the earlier part. I could have stood several pages more, had you condescended to write them.

To-day I met Lady Grove at Lady Burghclere's, where I happened to call, and she (Agnes G.) asked if I thought you would mind her writing to you, as she would like to do so, but was not sure if letters burdened you as yet. I said I thought you would be very glad to hear from her, and that you were quite well enough for letters. This brings me to what I have imagined that you are, after what you told me, and you know very well that I hope most earnestly that you are. We leave

403. In answer to a letter from Major-General Henniker, Hardy had written, 'it seems almost wrong to be out of physical pain oneself while another is bearing so much'.

404. He had to verify details in preparation for Part III of *The Dynasts*. For his other activities in London, in which music is prominent, see his *Life*, pp. 329–31.

London the 16th or 17th July. Possibly you may be here ere then? But don't run risks.

M. Jacques Blanche, the French painter, has painted my portrait (at his own request).[405] I think he is not quite satisfied with it, though I don't dislike it. He has been over these last last 2 months. But I am afraid I am retailing incidents to you which do not much interest you, owing to my having none of value in my commonplace life to describe.

I cannot tell you how heroic and patient I think you have been in this illness, and how much I feel that you deserve good health now as your reward. Believe me

Ever sincerely yours
Tho H.

98.   Max Gate,
                                          Dorchester.
                                        12: 9: 1906

My dear friend:

I am glad you liked my paper on Ancient Churches,[406] though I really wrote it only after repeated requests. Evidently we shall never agree about all things connected therewith, e.g., the high old Georgian pews, which I love.

I hope your stay in Hayling[407] has added still more to your strength as it was when you wrote. As you note, the French have been saying good things about me lately. Perhaps you saw the long article in the *Revue des deux Mondes*[408] for July 1? If you did not, I can lend it to you at any time you would like to read it.

405. Jacques-Émile Blanche, known as 'the French Sargent', painted two portraits of Hardy, one of which is in the Manchester City Art Gallery and the other in the Tate Gallery. For Blanche's conversations with Hardy, see his *Portraits of a Lifetime*, London, 1937, and Evelyn Hardy, *Thomas Hardy*, pp. 265–6.

406. 'Memories of Church Restoration' (Orel, pp. 203–17) was read in Hardy's absence at the annual meeting of the Society for the Protection of Ancient Buildings, and published in *The Cornhill Magazine*, August 1906. The first extant letter of Mrs Henniker to Hardy shows that she had her own views on the subject.

407. She was staying at Sea Field, Hayling Island (near Southsea), Hants.

408. In this Firmin Roz stresses the absence of passion from the English novel since *Wuthering Heights*.

Last Monday – apparently the last day of Summer – I
bicycled with my younger sister[409] to Yeovil by a route which
affords beautiful views over the Vale of Blackmore.[410] I wish
you could come down to the seaside near here, and drive out
that way. I am sure that Lulworth Cove would suit you, and
all the trippers are gone now. The people there let delightful
cottages and lodgings.

You knew by postcard of my visit to Lincoln Cath[edra]l. I
also went to Ely, Cambridge, and Canterbury.[411]

It is so provoking that where you are, or were, is so difficult
of access from this side. To get to Lincoln is less tedious than
the train to Hayling.

Were you not struck by the unexpected news of poor Pearl
Craigie's end?[412] We met her, for the only time this summer,
at the only evening party I went to in London – one at Stafford
House[413] – and she was looking better and fuller in the face
than when she called here in the Spring. I fear she broke down
through attempting too much. To keep three plates spinning,
literature, fashion, and the Holy Catholic religion, is more
than ordinary strength can stand. Perhaps it is rather unkind
to put it that way, but you will take me rightly.

The author of *A Man of Property*[414] sent me the book, and
I began it, but found the people too materialistic and sordid
to be interesting.

Always affec[tionate]ly yours
Tho H.

409. Kate (Katharine) Hardy.
410. The country seen at different seasons in *The Woodlanders,*
XXVIII, and *Tess of the d'Urbervilles*, XLIV. In his fiction Hardy had
written either 'Blackmoor' or 'Blackmore'.
411. He was accompanied by his brother (*Life*, pp. 331–2).
412. See note 3, p. 1. She died on 15 August 1906. Hardy attended
the unveiling of a memorial to her at University College, where she
had been a student and where a John Oliver Hobbes Scholarship was
founded in her honour (*Life*, pp. 331, 342).
413. Built for the Duke of York, son of George III, it was sold on
his death to the Duke and Duchess of Sutherland. In 1913 Sir William
Lever acquired it for the nation; it was renamed Lancaster House and
became part of the London Museum.
414. *The Man of Property*, the first of the Forsyte Saga novels by
John Galsworthy (1867–1933), was published in 1906. Mrs Henniker
thought it 'excellent'. Galsworthy's admiration of Hardy continued,
as the number of presentation copies of his novels in the Max Gate
library showed.

99.   Max Gate,
                                                 Dorchester.
                                                 21 : 12 : 1906
                                                 (Shortest day)
My dear friend:
  I have received your pretty reminder of the season. We get
plenty of such feathered choristers round our windows just
now, since the weather has got colder. I am sending a little
book for which I am not responsible, although only my words
are in it – so far as they can be called mine with so many misprints. It has been compiled by a young man lately, though
why he should have chosen such passages as he has, and not
any others that his eye lighted on, I do not know.[415]
  I have not been up to town of late, or I should have let you
know. Sundry little chills and aches have kept me indoors the
late autumn. I hope your visit to Lowestoft had the strengthening effect anticipated, even though I feel jealous that you
never condescend to try our air down this way – such a place
as Sidmouth, for instance; (I will not be so presumptuous as to
recommend a Dorset place.)
  How *could* you guess that those lines of mine in the *Daily
Mail*[416] referred to the Ilchesters' park? I happened to be
walking, or cycling, through it years ago, when the incident
occurred on which the verses are based, and I wrote them out,
though I had no intention of publishing them in a newspaper.
I think I may have told you that my interest in that park arises
from the fact that a portion of it belonged to my mother's
people centuries ago, before the Strangways absorbed it.
  Some verses of mine are coming out in the January *Fort-*

  415. A. H. Hyatt, *The Pocket Thomas Hardy,* London, 1906, contains many selections of prose and verse, most of them from novels,
among which it is interesting to note that *Desperate Remedies* and
A Pair of Blue Eyes are well to the fore, only *Tess of the d'Urbervilles*
and *Far from the Madding Crowd* being represented by more passages.
  416. 'Autumn in King's Hintock Park' (Melbury Park) was first
printed in *The Daily Mail* Books' Supplement, 17 November 1906.
See p. 58 for Hardy's previous reference to his ancestors' ownership
of land now belonging to the Fox-Strangways. (The first Lord
Ilchester, Stephen Fox, had adopted this family name; his wife,
mother of Lady Susan of Stinsford House, was daughter of Thomas
Strangways, formerly Horner, of Mells Manor House, Somerset.)

nightly Review,[417] but as I am *certain* that you will not like them I am not going to send you a copy. I have not read the Ronsard book.[418] Have you read the *Life of Leslie Stephen*?[419]

Best wishes from
Ever affec[tionate]ly yours
Tho H.

100.   Max Gate,
                                             Dorchester.
                                             8 : 8 : 1907

My dear friend:

I am sending this to Stratford Place, though I believe you are down at Aldershot. We have got back here and I am settling down to the somewhat mechanical work of omitting superfluous matter from *The Dynasts* (3rd part) as I don't want it to be over-long.

I have always regretted that I was not at home when you called with Miss Thornhill. I had to be in town for a few days after the flat was given up, and attended an interesting medical dinner, where I sat between two bright-minded friends, Sir J. Crichton-Browne, and Dr Clifford Allbutt[420] whom you know, I think.

417. 'New Year's Eve' (*Time's Laughingstocks*) would certainly have been heretical to Mrs Henniker.

418. George Wyndham, *Ronsard and La Pléiade,* Macmillan, October 1906.

419. Leslie Stephen (1832–1904) was a distinguished literary critic, philosopher, and mountaineer; he was the father of Virginia Woolf. He had known Hardy since 1873, when as editor of *The Cornhill Magazine,* he accepted *Far from the Madding Crowd.* In 1875 he invited Hardy to witness his renunciation of Holy Orders; the new scientific outlook had made him an agnostic. Hardy said that Stephen's philosophy influenced him more than that of any other contemporary. He contributed a notable section to F. W. Maitland's *The Life and Letters of Leslie Stephen,* which was published in 1906. (See Rutland, pp. 78–83.)

420. At this dinner, which was given by the Medico-Psychological Society, Hardy had scientific discussions with these two, not for the first time (*Life,* pp. 254, 336). Dr Allbutt was Regius Professor of Medicine at Cambridge. Sir James Crichton-Browne was an eminent authority on the treatment of mental breakdown. See p. 125.

The Wessex air seems to be much sought after this August. Sir F[rederick] and Lady Treves are neighbours of ours – having taken a house near here, and Francis Coutts writes to say that he is coming – also W[illia]m Watson – two poets. Mr and Mrs John Lane are staying at *The Antelope* in Dor-[cheste]r and came out here a day or two ago. Of course many motoring strangers are in the town whom I know nothing about. So you see that 'Nothing wanting is save she, alas!'

When is that book of yours coming out? You told me hardly anything, by the way, in your last letter. I am not really in such breezy spirits as a gossipy letter would seem to imply, and go along rather mechanically with the day's duties. I have just had a letter from Dorothy Allhusen, who is at Royat-les-Bains[421] doing a cure. She is not very strong. Nobody is, it seems to me nowadays – at any rate, nobody whom I come in contact with, though I gather from the newspapers that there are athletes in the world somewhere.

Ever affec[tionate]ly
Tho. H.

101.　　　　　　　　　　　　　　　　Max Gate,
　　　　　　　　　　　　　　　　　　　Dorchester.
　　　　　　　　　　　　　　　　　　　29: 9: 07

My dear friend:

I thought I would not write to thank you for your kind gift of *Our Fatal Shadows*[422] till I had read it, which I have now done (finishing it late last night).

In point of workmanship it shows I think a great advance upon your previous novels, and it is, in truth, a really literary production by a facile pen, which cannot be said of many novels nowadays. It is absolutely convincing – nothing in it *made up* to produce a melodramatic effect (my taste was depraved enough to make me wish there had been towards the end, to confess the truth; but please excuse me, it was late at

421. A spa, situated, in the words of the first Lord Houghton, 'under the shadow of the mountains of Pascal', who was born at Clermont-Ferrand, the neighbouring town in the Massif Central of France.
422. Mrs Henniker's novel, published in 1907.

night, when one can swallow anything). It is quite Trollopian, indeed, in its limitation within certain strict lines of natural-ness.

When one thinks that flirtations of that pattern are going on by the hundred every season, it shows your power that you should make us interested, unflaggingly, in that particular instance, as if it were quite exceptional. Of course *I* should not have kept her respectable, and made a nice, decorous, dull woman of her at the end, but sh[oul]d have let her go to the d—— for the man, my theory being that an exceptional career alone justifies a history (i.e. novel) being written about a person.[423] But gentle F. H. naturally had not the heart to do that. The only thing I don't care much about is her marrying the Duke's son – whom she did not love; an action quite as im-moral, from my point of view, and more so even, than running off with a married man whom she did love would have been. But convention rules still in these things of course.

There is really no reason why you should not go on writing scores of popular novels and making a fortune beyond the dreams of avarice, as poor Walter Besant used to say.[424]

Perhaps you have got back to London by this time, so I send this to Stratford Place. I have broken the back of *The Dynasts* at last, but have not quite finished it.

Yours Affec[tionate]ly Ever
Tho H.

I forgot to say that the situation before the story begins, that of the heroine having been engaged to Aurora's *first* husband before she flirted with her second, is very good, and might have made a long novel of the *whole* story.

T. H.

423. Compare this with Hardy's note of 23 February 1893 (*Life,* p. 252).

424. Sir Walter Besant had died in 1901. *Beyond the Dreams of Avarice* was the title of one of his novels. The title originated from Edward Moore's play *The Gamester* (1753).

102.   Max Gate,
                                          Dorchester.
                                    New Year's Eve 1907

I must just write a few lines, my dear, to thank you for that
pretty Christmas Card, and to wish you a happy New Year.
It was a relief to me to see your figure standing, apparently
hale and strong, in the view of your front door, for I was really
getting anxious about you, not having heard from you lately,
and forgetting that, strictly, it was my turn to write to you. I
hope you are as well as you look?

It is dreadfully dull here just now: raw, a little snow on the
ground, and descending from the sky something neither rain,
snow, nor hail, but what the almanack makers call 'downfall'.
It does not seem to me, however, that we are going to have a
very severe winter. I may be quite wrong, however.

I have almost finished the proofs of *Dynasts III*, and the
book will appear, I suppose, some time in Jan[uary].[425] I feel
like an old Campaigner – just as if I had been present at the
Peninsular battles and Waterloo (as they say Geo. IV imagined
of himself) It is a good thing to have nearly got rid of it, though
I shall miss the work.

I have had a ballad[426] – what I consider rather a strong one –
refused by the *Fortnightly* and the *Nation* (though they both
wanted something of me) on the ground that those periodicals
'are read in families' – The poem turns upon a tragedy that
'families' read about in the newspapers every week. But I
expected that it would be declined, so was not surprised to see
it come back. Yet people complain nowadays that the authors
of England have no strength like those of Elizabethan days. If
they had it they could not show it![427]

425. It was published in February 1908. Again a proportion of copies
was sent to be bound in the States, where it appeared in March.
Edmund Gosse continued his perceptive praise of his friend's great
work, stating that Hardy had invented 'something quite new' and
that his 'bigness and brevity of touch' and 'panoramic breadth' were
inimitable.

426. 'A Sunday Morning Tragedy' was written in 1904. It appeared
in *The English Review*, December 1908, nearly a year after this letter
was written. Hardy had thought of treating the subject dramatically
first, before realizing that it would never be accepted for the stage.
See Purdy, pp. 139–40.

427. Hardy had found this with the novel (Pinion, pp. 149–51).

I am just now hunting up old psalm tunes for the Society
of Dorset Men in London[428] – who, much against my wish,
have elected me as their President. I am about the worst they
could possibly have chosen.

Where have you been lately, and where are you going to,
if anywhere? Lady St Helier[429] writes from her new house near
Newbury. Is it not extraordinary that she should have had
the energy to build it after her troubles.

What did you think about Kipling being the Nobel prize-
man this year? It is odd to associate him with 'peace'.[430]

I repeat my wish for the New Year, both as to yourself and
to Gen. Henniker, and am, your affec[tiona]te and rather
gloomy friend

                                        Tho H.

103.   The Athenaeum,
                                            Pall Mall,
                                                S.W.
                                        21 : 5 : 1908

My dear friend:

I was glad to get your letter, and such a nice one too. I am
up here for a week or two, going back, I imagine, next week,
and thinking to come again after Whitsuntide. We have not
taken a flat this year, Emma being too weak to face house-
keeping in London, so I am staying by myself at a little hotel
I sometimes go to near Russell Square. I encounter people
here and there, and they are very kind, asking me to dinners
and luncheons, but I do not go to many. I did dine out last
night, however, at Lady St Helier's, and met a pleasant party –
some judges and their wives, the Gosses, the D[uche]ss of St
Albans (who by the way showed me a diamond pin that had

428. The tunes chosen are given in Hardy's *Life*, p. 337.

429. Formerly Lady Jeune. Sir Francis was created Baron St Helier
in the year of his death (1905). The new house was probably Poplar
Farm (cf. Weber, p. 66).

430. It may seem strange that the author of *The Dynasts* was never
awarded the Nobel Prize. His second wife had hopes that he would be
awarded it in 1914, but Hardy's heterodox views on the Immanent Will
had created too much hostility in the 'Establishment' for his full
recognition.

been worn by Nell Gwynne) etc., etc. She is in her new house, (Lady St H[elier]) in Portland Place, having sold the one in Harley St[reet]. Her dinners are not, of course, such as they used to be, but she is personally much the same – indeed, nicer and gentler than before her afflictions, which I don't think she will ever entirely get over.

You will be satisfied with the weather by this time. It is most good of you to tell me you like so many things in *The Dyn[as]ts*. The publishers are much pleased that it is taking so well: never before in my experience (if I remember) have I had my pub[lishe]r enthusiastic about a book he has brought out for me.

Morley in the Lords is an odd idea to me still: but I suppose he will shake down in time, and we shall get accustomed to him there. But upon the whole I wish that he had remained the scribbler he began by being: authorship was his natural profession.[431]

I am correcting proofs of a selection from Barnes's Dorset Poems.[432]

Yours ever affect[ionate]ly
Tho H.

104.   Max Gate,
                                             Dorchester.
                                          Dec. 23. [1908]

My dear friend:

I cannot send you anything so attractive as your Christmas picture, so I will only send a humble letter. Your figure standing so naturally, and so unaltered, in the front of your house reminds me much of old times.

I was in London for the Milton banquet at the Mansion House on Dec[ember] 9th – not that I care for banquets, but

431. John, Viscount Morley (1838–1923), a Liberal in politics, and an eminent man of letters, had recognized talent in the first novel Hardy submitted for publication (*Life*, pp. 58–9, and Charles Morgan, *The House of Macmillan*, London, 1944, pp. 87–92). He edited *The Fortnightly Review*, the 'English Men of Letters' series (Macmillan), and *The Pall Mall Gazette*. He was made a peer in 1908.

432. For the Oxford University Press; see note 315, p. 98.

I felt that I owed such attention to John Milton[433]— and I intended to return next day, so did not let you know I could call — which I found afterwards I could have done, for I was detained one day longer. If I come up early next year I wonder if you will be there. We seem to have a knack of not seeing much of each other nowadays.

Perhaps you saw in the papers that the energetic young burghers of Dorchester dramatized and acted *The Trumpet-Major*[434] here last month. The performance excited extraordinary interest, and a row of London critics sat in the front stalls as at a London first night. As it happened I had influenza that week, and could not go: so that I have not yet seen the play.

I think when you go to the seaside for change of air you might patronize Dorset just once. But you never do.

I found that circular you sent about the poor would-be novelist. I could not conscientiously have encouraged him: it is a hopeless business when publishers will not take the risk themselves, and wrong to pay for publication.

Our very old cat 'Comfy' died two days ago, over 20 years of age we judge. He is buried in our pets' cemetery. Best, *very best,* wishes.

Ever affec[tionate]ly
Tho. H.

105.   Max Gate,
                                           Dorchester.
                                           24 : 5 : 1909

My dear friend: How strange — I was thinking of either writing or calling to see if you were in London (where I was last week) when your nice letter came. It was purely by accident

433. Hardy also attended the Milton tercentenary celebration at Cambridge (where he met the Poet Laureate Robert Bridges for the first time at Sir Clifford Allbutt's; see *Life,* p. 342). His novels illustrate how closely he had read *Paradise Lost*; he honoured Milton also for his views on divorce, and his championship of truth, whatever the opposition (cf. the epigraph to *Jude the Obscure,* IV; 'Lausanne, In Gibbon's Old Garden: 11–12p.m.'; and *Life,* p. 294n.)

434. The novel was dramatized by A. H. Evans and performed at Dorchester on 18 and 19 November 1908. This was the first of many dramatic productions of Hardy's novels by Evans and, later, by T. H. Tilley. (See Purdy, pp. 351–3.)

that I was up there when Meredith died: [435] I turned the corner
at the top of St. James's Street that morning, and saw the
announcement on a placard before me. It was a sad shock, for
he sent to ask if I would run down and see him some time ago,
and I was intending to this summer. I send a few lines of verse
I was moved to write about him, in case you did not see them
in the *Times*.

I am not surprised that you got stuck in *The Egoist*.[436] It is
awkward for me, of course, to criticise the work of a man I
liked and admired so much, but I may say that the difficulty of
reading – or at least enjoying – some of his books arises entirely
(as I think) from his errors of method. Why he was so perverse
as to infringe the first rules of narrative art I cannot tell, when
what he had to say was of the very highest, and what he discerned in life was more than almost any novelist had discerned
before. A child could almost have told him that to indulge in
psychological analysis of the most ingenious kind in the crisis
of an emotional scene is fatal – high emotion demanding simplicity of expression above all things – yet this was what Meredith constantly did. Wordsworth knew better: and so I believe Meredith did, only he would not practise what he knew
because he was so exasperated by bad criticism.

This is what makes Swinburne[437] the greater writer, though
he is much the smaller thinker: he knew so well how to
appeal.

I, also, read the novel *Maurice Guest*,[438] the author having

435. Meredith, the poet and novelist, whose advice on Hardy's *The
Poor Man and the Lady* had great influence on the plot of *Desperate
Remedies* (*Life*, pp. 60–63), died on 18 May 1909, forty years after their
first meeting at Chapman and Hall's, where Meredith was reader. Hardy
visited him at his home near Box Hill in 1894. After seeing the
announcement of Meredith's death, he went on to the Athenaeum
Club and wrote the poem 'G. M.' ("George Meredith" in *Collected
Poems*), which appeared on the day of the funeral. Hardy attended a
memorial service in Westminster Abbey (*Life*, pp. 345–6).

436. It was published in 1879, and is probably the most brilliantly
tedious of Meredith's novels.

437. Swinburne had died in April 1909. Hardy was not able to attend
his funeral, and wrote his tribute 'A Singer Asleep' (*Satires of
Circumstance*) after his visit to the grave at Bonchurch in March 1910.

438. By Ethel Florence Lindesay (1870–1946), an Australian who
wrote under the pseudonym of Henry Handel Richardson. The novel
was published in 1908.

sent me a copy. Yes the characters are a bad lot, but the woman is well done (utterly unattractive to me personally: — there are scores of them about; but attractive as a drawing, because of its accuracy).

I knew John Davidson[439] very slightly. I think he might have rubbed on, if he had had a little more ballast. I am not doing much just now, and think of going to Aldeburgh[440] for Whit-suntide.

It is announced that *Tess* is to be produced at Covent Garden this season as an Italian opera: [441] I gave permission some time ago, and it has already been done in Milan, Venice, Naples, etc., with much success. Let me hear from you again.

Your affec[tiona]te friend
Tho H.

106.   Max Gate.
                                            19 : 7 : '09

My dear friend:

I fear I shall never win your forgiveness for not entering into that vivisection question, and agreeing to be a Vice-president at the Congress.[442] But I find myself almost unable to do anything at all by reason of innumerable worrying difficulties on outside matters, and I have to decide either to neglect these important though not well understood questions (by me), or to give up writing a single page more. I cannot boast of the manysidedness possessed by some men, and am but a poor creature in practical things.

It has just occurred to me that your house at Hinstock must be near Farnborough,[443] which, as I pass there in going to and from London, I could perhaps stop at, and see you?

439. The poet John Davidson (1857–1909) committed suicide.
440. As a result of the 'influenza' which as usual afflicted him in London, Hardy had to postpone his visit until July (*Life,* pp. 346–7).
441. The opera, by Baron F. d'Erlanger, was a great success. Hardy and his wife were present at the first Covent Garden performance on 14 July (*Life,* p. 347).
442. For his views on vivisection and cruelty to animals, see *Life,* pp. 346–7, and the letter to the Secretary of the Humanitarian League, p. 349.
443. And Aldershot, where Brigadier-General Henniker commanded the First Guards Brigade.

I came down here Saturday evening – very much depressed with London, and, alas, with life generally, which I should not be particularly sorry to take my leave of. Yet I suppose I ought to have felt lively last week, for, as you may have seen in the papers, *Tess* was produced as an opera at Covent Garden, with such success as (so the management tell me) they have not had for years. It is to be done again to-morrow night. I wish you had been in town and could have accepted a stall or stalls that I could have offered you. When are you going to be living there regularly again?

I am hoping soon to hunt up my fugitive poems in the papers, and bring them out.

Your affec[tiona]te friend
Tho. H.

107.   Max Gate,
                                        Dorchester.
                                        Nov. 28. 1909

My dear friend:

I wonder if you are again in London, or down at Farnborough still, and if you are keeping quite well, as I hope? I like you to be in London best for my own convenience in seing you, but country air does, after all, keep up one's strength better, and therefore you should have it.

In about a week some poems of mine are to be published under the title of *Time's Laughingstocks*.[444] I imagine that you don't like the title, and fear that you will like some of the verses still less than the title – indeed I may say I am sure you will. So, shall I send you a copy, or not. I don't quite like to do so unless you say you really want to see them, and I shall not be offended if you say you don't. To be sure, it is possible to continue to like a person even if you disapprove of some of his writings. I am thinking of sending a copy to your brother, as it is so very long since I have done such a thing, though I

---

444. *Time's Laughingstocks* was published on 3 December 1909. Its title, first used for 'The Revisitation', the first poem in the volume, derives from Tennyson's *The Princess* (IV).

suppose it is rather senseless to send verses to a Cabinet Minister at such a political moment as this![445]

Last week a company of amateur actors went up to London from here, and performed their version of *Far from the Madding Crowd*[446] before the Society of Dorset Men in London. It pleased them enormously, though I was not there to see the effect. Bathsheba was a very pretty girl of this county.

I retail such as this to you, but I am not in the brightest of spirits, to tell the truth. Still, who can expect to be at my age, with no children to be interested in.[447] I may be running up to town in a few days.

Ever your affect[iona]te friend
Tho. H.

Have you read Lady St Helier's reminiscences yet?[448]

108.   Max Gate,
                                        Dorchester.
                                      19: 12: 1910

My dear friend:

Yes: the poor cat was such a loss. She was 'the study cat', and used to sleep on my writing table on any clean sheets of paper, and be much with me. I might possibly have saved her life if I had known where to look for her.[449]

445. Resistance by the peers to Lloyd George's budgetary proposals had created much indignation and a move to 'hang the House of Lords'.

446. The second of Hardy's novels to be dramatized by A. H. Evans. In the London production, at the Cripplegate Institute, the part of Bathsheba was played by Miss Ethel Hawker.

447. A significant statement, which helps to explain Hardy's outlook. He voices the same thought in a letter to Gosse. See the note of 13 August 1877 (*Life,* p. 116) for an even more telling comment on the subject.

448. *Memories of Fifty Years,* London, 1909.

449. This was Kitsy, buried in the pets' cemetery at Max Gate, where Roman skeletons had been found (*Life,* p. 163), and the subject of Hardy's poem, 'The Roman Gravemounds'. The end of the paragraph suggests that Kitsy may have been the cat strangled in a rabbit wire on Conquer Barrow near Max Gate (see Purdy, p. 169, 'The Death of Regret').

Miss Dugdale[450] mentioned to me that she had been with you. It was a great enjoyment for her. *Nobody* but you does kind things like that, and I am sincerely grateful to you. I am so glad you like her: she quite loves you – indeed you have no idea what a charm you have for her. Her literary judgment is very sound.

By an unfortunate accident I never replied to your question if Mr Frank Lambert might set 'The Division'[451] to music. Please let him know, if he is still in the mind, that he certainly may, and that it will be a great pleasure to me.

A very happy Christmas to you.
Ever your affect[iona]te friend
Tho. H.

109.
Max Gate
Christmas Eve
[1910]

My dear friend:

Many thanks for your handsome Christmas card just come, and its genial texts. I was just beginning to copy out those lines on the loss of our cat that I promised to send: but on looking at them they seemed too elegiac to reach you on Christmas morning, so I will postpone them.

I have nothing else to send, for I have not been able to go out or see about anything lately. After returning here from London a cold developed, and I have been laid up with a sore throat for a week or more. It has nearly gone off now, but I

450. Florence Dugdale was introduced by Mrs Henniker to the Hardys in 1904. She was the daughter of the headmaster of St Andrew's National School, Enfield, wrote several children's books, worked as a reviewer, and occasionally typed for both Mr and Mrs Hardy; she had done research for Hardy in the British Museum when he was writing *The Dynasts*. Miss Dugdale was at Max Gate several times before Mrs Hardy's death. Afterwards Hardy invited her to take charge, and she did much to protect him from the intrusions of uninvited visitors and help him with his correspondence. They were married at Enfield in February 1914.

451. See p. xxxiv.

must stay indoors a few days longer; so my Christmas will be dull enough.

What a pleasant luncheon yours was: but yours always are. I was glad to see you looking just the same. To my great surprise the publishers tell me that they have to reprint 'T.L.S' – which is a very unusual event in the history of verse so soon – especially as a large first impression was printed.[452]

It is a fine sunny frosty day here, without a cloud. I hope it is so with you. Well: a merry Christmas to you and your house ('merry' is the old word, and I like it best). By the way, you would find that poem 'The Dead Quire'[453] apposite to the season.

Ever affectionately
Tho H.

110.   Max Gate,
                                                  Dorchester.
                                                  17 : 3 : 1911

My dear friend:

I will be a member, or on the Committee of, the Council of Justice[454] to animals, if you think it will be of any service to the cause. In that event please let them have my name. I fear I shall not be able to do much, but I will do what I can.

My trouble is that I am expected to support all sorts of Societies in which I take no interest, and which I don't much believe in, to the neglect of such movements as these.

I was going to write to you when I read the account of L[or]d Crewe's accident.[455] but when I found next day that it was not so serious as I had feared, I did not. I am glad to see that he is getting on well.

452. *Time's Laughingstocks*. It is interesting to note the rise in the number of copies printed for the first editions of Hardy's poems, from 500 (*Wessex Poems*) to 5000 (*Human Shows* and *Winter Words*). 2000 were printed for the first edition of *Time's Laughingstocks*.

453. In *Time's Laughingstocks*; first printed in the Christmas number of *The Graphic*, 1901.

454. In 1914 he was Vice-President of this Committee.

455. Lord Crewe, undoubtedly as a result of political strain and anxiety over a long period, had fainted at a dinner at Claridge's hotel, sustaining severe concussion. He was ordered to rest for eight weeks.

Miss Dugdale has written this week, and tells me she went to the play with you, and much liked going. My taste for the theatre is, I fear, weakening, which hers is certainly not.

How is that novel getting on? You said ever so long ago, if you remember, that you were doing one.[456] I think some verses of mine are coming out in the *Fortnightly*[457] soon, but I dare not send a copy to you, as I *know* you won't like them, or some of them. We have drifted so far apart in our views of late years.

They have asked me to Westminster Abbey to the Coronation,[458] but I am not going. All that week I am thinking of doing as good men did in the Scriptures, and going away into a desert place.

I am very lonely and dull down here, and wish I could be more in London: but I always get influenza or a putrid throat if I go.

> Your ever affec[tiona]te friend
> Tho. H.

111.   Max Gate,
                                              Dorchester.
                                            May 3: 1911

My dear friend: I wonder if you are in London now, or likely to be the week after next (May 15 to 22). I propose to be there then, and Emma wants me to take her to the reception at the Foreign Office (22d) so I suppose I must.

I have been asked to be present at the unveiling of the Victoria Memorial by the King and Queen on the 16th, but I am not going. Levée Dress at 12 o'clock in the day in the middle of a Park[459] seems to me a mistake – though I know it is the custom.

456. *Second Fiddle,* published in 1912.
457. See the next letter.
458. The Coronation of George V took place in June 1911. Hardy decided to avoid 'the Coronation circus', and went with his brother on a tour of the Lake District (making no effort, it seems, to visit the Owens at Belmount Hall); see *Life,* p. 355.
459. The Victoria Memorial looks down the Mall between Green Park and St James's.

I was in London for the last week-end, and went to the Academy Dinner, which is one of the few functions of the kind I care to attend nowadays. I sat next to Buckle of *The Times*,[460] and had an interesting talk with several other friendly people – Sargent,[461] Barrie, Kipling, and many R.A's.

In your last very charming letter (you *can* write them when you choose) you say you w[oul]d like to see those poems which appeared in the *F[ortnightly] Rev[ie]w* called *Satires of Circumstance*. Perhaps you have met with them by this time, but if not I have a copy here and will send it on your letting me know. You will remember, I am sure, that being *satires* they are rather brutal. I express no feeling or opinion myself at all. They are from notes I made some twenty years ago, and then found were more fit for verse than prose.[462]

I am pleased that you liked 'A Darkling Thrush', and 'Rain on the Windows'.[463] So do I. They were written quite off hand.

Your novel must be nearly ready by this time? I have been reading Mrs Craigie's *Life*[464] – indeed, have not finished it yet. A remarkable woman; and yet she achieved nothing solid or enduring.

Believe me

Your affectionate friend

Tho H.

460. G. E. Buckle (1854–1935) was the editor of *The Times* from 1884 to 1912.

461. John Singer Sargent, an American, became famous as a portrait-painter. Most of his work was done in England, and he was made an R.A. in 1897.

462. In *Satires of Circumstance* (1914) there is a series of fifteen poems entitled 'Satires of Circumstance'. Eleven of these (all but viii, xii, xiii and xv) were printed in *The Fortnightly Review*, April 1911, together with a twelfth which was discarded. They are dated 1910 in the MS. (Purdy, pp. 164–5.)

463. 'The Darkling Thrush' (the MS. suggests that it may have been written for the end of 1899) was printed in *The Graphic*, 29 December 1900, under the title 'By the Century's Deathbed'.

'The Division', which was written in 1893 and probably relates to the strain in Hardy's relations with his first wife about the time when he first became acquainted with Mrs Henniker, begins 'Rain on the windows ...'. Mrs Henniker included the last two verses of the poem in chapter xxvi of *Second Fiddle*.

464. *The Life and Letters of Mrs Craigie* (1911) was written by her father, John Morgan Richards. See Vineta Colby, *The Singular Anomaly*, New York and London, 1970.

112.   Max Gate
                                               Dorchester.
                                               May 26: 1911
My dear friend:

I have read your brief story with much interest. It is just
long enough for what it tells, and might be made one of a
series entitled *Unfulfilled Intentions*.[465] I think some other of
your short ones would go into such a series. The man is just
like a politician, or I suppose I ought to say a statesman, – a
sort of L[or]d Haldane[466] one fancies? The girl, though so
slightly sketched, is very distinct – the modern intelligent,
mentally emancipated young woman of cities, for whom the
married life you kindly provide for her would ultimately
prove no great charm – by far the most interesting type of
femininity the world provides for man's eyes at the present
day.[467] In fact, between ourselves, I don't quite believe she did
marry that other man.

I could not call, for I found I was getting a slight cold in
London and felt, too, rather fagged; so I came back Thursday.
I return the story.

                              Y[ou]r affec[tiona]te friend,
                              Tho H.

113.   Max Gate,
                                               Dorchester.
                                               22. Aug. 1911
My dear friend:

I don't quite know where you are just now, but no doubt
this missive will find you out. I was most interested in your

465. Although the phrase is used with no more than human connota-
tions here, Hardy uses it elsewhere with a wider, philosophical significance, which is explained in a note of 9 May 1881 (*Life*, pp. 148–9),
where Hardy, after 'trying to reconcile a scientific view of life with the
emotional and spiritual', argues that a Creator would not have made
man sensitive to suffering without eliminating evil. See also *Life*, p. 163
(17 November 1883). His most famous use of the expression occurs in
The Woodlanders, VII, and the whole novel is a comment on it, in its
human aspect.

466. Richard Burdon, first Viscount Haldane (1856–1928), lawyer
and philosopher, entered the Liberal Party, was Secretary of State for
War (1905–12), and subsequently Lord Chancellor.

467. Hardy held rather similar views about Sue Bridehead.

success in seeing the Coronation show by land and sea. Really your enterprise is becoming almost American. I felt myself a poor creature, for I went off to the Lakes to be away from the millions – who did not come to Town after all.

The only thing worth mentioning that I have done since then has been a little trip I took with my sister Kitty (the younger one) about a fortnight ago to the north coast of Somerset and Devon: to Minehead, across Exmoor by coach (a cruel climb for the horses – 1400 f[ee]t, six being necessary) to Lynmouth (where Shelley and Harriet[468] stayed), Lynton, Ilfracombe by steam boat, Exeter Cathedral, etc. No sooner had we got back than the railway strike began.

I have found an unexpected ally in the Slaughter-house reform work – Lady Hoare, of Stour Head (*sic*), Wilts. She, too, is getting the instruments sent about. She motors over here to tea sometimes, and knowing you are interested in the same causes, would like to make your acquaintance some day.

Steps are being taken to publish an *edition de luxe* of all my books.[469] (The publishers mark their letters on the subject 'private', so I suppose I must ask you to treat it as such). I did not feel altogether elated at the proposal, though it will be in some respects a good thing; for it involves re-reading old books of mine, written when my spirits were brisker than they are now, and full of artistic errors which cannot be altered.

I will inquire if the butchers, etc., will use the pig-killer hereabout. I ought to have done so before, but I have had no energy at all.

Will you be in London in the autumn, I wonder? I will try to see you if you are. It occurred to me the other day that this year completes the eighteenth of our friendship. That is rather good as between man and woman, which is usually so brittle.

Ever affec[tionate]ly
Tho H.

468. Shelley's first wife, whom he married in 1811 and deserted. For Hardy's interest in places associated with Shelley, see, for example, *Life*, pp. 17, 42, 188–9, 192–3, and p. 66 of these letters.
469. The Wessex Edition was published by Macmillan and Co., Ltd., and began in 1912 with seventeen volumes of novels and short stories. For the first, *Tess of the d'Urbervilles*, Hardy wrote his important 'General Preface to the Novels and Poems', dated 1911 (Orel, pp. 44–50).

114.   Max Gate,
                                         3: 10: 1911

My dear friend:

At last I know where you are, which I have lately been in some doubt about. Mr Stewart, the Secretary of the Council of Justice, writing to inquire if I would have a 'painless killer' (at your suggestion) seemed to imply that you had returned from abroad. What with Harzburg and Scotland I shall expect to find you in rude health when we meet – which I trust may be at no distant date.

I am much interested in 'G. Worlingworth'[470] and all his works, and certainly don't mind receiving letters for him, or his MS. which shall be duly posted on. But I really think your own name would have accelerated the reading of a play rather than otherwise. – Whether there is a prejudice against a woman-dramatist I don't know: I should hardly have thought so.

I was *much* interested in your criticisms of *The New Machiavelli*,[471] and have been saving up powder and shot for replying to your arguments, or rather the assumptions involved in your queries. I have not read Wells carefully enough to discern his exact theories on the marriage question (if he has any), but you know what I have thought for many years: that marriage should not thwart nature, and that when it does thwart nature it is no real marriage, and the legal contract should therefore be as speedily cancelled as possible.[472] Half the misery of human life would I think disappear if this were made easy: where there were no children at the wish of both or either: where there were children after an examination of the case by a court, and an order for certain provisions to be made.

There would, of course, be difficulties, as you point out, but they would not be insuperable. Every kind of reform is met with the objection that it would be impossible, would have monstrous results, etc., yet the reform takes place, and the impossibility vanishes. However, as I said, I am not sure what

470. The name which Mrs Henniker proposed to assume for dramatic writing. For its link with her family, see note on p. 202.
471. By H. G. Wells (1866–1946), published in 1911.
472. In *Jude the Obscure* both marriages are against nature. Jude fails to realize that the second is against Sue's natural inclinations.

it is Wells advocates in this book, and I may really not be answering you. Anyhow we will discuss the question when we are together. But I know beforehand that I shall not move you to sympathize with my views any more than you do with Mr Wells's.

It is so kind of you to have Florence Dugdale sometimes, and she likes coming very much. She has just gone to Weymouth for a week or two's change: I am going to run down this afternoon to see how she is getting on.

I hope you will not find Scotland too cold, but I really should think it must be almost, judging from the weather here – why don't you come to Bournemouth sometimes: I am sure it would suit you.

I think that another ballad of mine will appear in print in a month or two – this time in the *Fortnightly*. I *fancy* you may like it – though it is tragic.[473] I will let you know about it in due time.

If I read another novel in the immediate future I think it shall be *Hilda Lessways* – the continuation of *Clayhanger*[474] by Bennett.

Affec[tionate]ly yours
Tho H.

115.   Max Gate,
                                              Dorchester.
                                   Sunday: 21:4:12[475]

My dear friend:

I must seem a bad and neglectful person in not having written to acknowledge your kind gift of your new novel: and to answer your letter. But I have had a chill which though it only kept me in bed two or three days pulled me down rather much, and took away all my energy – even that for reading. All this time there were heaps of proofs waiting for me to

473. 'The Sacrilege', published in November 1911.

474. *Hilda Lessways*, the second volume of the Clayhanger trilogy by Arnold Bennett (1867–1931), was published in 1911.

475. Mrs Henniker had travelled to Dorchester (in November 1911) to attend with Hardy and his wife a performance of 'The Three Wayfarers' and 'The Distracted Preacher'. See pp. 155 and 180–1.

Major-General the Hon. Arthur Henry Henniker-Major, C.B.
(probably 1911)

Thomas Hardy and Edmund Gosse at Max Gate in 1927,
after a friendship of more than fifty years

correct (of a new definitive edition – *edition de luxe* some call
it – of all my awfully imperfect books, that you may have seen
announced).

At last I feel about as usual, and have tackled most of the
proofs, and yesterday and to-day have given myself the holiday
of reading *Second Fiddle*.

It is one of your best novels, I think, with more matured
insight and thought in it than were in your earlier ones. The
character drawing is firm and distinct, and the action unforced. Florence Dugdale told me before I began it that she
thought it a very good story, but though she is a good judge I
would not be influenced, and formed my own opinion.

I notice that you are quite up to date in the mode of
constructing your narrative. I had left off writing novels before the mode came in – or rather was revived – and should
not in any case adopt it: I mean, the making the story a
chronicle covering a good many years – so many yards cut off
the roll of life, without any attempt to make an organic whole
of the piece, as in a drama. Your method has the attractive
swiftness of movement which stories preserving the unities
do not possess, and so leads one on skippingly: though it has,
on the other hand, the defects of its qualities, unavoidably.

George is *excellently* portrayed. Women's men are usually
such unreal duffers that it is rather remarkable you should
have drawn such a real man. Elizabeth is, also, vivid; but of
course you could draw her. Yet I don't see why she should
have been so upset by that telegram, as it did not distinctly
convey information of the relations between Mrs Vance and
her husband – whatever those relations may have been, which
you leave rather vague. However I admit that you know best
in that matter.

I am rather sceptical about that wonderful garden of Uncle
Charles's – in the dust and smoke of London. To me London
gardens *always* seem faded and dirty.[476]

How ungrateful of me to be so carping, when you do me
the honour of quoting some of my verses. But you would not,
I know, have cared for me to write about the book except just
as I felt.

476. He had thought so much earlier: compare the poem 'To a Tree
in London' (*Winter Words*) with the description of the same tree in
A Pair of Blue Eyes, XIII.

G

The motor-car by the way, 'as large as a drawing room' is nicely descriptive. Those huge fashionable structures come to our door sometimes and fill us with awe as they super- ciliously encounter the difficulties of our narrow drive.

I hope you feel more settled and cheerful now? I was thinking – the immediate cause of the thought being the disaster to the *Titanic*,[477] in which I have lost two acquain- tances – that we feel it such a blow when friends go off before us, as if we were never going ourselves at all:[478] when the same journey is only postponed for us by a few years.

Believe me
Ever your affect[iona]te friend
Tho H.

116.   Max Gate,
                                             Dorchester.
                                          22:5: 1912

My dear friend:

I was so glad to hear that you liked the verses.[479] I posted them directly I had finished them, and had no time left to

477. On 15 April 1912. See Hardy's poem 'The Convergence of the Twain', first printed in aid of the *Titanic* Disaster Fund.
478. Hardy was thinking of Mrs Henniker's loss. Major-General Henniker had died of heart failure at 13 Stratford Place on 6 February 1912, after being kicked by a horse and sustaining a broken leg.
479. Written by Hardy in memory of Major-General Henniker:

A. H., 1855–1912

A laurelled soldier he; yet who could find
In camp or court a less vainglorious mind?
Sincere as bold, one reads as in a book
His modest spirit in his candid look.

At duty's beckoning alert as brave,
We could have wished for him a later grave!
A season ere the setting of his sun
To rest upon the honours he had won ...

Yet let us not lament. We do not weep
When our best comrade sinks in fitful sleep,
And why indulge regrets if he should fall
At once into the sweetest sleep of all?

write a letter. I am afraid they are not very good – not so good as he deserved, but they were at any rate spontaneous, and not made up. I must be frank enough to own that, though I had *thought* of doing some myself, the immediate cause of their being written was dear F.D.,[480] who assured me that you would like them – which I had not felt certain of till then.

I am immersed in this drudgery of correcting 20 vols. of proofs. I am now doing the sixth volume: this keeps me here, for if I had gone to London to stay as formerly I must have got on with them just the same. On this account though I run up for a day or two I have to come back again quickly. I go up early to-morrow but return next day to escape Whitsuntide.

I shall be glad to see the little book[481] when it comes out. I am sure you are preparing it beautifully and devotedly.

If you should see the *Fortnightly* for June, which comes out next week, you will find some lines in it by me on the loss of the *Titanic*. I wrote them for the matinée in aid of the bereaved ones, and the editor asked me to let him have them.

I hope you will keep in the country as long as you can. It has every advantage over town at this time of the year except one – that when it rains it seems gloomy.

Ever y[ou]r affect[iona]te friend
T.H.

In March 1922 when she heard that Hardy was preparing *Late Lyrics and Earlier* for publication, Mrs Henniker expressed the wish that he would include the poem he wrote 'so sympathetically in memory of Arty'. It may have been too late, but Hardy, probably aware of its syntactical blemishes and the disapproval its concluding borrowed sentiments (see *Life*, p. 336) would meet, did not include it in his later volumes of poetry.

480. Florence Dugdale.

481. *Arthur Henniker*, described as 'A Little Book for His Friends', contains obituaries and many reminiscences and tributes (including Hardy's poem), all remarkably consistent in his praise. It was arranged by Mrs Henniker with the help of Florence Hardy, and published in 1912.

117.   Max Gate,
                                             Dorchester.
                                             3 : 6 : 1912

My dear friend:
  Sincerest thanks for your good wishes. Alas, birthdays are
not so attractive as they were when I was 7, but I was so glad to
hear from you.

                               Affect[ionate]ly yours
                                    T.H.

118.   Max Gate,
                                             17 : 12 : 12

My dear friend:
  It was a great kindness in you to write to me, and I have
been going to tell you so before, but I have felt so inert that I
have been able to do very little, and this will be a mere
apology for a letter. Emma's death[482] was absolutely unexpected by me, the doctor, and everybody, though not sudden,
strictly speaking. She was quite well a week before, and (as I
fancy) in an unlucky moment determined to motor to some
friends about 6 miles off.[483] During the night following she
had a bad attack of indigestion, which I attributed to the
jolting of the car. She was never well from that time, though
she came down to tea with some callers[484] on the Monday
evening before her death on Wednesday morning. I was with
her when she passed away. Half an hour earlier she had told
the servant that she felt better. Then her bell rang violently,
and when we went up she was gasping. In five minutes all was
over.
  I have reproached myself for not having guessed there
might be some internal mischief at work, instead of blindly
supposing her robust and sound and likely to live to quite old

  482. Emma Hardy died unexpectedly on 27 November 1912. See
Life, pp. 359–60.
  483. The Wood Homers of Bardolf Manor (Christine Wood Homer,
'Thomas Hardy and his Two Wives', Toucan Press, 1964, p. 10 and
footnote).
  484. Rebekah and Catherine Owen. They had travelled down from
the Lake District to see the play *The Trumpet-Major*.

age. In spite of the differences between us, which it would be affectation to deny, and certain painful delusions she suffered from at times, my life is intensely sad to me now without her. The saddest moments of all are when I go into the garden and to that long straight walk at the top that you know, where she used to walk every evening just before dusk, the cat trotting faithfully behind her; and at times when I almost expect to see her as usual coming in from the flower-beds with a little trowel in her hand.

I think I have told you before that her *courage* in the cause of animals was truly admirable, surpassing that of any other woman I have ever known. I have nothing at all approaching it myself. In town or country she would, when quite alone among the roughest characters, beard any man ill-using an animal and amaze him into a shamefaced desistence: and she would carry lost or injured cats in London into a house or to some home and insist on their being looked after.

I have her niece Lilian Gifford here with me attending to the house affairs. Florence Dugdale has also come to help me with the proofs of the American edition of my books, which happen to be in full swing.[485] By a strange coincidence, after not having been here for a long time, she was in the train on her way down to see Mr Evans's dramatization of *The Trumpet-Major*, at the very hour Emma died, and on her arrival at Weymouth, where she was going to stay for the sea air, was met by my telegram. So she did not see the play after all, and went back in a day or two.

I hope you are keeping well. People have been very sympathetic here. I feel so glad that you came last year to the other play.[486] It gave her so much pleasure to have you here.

Your ever affectionate friend
Tho H.

485. A very limited edition, published by Harper and Brothers in 1915.

486. See note, p. 150.

G

119.   The Lodge,
                                        Magdalene College,
                                              Cambridge.
                                            Nov.2.1913

My dear friend:

I was glad to receive your letter telling me that you like to
have the book,[487] but you must not expect much from it: most
of the stories were written so very long ago, as mere stop-gaps,
that I did not particularly care to reprint them. Readers seem
to be pleased with them, however.

You are by this time, I think, at your new house in Shoreham.[488] I hope you do not feel dull there when the weather is
bad. That makes an enormous difference to my feeling about
places.

I am here for the week end, leaving to-morrow, and what
instigates me to write at this especial moment is to tell you
(I don't think I have mentioned it before?) that I am now an
honorary Fellow of this College,[489] which was General Henniker's, and the association is pleasant. I don't suppose I shall
be coming to Cambridge very frequently, but there is a foot-
hold for me on this account, if I do come at any time. Believe
me still, affectionately yours

                                              Tho H.

120.   Max Gate,
                                            Dec 21: 1913

My dear friend:

I had reserved my reply to your last kind letter till to-day,
in order to make it a Christmas greeting, and now I have a
double impulse to write, having received the picture-card and
words on it this morning. It seems, so far as I can judge, a very

487. *A Changed Man*, consisting of twelve uncollected stories which
had appeared in magazines from 1881 to 1900, was published in October
1913.
488. The Little Orchard, Shoreham, Kent.
489. In June 1913 Hardy was awarded the honorary degree of Doctor
of Letters by the University of Cambridge. The Vice-Chancellor was the
Master of Magdalene College, A. C. Benson, with whom Hardy was
now staying.

pretty place, but I cannot tell the sub-soil from the view. However I hope it is dry, and will suit you.

The new Christmas does not exhilarate me much. But of course I cannot expect it to. The worst of a sad event[490] in middle life and beyond is that one does not recover from the shock as in earlier years; so I simply say to myself of this Christmas, 'Yet another!'

The alliance with Cambridge, to which you allude, is pleasing: it gives me a fresh centre of interest, and they are all such nice friends to me there. I am intending to visit it very often, but whether I shall is doubtful.

I read Miss Wedmore's poems[491] that you were good enough to send, and liked best those you had marked, as was natural. The half-page of *The Sphere* of this week, which I enclose as a sort of Xmas card, gives a few verses[492] I was asked for by the editor, but a periodical is a chilling atmosphere for poems: the mood induced by a newspaper is just the wrong one, and puts them out of tune.

Do you ever see a quarterly magazine called *Poetry & Drama*.[493] It is written by a group of young men whose idea of

490. Hardy had to suffer more than the 'sad event' of his wife's death; he had discovered the diaries which she had kept and in which for more than twenty years she had denounced and vilified him. Though aware that he was the victim of her delusions, he continued to harbour self-condemnation for neglecting her, and the process was intensified when he read the reminiscences of her early years which she wrote towards the end of her life. (See Emma Hardy, *Some Recollections*, ed. Evelyn Hardy and Robert Gittings, London, 1961.) He realized once again how happy she had been, and how genuine was the love for him which irradiated her memories; he now recognized in full that her hereditary afflictions made her the innocent victim of the Crass Casualty which, as a philosopher, he had been quick to see throughout the universe. Remorse for lack of charity at home prompted 'Poems of 1912–13' and the scores of expiatory poems that were to follow. For the former, see Hardy's remarks on p. 163.

491. Millicent Wedmore. *Chiefly of Heroes* (1913).

492. 'To Meet, or Otherwise' (addressed to Florence Dugdale) was published in *The Sphere* on 20 December 1913. The editor was Clement Shorter.   ,

493. The June number included an article on Hardy's poems and *The Dynasts* by Edward Thomas, who expressed his surprise that a man 'who can write prose' could allow some of his rhymes to be published. The December number includes Hardy's 'My spirit will not haunt the mound', and poems by Bridges, de la Mare, Rupert Brooke, Robert Frost, W. H. Davies, Frances Cornford, and Harold Monro.

verse is that nobody has ever known how to write it in the whole history of literature till they came along to show the trick to the world; so it is amusing reading, which I think you would like.

A young lady came this week to photograph me in colour, at the request of a friend of mine. The specimens she showed me were extraordinary in their reality. But I am getting tired of it all. My niece and Miss Dugdale are here ministering to my wants: I don't know what I should do without them, and I am sorry to say that just now Florence has a bad cold. I want her to stay in bed, but cannot get her to. I do not see many people. Mrs Sheridan[494] says she is coming, but she has not come. Lady Ilchester is at Melbury, and tells me she will be there if all's well till June. Mrs Asquith[495] tells me she is ill, and going away – not for a 'rest cure' – she is too weak for that she says. I am sorry for her. Sir H[ubert] Herkomer[496] is doing films of *Far from the Madding Crowd,* for the picture palaces: [497] young Herkomer came here a few days ago to get local colour, and has photographed the *real* jug used in the malt-house.[498]

There: that is about all the social and artistic intelligence I can think of – a poor supply. One thing more: did you see my letter in the *Times*[499] about performing animals? You may not have done so, and I send it on. But the words 'Performing Animals' do not clearly indicate the matter: what I object to most are performances *with* animals – in which they are passive – e.g. bringing live canaries, rabbits, pigeons, etc., out

494. See note 192, p. 59.

495. Hardy met her for the first time in July 1894 (*Life,* p. 265) when Asquith was Prime Minister. He had met Mr and Mrs Asquith in London in July (*Life,* p. 362).

496. Sir Hubert von Herkomer, British portrait-painter (1849–1914), was born in Bavaria. He became Slade Professor at Oxford in 1889 and an R.A. in 1890. He illustrated *Tess of the d'Urbervilles,* and painted Hardy's portrait.

497. The film, made by Turner Films, Ltd., was released in February 1916.

498. Described in *Far from the Madding Crowd,* VIII. The jug is now in the Dorset County Museum.

499. Published on 19 December in reply to the article, 'Performing Animals, The Psychology of Pain in Man and Beast', which appeared in *The Times* on the 17th.

of the sleeve or handkerchief. Every spectator can see that the wretched creature is in the greatest misery, and I believe that a great many are 'used' in these tricks – that is, tortured to death.

I wonder when I shall see you. Not very soon I suppose; and you have many interests outside my life.

Your affectionate friend
Tho. H.

121.

Max Gate,
Dorchester.
Wednesday. 11 : 2 : 14

My dear friend:

I wanted to tell you by letter before you could have learnt it from the papers that Florence Dugdale and I were married yesterday at Enfield. But somehow, although nobody seemed to know anything of it, the news was telephoned to London immediately. If I had foreseen this I would have written beforehand to you, my best friend. However, we thought it better in the circumstances to inform nobody, not even relations.

Beyond the parties and the officiators there was not a soul present but my brother and her father and sister. And although the church door stood wide open nobody walked in. It was a lovely morning, and the ceremony was over by 8.20![500]

You do like her I am sure, and I want you to like her better still, if you will be so kind – though as you *always* are kind I needn't have said that, and I am sure you will go on liking her.

Let me hear from you soon. I don't know when we shall go to London. I rather shun it at this time of the year because it gives me such colds. Thank you for your last nice letter. I am glad to know you are on chalk. My experience is that chalk is the healthiest subsoil of any.

Believe me
Your always affect[iona]te friend
Tho. H.

500. Hardy had been as astute as old Lord Mountclere (*The Hand of Ethelberta*, XLV).

122.
                       Max Gate,
                          Dorchester.
                              6: 3: 1914

My dear friend:

I am writing again to you to answer some points on which you say you are curious (as indeed I should have guessed you were), and also because your letter was so kind as to make me wish to write.

It has been a great delight to me all through that you know Florence quite well, and like her. As you say she is very sympathetic – so much so that her own health is largely dependent upon the happiness, or otherwise, of her friends. One thing you may be sure of – her intense love and admiration of yourself: she often settles points by saying or thinking what *you* would do in the circumstances, assuming invariably that that is absolutely the right thing.

I rather am surprised that *you* were surprised at the step we have taken – such a course seeming an obvious one to me, being as I was so lonely and helpless. I think I told you in my last letter that I am very glad she knew Emma well, and was liked by her even during her latter years, when her mind was a little unhinged at times, and she showed unreasonable dislikes. I wonder if it will surprise you when I say that according to my own experience a second marriage does not, or need not, obliterate an old affection, though it is generally assumed that the first woman is entirely forgotten in such cases.

We are going to London next week, but only for a day or two. I will let you know when we go up later (if we do) for a longer stay, so that we may contrive to see you somehow.

Even now I have not answered your question on what people wrote about our marriage. Well: they all say they foresaw it, except one besides yourself – I forgot who. Of course they *might* say so to show their penetration or to claim it. But perhaps they really did. With all affection I am, your sincere friend
                        Tho. H.

I enclose 2 little poems of mine you may like to see. They have appeared in magazines.[501]
                        T.H.

501. Mrs. Henniker's letter of 20 March 1914 suggests that one of them was 'Beyond the Last Lamp' (*Satires of Circumstance*).

123.   Max Gate.
                                                                        Dorchester.
                                                                       11 June 1914

My dear friend:

What a strange thing. This morning when I was dressing it flashed into my mind that I had been going to write to you for several days, and that I would do it this very day: when lo, there was a letter from you. This has happened I think once or twice before in our correspondence. Still I suppose I must knock the romance out of it and say it was only a coincidence.

We intend to be in London from Wednesday to Saturday next week, and we shall I believe be staying at Lady St. Helier's. I was in hopes you were at Stratford Place. I fear there will not be time to run down to you,[502] in the event of her having arranged things to do; but I don't know. I am thinking we may be able, however, to go to London again for a day or two during July, in which case we will make a point of visiting your little orchard. Meanwhile cannot you come here for a week-end or week-middle, just as you choose. I really think you ought to honour Max Gate by sleeping in it just once at any rate. F. will write to you about this.

The vein, or veins, do not trouble me, unless I walk too far. How kind of you to bear in mind that inconvenience of mine. I think bicycling was the original cause.

As you ask what I am doing in poetry I am sending the *Fortnightly* for May, containing the last thing I published.[503] I have a lot of loose poems in MS. which I must, I suppose, collect into a volume. Of course I shall send you a copy, whenever it comes out.

We are going on very quietly. Florence works at flower-gardening – rather too hard, I think; but she is quite devoted to it. About three weeks ago we motored to Plymouth, partly because I wanted to clear up a mystery as to the Gifford

502. Mrs Henniker was still at Shoreham in Kent. One wonders whether she heard of the landscape painter Samuel Palmer (1805–81), who had been influenced by Blake, and had lived at a cottage called 'Waterhouse' in Shoreham for about seven years (from 1825 to 1832 approximately).

503. 'Channel Firing' (*Satires of Circumstance*).

vault there.[504] We came back over Dartmoor. It was cold, and
the gradients were high, but the views beautiful.

I, too, have felt uneasy about that physiological laboratory.[505] But I suppose one must take the words of vivisectors
as honest when they assure us that they never torture animals.
Altogether the world is such a bungled institution from a
humane point of view that a grief more or less hardly counts.
Wishing one had never come into it or shared in its degrading
organizations is but a selfish thought, as others would have
been here just the same. But this sounds gloomy to you I know;
and I am after all not without hope of much amelioration.
Ever your affect[iona]te friend

Tho H.

P.S. 'Wessex', 'Wessie', or 'Wess'[506] is thriving, but he is pro-
nounced a spoilt dog. He is fond of other dogs, and
w[oul]d not object to your bringing Milner.[507]

T.H.

I enclose something else I have lately printed – quite a
trifle as you see.

504. Hardy's first wife (*née* Gifford) had been born in Plymouth. She
had changed her mind about being buried there when she heard that
alterations had taken place in the churchyard (cf. Evelyn Hardy,
Hardy's Notebooks, p. 80).

505. Newly opened at Cambridge by Prince Arthur of Connaught.
Mrs Henniker had been disgusted, and wished some mad woman
would burn it down!

506. 'Wessex' has an interesting history. He was brought to Max
Gate by Florence Dugdale, was unwelcome at first to Hardy but
gradually won his affection and was completely spoilt. He was the
terror of many callers and visitors, liked J. M. Barrie but not John
Galsworthy, bit the postman three times and had two of his front teeth
kicked out in consequence, and, though often the despair of his mistress
and in danger of being 'put to sleep', was always reprieved. Lady
Cynthia Asquith recalled visiting Max Gate in 1921, when she was Sir
James Barrie's secretary, and finding Wessex on the dining-table 'con-
testing every single forkful of food' she raised to her mouth. See
Cynthia Asquith, *Portrait of Barrie*, London, 1954, pp. 108–11, or *The
Listener*, 7 June 1956.

507. Mrs Henniker's dog.

124.   Max Gate,
                                 Dorchester.
                              July 17: 1914.

My dear friend:

As you are kind enough to write about that little poem called 'Before and after Summer'[508] I remember to tell you that I am collecting the pieces in verse that I have written since the last volume of poetry was published and looking them over with a view of bringing them out some when (sic) towards the end of the year.[509] Some of them I rather shrink from printing – those I wrote just after Emma died, when I looked back at her as she had originally been, and when I felt miserable lest I had not treated her considerately in her latter life.[510] However I shall publish them as the only amends I can make, if it were so.[511] The remainder of the book, and by far the greater part of it, will be poems mostly dramatic or personative[512] – many of which have been printed in magazines, etc. (I have let nobody but you and Florence know as yet that I purpose this.)

We are going on calmly enough here as you guess. She is a very tender companion, and is quite satisfied with the quietude of life here. But we flit about a little. Last week-end we spent at Sir Henry Hoare's at Stour-head (sic) in Wiltshire – a beautiful spot.[513] Lately they have had a visitor by aeroplane: they saw him in the air over their park, and he descended, being unable to get further. He had come from Paris. They gave him a night's lodging, and next morning he flew away, after entering his name in the visitors' book. He was a total stranger, and they think he must be the first entertained in that way and written down as a guest.

The Irish question is perplexing, and gloomy, but I can

508. It appeared in *The New Weekly*, 4 April 1914.
509. *Satires of Circumstance* was published in November 1914.
510. These are the poems of the section 'Poems of 1912–13, *Veteris vestigia flammae*'; only the first eighteen of those under this heading in *Collected Poems* were in the original group. Hardy had revisited some of the places associated with Emma in Cornwall (*Life*, p. 361).
511. Hardy called them an 'expiation'.
512. He uses the same expression in his preface to *Wessex Poems*; in the preface to *Poems of the Past and the Present* he preferred 'dramatic or impersonative'.
513. Noted for its gardens, trees, classical temples, and lake.

hardly think there will be bloodshed. I wish Mr Gladstone had never opened it up.[514] The Irish temperament, I fear, will not be satisfied for long with *any* rule, and probably the new rule will work no better than the old.

We had a pleasant time at Lady St Helier's. She got up a big dinner mainly on our account, and Mr and Mrs Winston Churchill[515] came. I had her next me. He has promised her not to fly again till after a certain event, but he won't promise *never* to fly again.

I am so glad to think you mean to be more in London: I so regretted that you were not there when we were. My impression is that you would have done better by coming to the south coast instead of going to Kent, but probably you don't think so. F. still thinks you the dearest friend she has in the world.

I *may* send you a new magazine later on (if it really comes out) containing a very small poem – two stanzas only[516] – of mine, which I think may interest you, as it refers to so long ago as 1894.

Your neighbours are probably like most country folk – rather stolid. Yet that sort of person does really feel a sincerer regard for one's welfare than town people, I consider.

Ever y[ou]r affectionate friend
Tho H.

125.   Max Gate,
                                        Dorchester.
                                        23 Dec. 1914

My dear friend:

I have not written till now to thank you for your letter about the volume of poems,[517] and I am glad that I combine

514. Gladstone had been in favour of Home Rule for Ireland. Mrs Henniker was very worried about the strain of 'all this political work' on her 'highly strung' brother.

515. Sir Winston at this time was First Lord of the Admiralty. He began flying in 1913. Throughout the First World War (1914–18) he frequently travelled by plane between England and France. He gave up his ambition to become a qualified pilot after a crash in 1919. See the chapter 'In the Air' in his *Thoughts and Adventures*, 1932.

516. It has been *suggested* that this is 'Last Love-Word', written in 189– and published in *Human Shows*. See p. xxxv.

517. Hardy had sent Mrs Henniker a copy of *Satires of Circumstance*.

with it by my delay a Christmas greeting which I wanted you to have from me.

I sent the poems through the publishers because by doing so you received them 2 or 3 days sooner than they would have reached you if they had come here first. Of course I will write your name in them when I have opportunity.

At first I thought I would not send any copy to any friend owing to the harsh contrasts[518] which the accidents of my life during the past few years had forced into the poems, and which I could not remove, so many of them having been printed in periodicals – those in fact that I liked least. And unfortunately they are the ones the papers have taken most notice of. My own favourites, that include all those in memory of Emma, have been mentioned little. The one to Florence was written when she was a mere acquaintance: [519] I think she likes it. I am so glad that you like 'When I set out for Lyonnesse.'[520] It is exactly what happened 44 years ago.

We went to London last week to see *The Dynasts*.[521] I had not seen it till then, except in an early rehearsal. It is much more impressive than I thought it would be: perhaps the present war makes one feel it more. Some people have been three times, they tell me. The actors themselves are very keen about it, and there are understudies 2 or 3 deep, on the chance of their being required.

'Wessex' has developed a tendency to fight other dogs, quite to our surprise. We fancy he will get a nip from a big dog who lives near here, which will make him less bumptious.

Gosse's poem[522] was among the few good ones that have been brought out by the war. At night here the sky is illuminated by the searchlights in Portland Roads, so we are kept in mind of the slaughter in progress. Mr Asquith went to *The Dynasts*

518. Hardy is more explicit in his *Life*, p. 367.

519. 'After the Visit' (to F. E. D.) was published in *The Spectator*, 13 August 1910.

520. The lyric describes Hardy's first visit to Cornwall in March 1870, when he met Emma Gifford, whom he married in 1874.

521. Hardy had adapted scenes from *The Dynasts* for Granville-Barker's production at the Kingsway Theatre. He had been to a rehearsal, but was deterred by a cold from attending the opening performance. He saw the play two or three weeks later (*Life*, p. 367).

522. 'To Our Dead', *The Times*, 20 October 1914.

one afternoon, and liked it much. I hope you keep well, and
will have a cheerful Christmas.

Y[ou]r affectionate friend,
Tho H.

F. has gone to see my sisters,[523] she would send her love if she
were here I know, and good Christmas wishes.   T.H.

126.   Max Gate,
                                                 Dorchester.
                                                 23: 3: 1915

My dear friend:

In your last letter you asked me, I remember, what I
thought about the duration of the war, which question I did
not answer, to my shame, though my reason was my perplexity
on the point. I can only make guesses, and the one I think
the most probable is that it will last till one of the combatants is exhausted and sues for peace without being beaten,
or till one or more country is bankrupt, or starved, or till
there is a revolution in Germany: a rupture between the dual
monarchies of Austria might, too, help on peace. I hardly
think it will end by the sheer victory of one side or the other
in the field – unless Italy joins the allies, in which case it
might.

I, too, like you, think the Germans happy and contented as
a people: but the group of oligarchs and munition-makers
whose interest is war, have stirred them up to their purposes –
at least so it seems. I have expressed the thought in a sonnet
that is coming out in the *Fortnightly*.[524] I enclose a proof of
it, which, as I have no other copy, you can return at your
leisure.

As you say, and as it also has struck me, how can we consistently crush German militarism without reducing arm-
aments and armies all round: and diminishing our navy?

523. They and their brother Henry had left Higher Bockhampton,
and were living at Talbothays, West Stafford, less than two miles from
Max Gate.
524. 'The Pity of It' (*Moments of Vision*).

You have no doubt read in the papers to-day Sir E[dward] Grey's[525] synopsis of the beginning of the war. England has been so often the arrogant aggressor in past wars that it would have been quite in keeping with her history if she had been in this: but really, when you honestly look at the facts marshalled by Sir E[dward] G[rey] England is innocent for once. They show that the war began because the Germans wanted to fight.

In this connection I am much puzzled as to the attitude of Lord Morley and John Burns in resigning office – particularly the former.[526] When I saw him last he had aged much, and was getting deaf, so at first I thought he had given up on those accounts. But if so, it would have been stated, to strengthen his colleagues' position: on the other hand, how can he hold that we ought not to have fought? Perhaps you can solve this conundrum?

I am so glad you liked the play, which though not *The Dynasts* as I wrote it, was interesting to me also.

Florence sends best love. I am sorry to say she has been confined to her bed with *sciatica,* left by some chill she caught. She is better, and would much like to see you again – as should I also.

Your affect[iona]te friend
Tho. H.

127.   Max Gate,
                                   Tuesday morning.
                                   [25 May 1915][527]

My dear friend:

I send off the enclosed in a hurry; otherwise you may not get it to-morrow morning. If the words are not quite what is

525. Foreign Secretary when war was declared in August 1914. He was later Viscount Grey of Fallodon and a distinguished author.
526. From 1910 to August 1914 Lord Morley was Lord President of the Council. Edmund Gosse expressed the view that Morley's 'nerves gave way'. John Burns resigned from his office as President of the Board of Trade, and took up Red Cross work.
527. Mrs Henniker's letter requesting testimony for the Home Office that her German servant Anna Hirschmann could safely be allowed to stay in England was written to Hardy on 23 May.

required I will write another. Don't mind asking me to. F is going to London this week to see a surgeon about a little nasal catarrh that she has been suffering from. I am staying here. Thanks for your kind wish to see me at Shoreham, but I cannot very well leave just now. I have to be in London for one day a little later on, not for longer, thank Heaven, for I dislike being there more and more, especially with the incessant evidences of this ghastly war under one's eyes everywhere in the streets, and no power to do anything. However I hope that the entrance of Italy upon the stage will shorten hostilities.

I am still puzzled at the attitude of L[or]d M[orle]y, etc. Surely, even if they believe the gov[ernmen]t wrong in the steps they took, they should stand by it now to help us out of our peril?

Ever affect[ionate]ly yours
Tho H.

Also, I have misgivings on the sending Mr Balfour to the Admiralty, which seems to be decided on?   T.

128.   Max Gate,
                                           Saturday.
                                   [June or July, 1915]
My dear friend:
    Here is a letter from America, and I hope it contains good news.
    We expect to be staying at Lady St. Helier's[528] from Tuesday to Thursday next week – merely lodging there while we attend to prosy London matters which will leave no time for running down to see you, pleasant as it would be. Why not meet us there at lunch or tea: she said last time that she would be so glad if you would; and, as you know, I can invite anybody there at any time.
    We almost wish you were not in Kent, as you may be in the track of some Zeppelin on its way to London. Still, you are

528. 52 Portland Place. For the date of this letter and the next, see *Life*, p. 371.

not so badly off as some. A friend of ours – Colonel Inglis, stationed here – has his home but 2 miles from Dover. My cousin Frank George – Lieut. 5th Dorset Battalion – sailed for the Dardanelles or Egypt this week.[529]

Your affectionate friend
Th. H.

129.   Max Gate,
                                           Thursday.
                                         [July 1915]

My dear friend:

I think you must mean 'The Society of Architects'. It is not absolutely new, but since my time. Its address a year or two ago was 28 Bedford Square, and the Sec[retar]y, C. M. Butler. I know nothing about its standing.

There is, of course, the 'Royal Institute of British Architects' – a dignified and venerable body[530] – and the chief architec-[tur]al Society in England. The President is a well-known architect. I cannot for the moment remember his name – the sec[retary]y is Ian MacAlister, B.A. and its address 9 Conduit Street.

There is also a junior society called 'The Architectural Association' – 18 Tufton St. Westminster: sec. F. R. Yerbury.

We have just come back from a motor ride to Seaton, and Beer,[531] a little beyond. The views along the route have been beautiful.

I was so sorry to let you go in the rain from Lady St. Helier's. I wish, if you get rid of your house, you would take or buy one down this way: I think the air would suit you.

We have a huge cavalry camp here, and hear the reveillé

529. Frank George was a favourite with both the Hardys, who looked upon him as a son and had agreed to leave Max Gate to him; he called on them for the last time in April 1915 (*Life*, p. 370).

530. Hardy had been associated with the R.I.B.A. for more than fifty years. In 1920 he was elected an Honorary Fellow; in 1863 he had won the R.I.B.A. prize for an essay on an architectural subject (*Life*, pp. 403–4).

531. Probably to see Frank George's mother, who lived at Beer.

sounded at 5 in the morning. We have also foot: so that the town sometimes is a surging mass of soldiers. F. sends love.

Affect[ionate]ly yours
Tho. H.

The post goes in a few minutes, wh[ich] is why I am so brief.

T.H.

130.   Max Gate,
Sept 2: 1915

My dear friend:

I am sorry not to have acknowledged your letter and the enclosure sooner. As to the enclosure, upon the whole I would rather not take part in any movement of a spiritual or even ethical nature: it would in fact not quite accord with my feelings – at any rate just at present – to do so. My 'faith in the good there is in humankind' – except in isolated individuals, of whom happily there are many – has been rudely shaken of late.[532] I mention this parenthetically – not as my reason for abstention which is purely owing to circumstances of a personal nature.

We were much distressed on Monday morning by this brief telegram: —

'Frank was killed on the 22nd.'[533]

This referred to a very dear cousin of mine, Frank George, 2d Lieut. in the 5th Dorsets, who has fallen in action in the Gallipoli peninsula – almost the only, if not the only blood relative of the next generation in whom I have taken any interest. The death of a 'cousin' does not seem a very harrowing matter as a rule, but he was such an intimate friend here, and Florence and I both were so attached to him, that his loss will affect our lives largely. His mother (who was a Hardy) is a widow, and we don't know how she is going to get over it.

532. It was a faith (or hope) which he had dared to express at the end of *The Dynasts*. The First World War, however, gave 'the *coup de grâce*' to any belief he had held of an 'ultimate Wisdom at the back of things'. (See *Life*, p. 368, and the poem 'Thoughts at Midnight', part of which was written in 1906.)

533. Frank George was killed in an advance at Gallipoli. Hardy's poem 'Before Marching and After' was written to his memory.

We shall be glad to know when you move into your new Kensington House,[534] though I fear we shall not be much in London for some time. I have many requests for war poetry, but what good comes of writing and publishing it I don't know, though the different charities ask for it.

We are just going to take a walk entirely for the sake of our dog 'Wessie' – who *lives* for these little rambles. F. sends her love, and I am

> Your affect[iona]te friend
> Tho H.

131.   Max Gate,
                                                              28:6:1916

My dear Friend:

Florence has written to ask for Sir F. Wedmore's[535] book for review, but she does not know whether it may have been sent out to anybody else. She has just finished and posted off six reviews of other books. I cannot think how she gets through them so fast. It would take me a week to do one I am quite sure. A few days ago she told the editor that he need not send any more, but he would not let her off, saying that hers are more trustworthy than any he can get elsewhere.

We had a mild excitement last week – the *Wessex Scenes from the Dynasts* having been performed by the Dorchester players at the Weymouth Theatre.[536] The house was crammed – many wounded men and officers being present – and the money raised for the Red Cross and Russian wounded – was a substantial sum. Of course the interest to us lay not in the artistic effect of the play – which was really rather a patchwork affair, for the occasion – but in the humours of the characters whom we knew in private life as matter-of-fact

534. 15 Kensington Gore, S.W.

535. *Brenda Walks On*, a novel published in 1916. For Wedmore, see note 131, p. 43.

536. Not to be confused with Granville-Barker's production of *The Dynasts*. The Wessex scenes were selected by Hardy for the local 'Hardy Players'. Hardy attended a rehearsal in Dorchester, a fortnight before the play was produced at Weymouth.

shopkeepers and clerks. However, the *Times* thought it worth while to send down a critic.

We were at Melbury on Monday. Lady Ilchester had her sister-in-law, young Lady Londonderry staying with her. L[or]d Ilchester comes home for a day or two now and then, and disappears again (he is King's Messenger). She has shut up the large rooms and covered up the furniture with ghostly white cloths, and lives in the smaller ones. At the next performance of *The Dynasts*, which is to be in Dorchester,[537] she is going to make a speech before the curtain rises. She asked very warmly for you, and if we had heard from you lately.

I daresay you get rumours of war news which don't reach us here. People seem to think we shall do something decisive soon, but I don't know. Mr Jeune[538] comes often to see us (he is the father of Mrs Hanbury our neighbour at Kingston House–)[539] and as he comes from the House of Lords he brings us all sorts of reports. I have been invited to visit and address the wounded soldiers at Netley Hospital,[540] where they also want us to perform the play: perhaps the latter may be done: but I cannot go.

Always affect[ionate]ly
Th. H.

F. sends love: she will write.

Th.

537. *Wessex Scenes from 'The Dynasts'* was presented in Dorchester the following December; see p. 175.

538. Mr Symonds Jeune was Lord St Helier's brother and Clerk of the House of Lords.

539. Kingston Maurward House, which Hardy had known since his boyhood (see Evelyn Hardy, *Hardy's Notebooks*, pp. 18–22, 123–31, and *Life*, pp. 18–20). It is the centre for the story of *Desperate Remedies*.

540. On Southampton Water. It was founded for soldiers wounded in the Crimean War.

132.   Max Gate,
                                        Dorchester.
                                        4 Sept. 1916

My dear friend:

Herewith I send 'Worlingworth'[541] results so far. The post-card is a mystery, as I did not mention the Christian name of Mr W. to Sir G. Alexander,[542] and it came at the same time as this letter this morning.

We propose, D.V., to go to Cornwall for 3 or 4 days this week, starting I believe Thursday. The memories it will revive will of course be rather sad ones for me, but I want to see the tablet that has been erected in St Juliot Church, near Boscastle, to Emma, recording that she lived there, played in church, laid the foundation stone of the new part, etc., and Florence wants to see the place and the cliff scenery, never having been there. We mean to stay at Tintagel 2 or 3 days, and a day or two at Boscastle. But perhaps she has already told you of this.

The Macmillans are going to include a selection from my poems in their Golden Treasury series:[543] but when it will come out I do not know. We have been to Melbury since I last wrote – and we met Lady I[lchester] last week at a bazaar. She is going to preside at a performance of the *Wessex Scenes from The Dynasts* at Dorchester some time this autumn – that is, she will, as I understand, make a little speech at the beginning, stating the objects of the performance, etc. She makes those little speeches very well. The people here are getting much attached to her – as, indeed, they ought to be.

The morning papers have this moment arrived, telling us that a Zeppelin was brought down near London on Saturday. The war news is exciting almost every day: but I think our papers rather too sanguine. We have not beaten the Germans by any means yet.

F. is not here this moment or she would send her love with mine.

                    Always yours
                    Th. H.

541. See notes, pp. 149 and 202.
542. Manager of the St. James's Theatre.
543. Hardy's selection was published in October 1916.

133.   Saturday 9. 9. 16[544]

Thanks for 2[n]d letter, which was forwarded here. Hope Worlingworth will achieve his attempt.

We have been to St Juliot – and return to D[orchester] Monday.

134.   Max Gate,
                                                       Dorchester.
                                                      22 Dec: '16

My dear friend,
    I am writing a line to reach you at Christmas, though I don't know that it will, our post-office having behaved eccentrically of late. I am rejoiced to find that you liked the Golden Treasury Selection. Of course friends say – almost every one – that they miss so and so, but they could not all be got in.[545]
    I agree with Watson[546] about the writers of *vers libre*, etc. I suppose it is only a passing fashion, the original sinner being Walt Whitman, who, I always think, wrote as he did, formlessly, because he could do no better.
    Our blackbirds and thrushes have had a hard time on account of the frost and snow, but they are recovering now. We, like you, have plenty of tits. Florence knows their varieties better than I do.
    We have been reading Sir Oliver Lodge's *Raymond*[547] – which you also probably have read. We found it unconvincing, particularly the 'medium' business, all of which I remember going on 40 or 50 years ago, when they were treated as imposters. There will be one in every street after this. I

544. This is an unsigned postcard of Tintagel Castle. For the visit, see *Life*, pp. 373–4.
545. Edmund Gosse was disappointed to find that Hardy's selection did not contain some of his favourite poems. The selection, which may be seen in Purdy (pp. 179–87), was made for the general reader.
546. William Watson; see note, p. 101. He was knighted in 1917.
547. Sir Oliver Lodge (1851–1940) was an eminent physicist, who in his later years devoted himself to psychical research. *Raymond, or Life after Death* was inspired by the death of his son.

daresay Lodge is sincere enough, but he is vilely victimized I think.

In the *Sphere* for Jan 6th there will be, I believe, a poem of mine called 'A New Year's Eve in War Time'. It is concerning an incident that happened here on a New Year's Eve not so long ago.[548] I am glad to hear of Gerrie.[549] F. Harrison[550] told me that he tried to talk old Greek to the inhabitants when he was over there, but could not get on. We have had a performance of *Wessex Scenes from the Dynasts* here, for Red Cross purposes, and Lady Ilchester was to have made an introductory speech; but as she could not get here her daughter Mary delivered it faultlessly, it being her first appearance as a public orator.

Wessie is well, but has the defects of his qualities. F. has just come back from Weymouth, where she has a nice friend, a Mrs Inglis,[551] wife of Col. Inglis.

With all best wishes, and F's love, I am

Y[ou]rs ever

Th. H.

135.   Max Gate,
                                             Dorchester.
                                          March 4: 1917

My dear friend:

I have earned by the sale of an autograph the enclosed 1/1/– for the Blue Cross, and Florence suggests I should send it to the Fund through you, as you collect for the Society,[552] so I do so, making it the excuse for a letter, though a poor one,

548. The poem is dated 1915–16. The 'incident' of the horseman careering past exactly at midnight happened at Max Gate.

549. Gerald FitzGerald, Mrs Henniker's nephew, was a soldier throughout the First World War. At the end of 1916, his company was moved from the Suez Canal area to the Salonika front in northern Greece.

550. See note, p. 126.

551. Florence Hardy described her as her best local friend.

552. The Blue Cross began as Our Dumb Friends League in 1887, and was very active in the medical care of horses during the First World War.

as all my letters get to be somehow. We are living uneventful lives here (if the news of war events are not reckoned) feeling no enterprize for going about and seeing people while the issue of the great conflict is in the balance – and I fear that by the time the issue is reached I shall be too far on to old age to care to do so. The actual reminder in this house that the struggle is going on is that I have some German prisoners at work in the garden, cutting down some trees, and clearing the ground for more potato-room. They are amicable young fellows, and it does fill one with indignation that thousands of such are led to slaughter by the ambitions of Courts and Dynasties. If only there were no monarchies in the world, what a chance for its amelioration! [553]

I am so glad you like some of the poems in the Golden Treasury Selection. They were not, inclusively or exclusively, those I should have put there had I chosen them *entirely* for myself: but many of those I like best were included, my favourite lyric being the one called 'When I set out for Lyonnesse', I think, as it has the qualities one should find in a lyric.

Florence's youngest sister Marjorie was married about a week ago to a young Lieutenant in the Royal Flying Corps, on duty every day in the air above the fighting line in France. We think it a hazardous marriage, not on account of the young people's characters, for they are much attached to each other, nor for possible lack of income, for his father is well-off, and he is an only son, but because of his dangerous post. He has only had ten days' leave for the whole business of getting home and back, marriage, and honeymoon, and it will be rather a sad parting for them next Wednesday.

Did I tell you that Sir J. Barrie[554] came and stayed here for the play of *The Dynasts*?

Believe me your affectionate friend

Th: H.

553. A Shelleyan thought.
554. The previous December; see *Life*, p. 374. Mrs Henniker wondered whether Hardy had found him a pleasant visitor; she had found him 'very silent', and thought his writing much overrated.

136.   Max Gate,
                                                May 20: 1917

My dear Friend:

I am so sorry to learn that you have not been at all well, and so is Florence, as you will know. Somehow you have seemed to be so much in the active world, owing to you living in London, and I to be so entirely out of it, that it never occurred to me you might be ill. I wonder if you ought not to get away from Town? We have at last discovered the ideal place for making recoveries in. It is *Dartmoor,* the air of which is really wonderful. You may remember that Louis Stevenson was on his way there, as a last hope, when he was taken ill on the road, and could not get there.[555] Mr Eden Phillpotts,[556] who lives near it, would find you a place if you think anything of it. Mr Galsworthy[557] lives close to it, but he is now away in France.

The war has taken all enterprize out of me (I should add that it is partly because of the practical difficulties of getting about), and I have almost registered a vow that I will not see London till the butchery is over. Another of my cousins has been killed, and though his mother is but a distant cousin I sympathize deeply with her, as she is herself dying.

People are in strangely irritable moods I fancy. I said very harmlessly in a poem (sonnet) entitled 'The Pity of It' that the Germans were a 'kin folk, kin tongued' (which is indisputable) and letters attacking me appeared, denying it! The fact of their being our enemies does not alter their race.

Did I tell you that some time ago we had a visit from a cousin of Emma's,[558] who is also a cousin of our neighbours the Hanburys here who bought the Kingston estate lately a mile from here – and is a niece of the late L[or]d St. Helier?[559] She

555. In 1885. See *Life,* p. 175.
556. Eden Phillpotts (1862–1960), novelist and playwright. The Hardys visited him at his home in Torquay in June 1915 and October 1917.
557. See note 414, p. 130. His home was Wingstone, near Manaton, Moretonhampstead.
558. Evelyn Gifford, daughter of the archdeacon who married Hardy and Emma Gifford. She lived at Oxford, where Hardy met her – 'his bright and affectionate cousin by marriage' – for the last time when he received his honorary degree of Doctor of Letters in February 1920. She died the following September, and Hardy commemorated her in the poem 'Evelyn G. of Christminster'. See *Life,* pp. 397–8, 407.
559. See note 22, p. 7.

is much like Emma, and I felt so sorry that the Hanburys did not come here till after Emma's death, as it w[oul]d have been pleasant for her.

Gosse's *Swinburne*[560] book has been a great success I believe, which I am glad of, as it must have cost him much labour.

The young poets you allude to – I imagine you mean the 'Georgians' (an absurd name, as if the Georgians were not Shelley, Scott, Byron, etc.)[561] – are I think, or some of them, on a wrong track. They seem to forget that poetry must have symmetry in its form, and meaning in its content.

I have read young Sassoon's book dedicated to me.[562] I think the poems show much promise.

We have just heard that F's sister's husband, Commander (I think that's his title) in the Royal Flying Corps, came home from the front at 1.30 a.m. two nights ago to her great surprise. He has been in a position of much danger over the German lines and rear, and has been shot at and nearly brought down several times, and most of his comrades have been killed.

Florence says I am to tell you that she is looking eagerly forward to the issue of your book.[563] She is hoping to be in London after Whitsuntide, and to call and see you. She still keeps up her reviewing, but will soon drop it; not having quite sufficient spare time with the household to look after, and the garden also, which she has taken upon herself, much to my relief. She sends her love, and I am

Always y[ou]rs affectionately
Th: H.

560. *The Life of Algernon Charles Swinburne*, London, 1917.
561. The same view is expressed in Hardy's *Life*, p. 370. Mrs Henniker had been reading *Wheels* (1916), a selection from Miss Cunard, Miss Iris Tree, the Sitwells, and others.
562. *The Old Huntsman* (1917). Siegfried Sassoon (1886–1967), nephew of Sir Hamo Thornycroft, the sculptor, organized a tribute from forty-three poets to Hardy on his seventy-ninth birthday, and took the gift to Max Gate. See later.
563. It is not clear what happened to Mrs Henniker's novel, which she mentioned in her letter of 5 March 1917, stating that she thought it better than *Second Fiddle*. No subsequent publication of a novel by her has been found.

137.   Max Gate
                                                  Dorchester.
                                                  Feb. 7: 1918

My dear friend:

I have a guilty feeling that I did not reply to your previous letter. If I did not it was, at any rate, not from disinclination. I write much less promptly than I used to do, and if a letter gets covered over I sometimes do not remember that it is unanswered.

I am glad to find that you have gone away from the London atmosphere for a time: also from the contingency of bombs and shrapnell (*sic*), the latter protective seeming more endangering, though in a smaller way, than the enemy's attack. But the defence is getting far more expert and thorough than at first I think.

I did not myself attend the performance of 'The Mellstock Quire',[564] though I was at the rehearsal of the dances, which I remember seeing footed in country places when I was a boy. Florence and some friends however were there: and she entertained the actors at a tea in the Town Hall between the two performances, and had a speech made in her honour on account of it. Strange to say the man who played the parish clerk of 80 years ago is the clerk there now. Twelve of the present 'Mellstock' (Stinsford) quire attended, to see the ghosts of their predecessors.

I gave very few of the copies of the poems[565] to friends, as I thought they might not like them. As you have bought the book I am not responsible if they trouble you. I begin to think I shall never present any more of my own poems to anybody. I myself (naturally I suppose) like those best which are literally true – such as 'At Lanivet', – 'At the word Farewell', – 'Why did I sketch',[566] etc., etc., which perhaps are quite unattractive to readers, and may have little literary merit.

Did you see the super-precious review of the verses[567] in the

564. This adaptation by A. H. Evans of *Under the Greenwood Tree* was first performed in 1910–11 in Dorchester, London, and Weymouth. It was repeated at the end of January 1918 (*Life*, p. 384).

565. *Moments of Vision*, published 30 November 1917.

566. All three poems are related to Hardy's first wife and their courtship.

567. *Moments of Vision,* in which 'The Pink Frock' appeared. The lady of the poem was Marcia, Lady Yarborough (*Life*, p. 264).

Westminster Gazette? It amused me much (having no weight or value in criticism) as it was obviously written by a woman. It condemned the poem entitled 'The pink frock' because the frock described was old-fashioned and Victorian! The publishers have sent me some fifty reviews – all of them, save 5 or 6, deplorably inept, purblind, and of far less *value* than the opinion of one's grocer or draper, though they were friendly enough, I must say. I always fancy I could point out the best, and the worst, in a volume of poems, which none of these did. But perhaps that is my self-conceit, for I have had no experience as a reviewer.

If what you call sad poems do preponderate, it may be owing to the fact that they were selected from many more, and the rejected ones were of the less solid kind, and considered not worth printing. The 'Lalage' one,[568] 'Sitting on the Bridge',[569] 'Lyonnesse', etc., were of that sort which *were* thought worth retaining.

All our blue-tits, and other tits, have disappeared. We used to have great numbers. Our 3 magpies have also disappeared. Wessex still has the defects of his qualities.

Ever affectionately
Th: H.

138.   Max Gate,
                                           Dorchester.
                                        June 5: 1918

My dear friend:

It was so sweet of you to let me know of your good wishes,[570] and it affords me an excuse for writing. I don't know how you stand this weather in London, but it must be trying, as you probably don't get the breeze we get here, except when we sit in the shelter of our trees, and then the sun is scorching.

I was thinking of you Saturday for another reason than your telegram. We were dining in the large room of the King's

568. 'Timing Her' (inspired mainly by Horace, but originating from the name of a local girl who visited Max Gate).
569. Grey's Bridge, just outside Dorchester.
570. Hardy's birthday was 2 June. See p. 154.

Arms here, and I remembered that the last time I was in it was when you came to Dorchester to see one of the performances of the local society.[571] I wonder if you will ever come again.

I had an interesting letter from Mrs John Fortescue. I wonder if you know her, or him – the Librarian at Windsor Castle. Theirs is an extraordinarily happy marriage, and my poor Emma's last garden-party was the means of bringing it about. They met at it for the first time, as total strangers, and she says[572] we were those who helped her to realize her ideal and make all her dreams come true. I wish Emma could know it. She and her husband have been staying at Melbury. Lady Ilchester and her mother[573] came here to tea last week, and Birdie said she would so much like to have you at Melbury if you would come. If you were to go there I could get them to show you the house from which the two sisters of my maternal ancestor ran by the back staircase when pursued up the front stairs by the King's soldiery in the Monmouth Rebellion.[574]

Mr Gosse was kind enough to review my poetry in the last number of the *Edinburgh Review*. If you cannot lay hands on it and would like to read it I can lend it to you at any time.[575]

To-morrow I have the tedious duty to perform of adjudicating on food profiteers. How I come in for the job is owing to the difficulty of getting magistrates who are absolutely detached from and uninfluenced by local interests.

Always y[ou]rs affect[ionate]ly
Th: H.

Florence sends love, and will be so glad to hear from you.

Th: H.

571. See note, p. 150.
572. Mrs John Fortescue had sent birthday greetings to Hardy, and reminded him of the good fortune which came to her from Emma's garden-party. Hardy alludes to this in his *Life* (pp. 359 and 387).
573. Lady Londonderry. Hardy never saw her again (*Life*, p. 386).
574. See note 187, p. 58.
575. Edmund Gosse was the first important critic to champion Hardy as a poet; he twice compares his verse to that of Donne, and finds a parallel between Hardy and Crabbe. See Gosse, *Some Diversions of a Man of Letters*, London, 1919, or *Selected Essays* (First Series), London, 1928.

139.   Max Gate,
                                Sunday, 27: 10: '18

My dear friend:

I was much gratified to hear that you liked 'Jezreel', though I have not hurried to tell you so: this however you must put down to my indolence. It was written very rapidly, and was published the day after,[576] it being just a poem for the moment. I thought people did not seem to realize that Esdraelon and Jezreel were the same. Well, as to my having any affection for Jezebel, I don't think I can admit that: I have the same sort of admiration for her that I have for Lady Macbeth, Clytaemnestra, and such. Her courage was splendid.

I am not doing much just now. I hope the influenza has kept outside your door so far. It is creeping about down here, and appears in villages in a mysterious way. We have taken two or three short bicycle rides lately – one to the scene of that poem 'The Revisitation',[577] another to Egdon Heath, etc.

Last week Florence's sister achieved a little boy – her first baby – which she thinks a wonderful performance. Her husband is a flying man, and has rushed home to see the baby, though he is compelled to do it at his own expense – all the way from Ireland. If I were a woman I should think twice before entering into matrimony in these days of emancipation when everything is open to the sex.

I hope your nephew[578] has got well of his wound by this time. We have large hospitals for the wounded here and at Weymouth, and trainloads of them come in quite unexpectedly.

I think Arthur Balfour made a fool of himself in stating on his own responsibility (apparently) that we were not going to let the Germans have their colonies back. But he was always a tactless man.[579] F. gets letters asking her to review books

576. It was written on 24–5 September, and published in *The Times* on the 27th (Purdy, p. 210). The sub-title 'On its seizure by the English under General Allenby, September 1918' was added when the poem was included in *Late Lyrics and Earlier*.

577. It is west of Puddletown, and best approached along a lane on the Dorchester side of the village.

578. Gerald FitzGerald's regiment was sent to France in the summer of 1918. He was wounded near Arras in August.

579. Arthur Balfour, statesman and philosopher (1848–1930), was Foreign Secretary at this time. Hardy no doubt remembered his tactlessness in April 1893 (*Life*, pp. 253–4).

(since she reviewed Mrs Shorter's[580] poems under her own
name), but she does not want to, as the house is enough for
her to attend to, she finds. Lady Ilchester consulted her last
week about getting up a Café Chantant here for Xmas. I am
afraid I cannot assist – except by giving advice. Let us hear
again when you can.

Affec[tionate]ly yours
Th: H.

While writing a golden-crested wren has come outside my
window: also a cole-tit.

Th. H.

140.   Max Gate.
Dec. 28: 1918

My dear friend:

I am aiming for this to reach you on New Year's day to wish
you many happy returns, but as you are flitting I am not sure
that it will. My best thanks for your nice letter. Alas, about my
writing fine poems next year! I fear I am past that; though
people who know seem to like some I write, and praise them.
But 'to what purpose cometh there to me incense from Sheba!'
I often say.[581]

As it is an exceptionally mild afternoon I have been garden-
ing a little, and had to tie up a rosebush planted by Emma a
month or two before her death: it has grown luxuriantly, and
she would be pleased if she could know and that I care for it.[582]

However this is a bad beginning for a New Year's letter. I
heard two or three days ago from Mr Birrell, who tells me he
is going to print a little book about his father-in-law Frederick
Locker,[583] and asked if he might insert a letter of mine in it,

580. Dora Sigerson married Clement Shorter in 1896 and died in
January 1918. Hardy's poem 'How She Went to Ireland' was written
to her memory.

581. Jer. vi. 20. Hardy quotes far more from the Bible that from
any other source; next come Shakespeare, Shelley, and Browning.

582. This is clearly the rose of the poem 'The Spell of the Rose',
which Hardy wrote in 1913.

583. Augustine Birrell (1850–1933) was Secretary of Ireland,
1907–16, and a writer of critical essays. His 'little book' Frederick

written so long ago as 1880. Of course I did not mind.

Two evenings ago we dined at the Cecil Hanburys who now own those beautiful gardens at La Mortola near Ventimiglia and live about a mile from us here.[584] F. enjoyed herself much, and as she did I did. An amusing naval commander was there, who had been all through the war, and told us queer experiences.

I quite agree that people ought not to be let tear the holly trees to pieces for decoration. There used to be a good many on the heaths here, but they have all been destroyed.

You mention John Fortescue. Did I ever tell you that he met his wife for the first time at a garden party here? I hope they are happy, but the meeting was by a stone we call the Druid Stone,[585] which sounds ominous, though perhaps it is quite the reverse.

I have received from a composer the music to 'When I set out for Lyonnesse'[586] – which seems good, but I don't know for certain yet. (The words are in the *'Golden Treasury' Selection*).

I don't attempt to understand how the League of Nations is to be accomplished, so can only wait. I am glad you liked Cockerell: he is a most sincere man, and devoted to his friends.[587]

I saw that Gosse read the lessons. *I* used to read them in my

---

Locker-Lampson was published in 1920. Locker-Lampson (1821–95) was best known for his *London Lyrics* (1857), a collection of clever *vers de société*, which was printed many times in Britain and the States before the end of the century. Hardy's letter is given in his *Life* (pp. 133–4).

584. At Kingston (Maurward) House. See note 539, p. 172.

585. The 'Druid Stone' was found underground in the garden at Max Gate, and it took seven men to move and erect it in March 1891 (*Life*, pp. 233–4).

586. The music was by C. A. Speyer. It was published about Christmas 1920 (*Life*, p. 411).

587. Sydney Cockerell (1867–1962) met many writers in his long career, and was early influenced by Ruskin and William Morris. He transformed the Fitzwilliam Museum, Cambridge, of which he was Director from 1908 to 1937. In 1911 he took charge of the distribution of Hardy's MSS. As his literary co-executor, he was annoyed with Florence Hardy for having 'Old Mrs Chundle' published in the States in 1928, and for issuing privately an edition of 'An Indiscretion in the Life of an Heiress' in 1934.

brother-in-law's church,[588] but I hardly thought that G. knew about such things – I mean such old-fashioned doings. I am sorry to hear he has had such a bad cold. We had a Christmas line or two from Lady St Helier, who seems to be well. Now where shall I direct this to find you?

Ever yours

Tho. H.

141.   Max Gate,[589]

5 June 1919

Sincere thanks for your good wishes, my dear friend, which I echo back towards you. I should care more for my birthdays if at each succeeding one I could see any sign of real improvement in the world – as at one time I fondly hoped there was; but I fear that what appears much more evident is that it is getting worse and worse. All development is of a material and scientific kind – and scarcely any addition to our knowledge is applied to objects philanthropic or ameliorative.[590] I almost think that people were less pitiless towards their fellow-creatures – human and animal – under the Roman Empire than they are now: so why does not Christianity throw up the sponge and say I am beaten, and let another religion take its place.[591]

I suddenly remember that we had a call from our Bishop and his wife two or three days ago, so that perhaps it is rather shabby of me to write as above. By a curious coincidence we

---

588. See the poem 'Quid Hic Agis?' (*Moments of Vision*) and the note on that poem (*Life*, p. 157) at the end of an account of his brother-in-law, the Rev. C. Holder, for whom Hardy occasionally read the lessons at St Juliot and Lesnewth, Cornwall.

589. The inclusion of this letter in Hardy's *Life* (p. 389), with slight improvements and the omission of the penultimate paragraph, is a reminder of the extent to which Hardy and Florence worked from letters and a variety of records in compiling and checking his *Life*.

590. Hardy had expressed similar thoughts in January 1910 in 'The Jubilee of a Magazine' (*The Cornhill*, which began in 1860 under the editorship of Thackeray). See *Collected Poems*.

591. For the same thought, cf. p. 92, and the poem 'Christmas: 1924'.

had motored to Salisbury that very day, and were in his cathedral when he was in our house.

Do you mean to go to London for any length of time this summer? We are not going again till I don't know when. We squeezed a good deal into the 4 days we were there, and I got a bad throat as usual, but it has gone off. At Lady St Helier's we met the Archbishop of Dublin (English Ch[urch]) and found him a pleasant man.[592] We also met several young poets at Barrie's where we were staying.

We do hope you will carry out your idea of coming. We can put you up, and Anna, without trouble, and you can stay in bed half the day if you like. (I think, by the way, that Birdie will be vexed if you don't go on to her too).

I hope you are very very well – in 'rude' health, as they call it. Florence sends her love, and I am

Ever affectionately
Th: H.

142.   Max Gate,
Nov. 7: 1919

My dear friend:

Your welcome letter came when I was keeping in bed for a day or two with a bad cold – well, rather bad – and now I am about the house again. It was developed, if not caught, by a visit we paid to Swanage a week ago to assist at the opening of a Children's Hospital by the Bishop. He is a very nice man, and you should have seen and heard me making a speech of thanks to him for coming. All went off very well, but Florence has now the cold – I knew she would get it. We got there and

592. A more detailed account of this brief London visit is given in Hardy's *Life*, p. 388. He went to the Royal Academy dinner with J. M. Barrie; and discussed the Coverdale translation of the Psalms, and the inferiority of the Latin Vulgate in some of them, with Dr Bernard, Archbishop of Dublin, at Lady St Helier's. Hardy had known Barrie at least as long as he had known Mrs Henniker. With Gosse, Galsworthy, A. E. Housman, Kipling, and Shaw, Barrie was one of his pall-bearers. Subsequently he advised Florence Hardy on the preparation of Hardy's *Life* for the press, and the possible publication of his letters to Mrs Henniker.

back (about 25 miles each way) with our neighbours the Hanburys – who have a big car. Lady Ilchester is the President, and she made a very good speech. She asked F. affectionately about you, and was on her way to Holland House.[593]

Those three and forty[594] took me by surprise. It seems that the 'tribute', as they call it, has been in preparation for some time. I fear I shall not be able to live up to it with due dignity. Some of them are charming poems. I hope you will see the collection one day.

Yes: I am a strange member of the Wessex Pig Society. I accepted the nomination entirely in the hope of helping to popularize the 'killer'. I have seen so much cruelty practised on those poor animals.

I regret to hear of Anna's cold: but it is impossible to go to London at this time of the year without getting one. We are much struck by Milner's hospital treatment: [595] he would hold up his head to Wessex, whose life is of a wild sort, though he has several bedrooms, and goes from one to another.

I thought the letters you allude to very charming and graceful.[596] Gerrie as an explorer[597] is a new idea, and rather attractive. By the way, those youngsters – I mean the poets – have made me a year older than I am, but it has this convenience, that if I ever do get to be 80 I shall be able to slip by the date without much notice, it having been discounted (I think that is the commercial word) already.

Emma will have been in Stinsford Churchyard seven years

593. Holland House, Kensington, passed to the Ilchester family in 1889. See note 602, p. 189.

594. The poets who paid their tribute to Hardy in a volume of holograph poems collected by Siegfried Sassoon, who appears to have anticipated Hardy's eightieth birthday in his zeal.

595. Milner had gone to hospital for massage and electrical treatment.

596. Lord Crewe's congratulatory letter to Edmund Gosse on his seventieth birthday appeared in *The Times* on Monday, 22 September, with the names of over two hundred signatories, including Hardy's. Gosse's reply was published in the same paper on Saturday, 18 October. A bust by Sir William Goscombe John was later presented to Gosse at Lord Balfour's, and was the subject of a delightful cartoon by Max Beerbohm, which may be seen in Charteris (facing p. 444).

597. Mrs Henniker's nephew was studying archaeology at Cambridge 'with a view to doing explorations', she wrote. (She meant 'excavations', of course.) His aims were realized in the Middle East.

this month. It does not seem so long. I am sending a short poem to the *Fortnightly*[598] which they asked me for a year ago. Believe me.

Always affectionately
Tho. H.

Florence sends love, and is going to write.

143.   Max Gate,
                                               Dorchester.
                                               Feb 28: 1920

My dear friend:

Yes: you conjecture rightly: we had a very pleasant time at Oxford. The undergrads who form the O.U.D.S. took us in hand and treated us as their property, putting a taxi at our disposal from morning to night all the time. There were improvements on the London performance[599] – notably in the scenery: and the fact of the characters (110 in all, I think, and all speaking ones) being young, and many of them handsome, lent a great freshness and vivacity to their exhibition. Professonal actors might have envied the breathless silence with which some of the scenes were followed, and the large use of handkerchiefs at points of tragedy.

We did not go by motor after all. The doctor said he could not sanction it, the roads being just at that time full of holes and mud: yet a man went from here by road a few days after and said the journey was comfortable enough. We stayed at Sir W[alter] Raleigh's, the late professor of English Literature,

598. 'By Henstridge Cross at the Year's End' was published in the December number under the title 'By Mellstock Cross at the Year's End', i.e. at Bockhampton Cross, the crossroads between Higher and Lower Bockhampton. The transfer to Somerset was an attempt to disguise the personal note that runs through this despairing poem.

599. The Oxford University Dramatic Society performed *Scenes from 'The Dynasts'* in honour of Hardy in February 1920, and Hardy was invited to receive the degree of Doctor of Letters during his visit to attend the play, as adapted for Granville-Barker's earlier production of it in London. For the Oxford visit, see *Life*, pp. 397–401.

though we might have put up at the Giffords. However we went to see them.[600]

So Milner requires a garage to walk about in on wet days. Our Wessex, too, is very exacting. He sleeps in a room which has an anthracite stove that burns night and day; but if it goes out by chance in the small hours he promptly comes scratching at the bedroom door to induce us to come down and light it for him, as if it were unreasonable to expect him to sleep without a fire.

I wonder if you will be a fixture at Sussex Place. It is certainly a better side of the park[601] to live on than the South. The Gosses came about 6 weeks ago and stayed at the Gloucester Hotel, Weymouth: they visited us here, and we them: I think the air strengthened Mrs Gosse, as Wey[mou]th air does many people.

We have had of late great trouble with servants: they come and picnic for a month or two, and then leave, to picnic in somebody else's house. We have been reading L[or]d Ilchester's book on Henry Fox[602] which he was kind enough to send. Lady I. wanted to know what I thought of it, and I have told her. It is a very thorough and sincere piece of work, and interesting. Best love from both.

Your affect[iona]te friend

Th: H.

600. See note 558, p. 177.

601. Hyde Park.

602. Hardy would certainly be interested in the early part of this book, for Henry Fox (1705–44) was the younger brother of Stephen, who became the first Earl of Ilchester and whose marriage is the subject of 'The First Countess of Wessex' in *A Group of Noble Dames*. In his *Henry Fox, Lord Holland,* 1920, the sixth Earl thought it worth while to dwell on the story of the marriage to arrest the confusion of fact and fiction.

Holland House, which Henry Fox bought, had been the home of Addison; it was here, at private theatricals, that Lady Susan, the daughter of Stephen Fox, met the actor William O'Brien with whom she eloped. Henry Fox became Lord Holland in 1763; the famous Whig statesman Charles James Fox was his son.

144.   Max Gate.

                                      June 4: 1920

My dear friend:

We are delighted to hear that you are coming to Weymouth on July 1. I should have written to-day in answer to your kind telegram on my birthday, even if you had not added this pleasant letter. I was going to write last night, but some people came in just at the moment. You know how I valued having it, I am sure you do!

Yes: it was amusing to have the deputation.[603] I had never been deputated (?) before, so I was not at all dignified. But, as you know, I never am.

Yes: they did come to lunch. I was rather tired – not by them, for no less tiresome people can be conceived – but by the messages, and by strangers unexpectedly entering. I may tell you, since you allude to the King's message, that he has sent another to-day, thanking me for my good wishes for *his* birthday, which I expressed in my reply.

I saw the paragraph about the publishers. I wonder if it was true. Will you kindly thank Anna for her message as well. How very good of her. I am so sorry to hear of her sprained arm. I use Eliman's Embrocation for such accidents, but a relative uses a much stronger application – Jacob's Oil, or some such name. However I need not tell you of these things.

Florence has gone to Weymouth this very afternoon for an hour, taking Wessex. He so implores to be taken that it is hard to leave him at home. We will do anything to help you get there, if you will let us know. F. is splendid in managing such things. She often finds rooms for friends. Some rooms are good there, and some bad. Weymouth air is very good in summer, and probably you will not mind a few trippers beginning to come. (August is their great month.)

Lady I[lcheste]r will be so glad to have you near. She always asks when we see her if we have heard lately. She and L[or]d I. sent a combined wire on Wedn[esda]y, which I must thank them for.

  603. On his eightieth birthday, Hardy received the representatives of the Society of Authors: Augustine Birrell, Sir Anthony Hope Hawkins, and John Galsworthy (*Life*, p. 405).

Barrie has just sent a note to say he is coming to-morrow night for the week end. Believe me

Ever your affectionate

Tho. H.

By a curious chance the printers are reprinting just now:[604] and you may imagine how full my hands are.   Th: H.

145.   Max Gate.

July 7: 1920

My dear friend:

Yes: Thursday afternoon at 2, or as soon after as you can manage, at the Dorchester Museum, an easy place for an appointment, as we can read the papers, etc. during a few minutes of waiting; and you can look at the relics[605] if you should get there a minute or two before us.

As to the weather, to-day it seems doubtful. If bad to-morrow morning a discussion can be carried on over the telephone on what is to be done. I would suggest that, if persistently wet up to, say 4 o'clock, and then fine, you might still come to Dorchester, and we could go across to Stinsford, etc. going to Lyme the next day, or some other.

I enclose an amusing cutting from *The Outlook* which a Press-Cuttings agency has sent to Florence. She gives you her love, and says she will be so glad to see you again.

Always yours sincerely

Th. H.

604. The Mellstock Edition of Hardy's works was published in thirty-seven volumes from 1919 to 1920.

605. Mrs Henniker was staying at the Royal Hotel, Weymouth, and had proposed to arrive with Anna at 2 p.m. or very soon afterwards. The Dorset County Museum housed then, as it does now, a fine collection of prehistoric, Roman, and medieval relics. It is the principal centre for Hardy MSS. and personalia.

H

146.   Max Gate,
                                              Dorchester.
                                           Aug. 5: 1920

My dear friend:

I have found a copy of *Two on a Tower* in the edition you
like, and I am sending it with this. But instead of assisting you
to make up your set of these novels I ought really to be making
you read my more serious and later books. However you must
have your own way, I suppose.

We were glad to hear that you and Anna got back com-
fortably, in spite of the mishap with the engine. It was rather
a pity that you had not many really fine days in Weymouth,
but if you had waited till now you would have fared no better.
I hope, and so does Florence, that you will find a place somewhere in this direction – not further from here than you could
compass in a day, and back. We missed you very much the first
few days after you left: that's the worst of seeing old friends.

A poet and his wife – two quite young people – are going
to descend upon us on bicycles this month, and stay a night –
so they tell us. But as she has lately had a baby it seems rather
a wild project of theirs. Their scheme is to bicycle from Oxford
into Devon.

Florence's mother is immensely improved by Weymouth
air. I wish she could stay longer.

                          Believe me, ever affectionately yours,
                                              Th: H.

We are reading Jane Austen: [606] but *you* are to read *T. on a T.*
On looking into it it seems rather clever.

                                              Th. H.

606. Since 1915, when Hardy expressed the view that Jane Austen
wrote about trivial matters only, Hardy had obviously become more
appreciative of her talents: by the end of November, Florence had
read all Jane Austen's novels to him. At this time they were reading
Emma, and Hardy was amused to find how much he had in common
with Mr Woodhouse (Meynell, p. 306).

147.   Max Gate,
                                              Dorchester.
                                              All Saints Eve.
                                              Oct 31. 1920

My dear friend:

My thanks for your very nice letter; but before entering into it I write at this particular moment to ask if you are going to the presentation[607] to Mr Gosse on Friday next at 3, at the Steinway Hall? Florence has to be in London the day before, and thinks she can go, as she is not coming home until the evening train of Friday. I cannot go, so she must represent me. As L[or]d Crewe and Mr Balfour are in it, and the recipient is Gosse, I daresay it will be an interesting ceremony. They say the bust is good, but I have not seen it.

Yes: I have thought of you in your loss of 'Milner'. I have gone through the same experience in respect of cats. What silly people we are to get so attached to pets whose natural lives, as we well know, must in every reasonable probability finish before our own!

I did not expect much from the electric treatment, but of course if it has made you much better my doubts are answered. I have had a bad cold, but have begun to go out again.

I do hope what you expect of the Council of Justice to be well founded. Here in this stock-breeding county one sees instances continually of what does not exactly amount to legal cruelty, and yet is cruelty.

Fancy your reading that old novel of mine *Two on a Tower* right through. History does not record whether Swithin married Tabitha or not. Perhaps when Lady C[onstantine] was dead he grew passionately attached to her again, as people often do.[608] I suppose the bishop did find out the secret. Or perhaps he did not.

We saw the announcement of Mr Shorter's marriage[609] in the *Times*, and he has written since to us about it. We do not

607. See note 596, p. 187. The presentation took place at Lord Balfour's house, 4 Carlton Gardens (Charteris, pp. 444–5).
608. Hardy was thinking of himself and Emma Hardy.
609. Clement Shorter, who published many of Hardy's poems and short stories in the magazines which he edited, married as his second wife Doris Banfield. See note 580, p. 183.

know anything of the lady, except from what he says, that she is young, and in his judgment pretty.

I want you to get this to-morrow morning, and must hastily wind up as the post is just going. I like this mysterious eve of saintly ghosts, and also to-morrow eve, of All Souls.[610]

Ever affect[ionate]ly

Tho H.

This is a mere scrawl. I will write a better letter next time, as I hope.

Th: H.

148.

Max Gate,
Dorchester.
Dec. 22: 1920.

My dear friend:

Fancy my not writing to thank you for that very pretty present, which is on my table at this moment. It shows what ungrateful man is capable of. However I do thank you for it, and think it considerate of you to have chosen it.

I wonder if you are staying in London all this Christmas. I am as stationary as a tree, and don't feel any the worse for it, though whatever moss[611] I may gather is taken away by the tax-collector.

Our Christmas threatens to be quite an old fashioned one. For some reason best known to themselves the Dorchester Mummers and carolsingers are coming here on Christmas night, and we have to entertain them after their performance. I wish you could see the mumming: it is an exact repro-duction of the Dorset mumming of 100 years ago, as described in *The Return of the Native*.[612] (By the way, the Company is going to London on Jan. 27th next, and will perform the dramatization *including* the mumming before the Dorset Men in L[ondon] at the Guildhall School of Music, wherever that may be – so that you could see it if you wished)

610. Hardy became less of a rationalist in his later years (see Pinion, pp. 158–9).

611. Hardy alludes to the English proverb about 'the rolling stone'.

612. See *The Return of the Native*, II v and vi; *Life*, p. 411; and Meynell, p. 307.

It was very kind of you to shelter Florence during her late visit. She was so pleased – there is nowhere she likes to go better than to you.

Yes: Mr John Drinkwater is good looking: I hope his poetry will turn out to be as good as his looks. I am glad you know Newbolt[613] – I have heard from him this very week. He would be the last to think your manner pushing: I know the much pleasanter word he would use, but I shall not tell you.

F's sister is coming here for Xmas. I think it is more to see the mumming than to see us. The cold has quite gone off here, and this morning was beautiful: we went to Stinsford and put flowers on 'our' graves,[614] as we call them. A poem of mine comes out in the *Athenaeum*[615] on the last day of the year (Friday week). I don't think you will like it.

Ever affect[ionate]ly
Tho. H.

I have omitted to mention best wishes for Christmas – which is why I wrote at this particular time.

Th: H.

149.   Max Gate.
April 14. '21

My dear friend:

I must write just a line to thank you for so kindly accommodating Florence, and allowing her to make a hospital of your house.

How I wish I could come and see you. When I shall get to

613. John Drinkwater, poet and playwright (1882–1937) and Sir Henry Newbolt, poet (1862–1938). Newbolt and W. B. Yeats had presented the gold medal of the Royal Society of Literature to Hardy at Max Gate on his seventy-second birthday (*Life*, p. 358). Mrs Henniker had attended a lecture by Newbolt, and introduced herself; they had then talked about Thomas Hardy.

614. Where Emma Hardy, and Hardy's parents and sister Mary were buried. See 'Looking Across', written in December 1915, shortly after Mary's death (*Moments of Vision*).

615. 'At the Entering of the New Year' (*Late Lyrics and Earlier*).

London I do not know, what with railway and coal strikes and other things. Those who died before 1914 are out of it, thank Heaven – and 'have the least to pay' according to the old epitaph.[616]

I am glad you liked my Keats poem.[617] But almost everything that can be said about him has been said.

F. says that you have a dear and affectionate dog. When are you coming to the Royal H[otel] at Weymouth again. I am sure it picked you up very much last time. I have now to walk a short way with this to catch the early post, and secondarily to give Wessex a run.

Believe me ever

Your affect[iona]te friend
Th: H.

150.   Max Gate,
                                              Dorchester.
                                              2 July 1921
My dear friend:

This continuous fine weather makes me think that you might do well in trying Weymouth again, before the August trippers come. We have been told this week that the Burdon Hotel, which was until lately used for war-purposes, is now restored to its original state, has had the drains overhauled, and is altogether very comfortable, while not so expensive as the Royal – which some people are beginning to complain of in point of charges.

This morning we have had an odd experience. The film-

616. It exists in various forms in different parts of the country. One runs as follows:

> *Our life is but a winter's day:*
> *Some only breakfast and away;*
> *Others to dinner stay, and are full fed;*
> *The oldest only sup and go to bed.*
> *Large is his debt who lingers out the day;*
> *Those who go the soonest have the least to pay.*

617. Hardy's 'At a House in Hampstead' was written in 1920, and included in *The John Keats Memorial Volume* of 1921. A copy Hardy made of the poem may be seen in the Keats House, Hampstead, formerly Wentworth Place. In March 1920 Hardy had become a member of the national committee for the acquisition of this as a Keats museum and centre.

makers are here doing scenes from *The Mayor of C[aster-bridge]*, and they asked us to come and see the process. The result is that I have been talking to The Mayor, Mrs Henchard, Eliz[abeth] Jane, and the rest, in the flesh. The company arrived here at 1 o'clock this morning, and leave again to-morrow. It is a strange business to be engaged in.[618]

I believe I never have thanked you for your kind telegram on my birthday. I don't send you messages on yours, which is rather mean of me, but I send them in a lump now. I remember that you are not far from Lady Randolph Churchill, of whose accident we heard at the time, but imagined it to be one she would get over. She has had a lively life altogether, so her shade must not complain.[619]

As you know, we did not go to London after all, and now it does not seem the sort of place to go to in the drought. We have had a few pleasant people calling – poets mostly. I am getting to know quite a lot of the young Georgians, and have quite a paternal feeling, or grandpaternal, towards them. Siegfried Sassoon has been, Walter de la Mare, John Masefield,[620] and next week Mr and Mrs Galsworthy are going to call on their way to London. We have also seen the Granville Barkers. All this by reason of the car fashion of travel, which seems to make us almost suburban.

I hope Lady Crewe got over her attack of measles. Our neighbour Mrs Hanbury is ailing, and her father Mr Jeune (Lord St Helier's brother) is ill at her house.

We have no Sunday post now, so I must send this off to-night.

Ever y[ou]r affectionate
Th: H.

The cinema actors have just called in a body to wish us goodbye.

Th: H.

618. Hardy drove through Dorchester with the actors to visit the prehistoric earthwork Maiden Castle where part of the film was made.

619. Lady Randolph Churchill, mother of Sir Winston Churchill, died on 29 June 1921.

620. The poet Walter de la Mare (1863–1956) was a frequent visitor at Max Gate; he was there in June 1921. John Masefield, poet and novelist (1878–1967), served in the merchant navy in his youth, and became Poet Laureate in 1930. In 1921, accompanied by Mrs Masefield, he brought to Max Gate a model of a full-rigged ship, which he had made himself and called *The Triumph*.

151.   Max Gate,
                                                       Dorchester.
                                                     19 Dec. 1921

My dear friend.

I have delayed my reply to your kind letter a few days, to
bring it into Christmastide, when I know you like to
receive missives, even of such a dull character as mine is likely
to be I fear. Thank you for your inquiries: we have recovered
and are now as well as two aged people can hope to be (F. will
thank me for putting it this way!) I fancy from the brightness
of your letter that you are already profiting from the country
air, even though you must miss the people you are able to see
in London. We are in a drizzle here to-day, though the weather
has on the whole been good.

Bognor I seem to know quite well from friends, though I
have never actually set foot in it – which is very stupid, as I
have been to Chichester, Worthing, and all about there
several times. The young architect who was the original of
Stephen Smith in *A Pair of Blue Eyes* (so far as he had any
original) used to be enthusiastic on Bognor and to go there
with his family.[621] 'Blake's cottage' makes Felpham[622] interesting: but which Blake does it mean? Since writing this question I
have discovered that it means Blake the poet. Hayley was a
poetaster, Blake's friend, and was ridiculed by Byron in
'English Bards'. I don't know what 'steyne' means,[623] unless it
is a paved way.

I have read very little on the Irish situation lately: it was
so worrying that I had to give it up. 'Irish Free State' does, as
you say, sound unromantic. The Ireland Free State, or Irish
Freeland would perhaps be less so.

621. See *Life*, p. 73. The 'original' was a nephew of John Hicks, the
architect for whom Hardy had worked in Dorchester.

622. Mrs Henniker was staying at the Manor House, Felpham, Sussex,
near Blake's 'thatched house'. She had read that Haley (*sic*) had also
lived at Felpham, and wondered 'what' he was.

William Blake, the poet and painter (1757–1827), was induced by
Flaxman, the sculptor, to go to Felpham while he was working on en-
gravings for *The Life of Cowper* by William Hayley, the poetaster,
who lived at Turret House. Blake stayed at Felpham from 1800 to 1803.

623. In the Sussex dialect, to 'stean' or 'steen' means to pave or line
with stone.

Walter de la Mare has sent us his new poems.[624] They are rather too obscure, I think: but many of them have his own peculiar beauty in them when you get to the bottom of their meaning.

We were at our neighbours, the Hanburys at Kingston Maurward yesterday afternoon. Her father, Mr Symons-Jeune, whom you met, is coming to them to stay over Christmas, so we shall see him. A very mild little poem of mine appears in the Dec[ember] *Fortnightly*,[625] and to save trouble I send a spare proof of it instead of the heavy magazine. I have also another – a longer one – in the Dec[ember] *London Mercury*. It would, I think, please you more than this trifling one, but I have neither proof nor magazine. The title is 'Voices from things growing (in a churchyard)'.

Now I come to wishing you a happy Xmas and New Year: as also does F., and many of them.

Yours affectionately
Th: H.

I had nearly forgotten to say that F. had a letter in last Friday's *Times* (Dec. 16) about squirrels – I wonder if you saw it.

Th. H.

152. Max Gate,
Dorchester.
March 1. 1922

My dear friend:

I am writing at (I hope) the end of a series of household calamities, which have thrown my doings out of gear for some weeks past. They began by my having a return of an old complaint – internal inflammation – which, though not violent, has been extremely tedious, and though not absolutely gone as yet, is practically so. Then the whole house had influenza, F's being a particularly sharp attack, her voice being very weak and husky still. But, as I say, I believe we are gradually getting

624. *The Veil and Other Poems* (1921). Mrs Henniker had found some of his poems 'a little too mystical and puzzling'.
625. 'An Autumn Rain-Scene' (written in 1904).

normal. I hope you have not suffered from any such visitation.

We had no echoes here of yesterday's wedding[626] – except an invitation to Lady Astor's party, which of course we could not accept. Siegfried Sassoon writes to Florence saying the bridegroom looked worried; but then, bridegrooms always look as if they had got the worst of it, don't you think?

I fancy you knew Lulu Harcourt,[627] did you not? I regretted to hear of his death. He used to come here sometimes, and I was at his wedding. But he never looked strong. Did you see in the papers also the death of Charles Gifford last week? – Emma's first cousin – whom you used to know at Southsea, and, I think, liked. So friends and acquaintances thin out, and we who remain have to 'close up'.

I have collected most of the poems of mine that have been written since the last volume came out five years ago, and they are to be published anon – about the middle of May, I understand. It is no pleasure to me to appear again in print; but I really did not know what to do with them: a good many having already been printed in magazines, etc., about which people were continually writing to know when they could be got in a volume. In the book there will also be some very old ones, which I had overlooked in making previous collections.[628]

I was sorry to hear that you had lost 'Brush' – but that is a frequent unhappy contingency with pets. Our Wessex is as ill-behaved as ever, and acts as if he were quite the master of the house, which indeed he is.

I am directing this to Felpham, where I imagine you still are, though I am not quite sure. Affectionate regards from F. and from me.

Ever yours

Tho. H.

626. Of Princess Mary to the sixth Earl of Harewood.

627. Lewis Vernon Harcourt (1863–1922), Viscount (1916), had been Colonial Secretary from 1910 to 1915. He was the son of one of the great Liberals of the Gladstone era. Hardy had met him nearly thirty years previously at the Sheridans', Frampton (*Life*, p. 259).

628. *Late Lyrics and Earlier*, published 23 May 1922, and prefaced with a very impressive 'Apology', in which Hardy takes issue with the critics, particularly on the score of his 'pessimism'.

153.
Max Gate,
Dorchester.
May 29: 1922

My dear friend:

I ought to have sent you a copy of the Poems.[629] But I don't send books to women nowadays – not because I despise the sex, far from it! but because I fear they will not like something or other I have written, and will be in the awkward position of having to pretend they do. I am sure some in the present poems will be against your taste, so you can let fly at me freely and without compunction, which you could not otherwise have done.

Yes, Edmund Gosse was very funny about that young man.[630] But then he always writes wittily. I wish he would give himself more time: he would out-Walpole Walpole[631] if he did.

But I am saying nothing on the most delightful part of your letter (received this morning, I ought to have mentioned) – that you are coming to D[orchester] on the 26th. We are both so glad, and will certainly show you the country of *The Woodlanders*, which is only about 12 miles from here. It is, in fact, just beyond where Gen. Henniker's aunt lived,[632] and Mrs Charmond's house is a sort of composite one.[633] However I

629. Mrs Henniker's views had always been eminently respectable, and Hardy did not wish to offend her susceptibilities, although in the early days of their friendship he had tried to modernize her outlook. On the previous day she had written to say she had ordered a copy of *Late Lyrics and Earlier*.

630. In *The Sunday Times*, 28 May 1922, Edmund Gosse, discussing Hardy's new volume of poetry, referred to the 'Apology', and made light of the 'knowing reviewer, apparently a Roman Catholic young man' who had written of ' "Mr Hardy refusing consolation", the "dark gravity of his ideas" and so on'. What did it matter, Gosse asked, what some young Catholic, or some old Protestant, had been silly enough to say?

631. See note 113, p. 37.

632. Possibly Up Cerne. See pp. 22, 25, 31. In her letter of the previous day, Mrs Henniker announced that she had taken rooms at the King's Arms from Monday to Saturday, 26 June to 1 July, and expressed the wish to see *The Woodlanders* country. Hardy's *Life* (p. 416) shows that this visit took place; elsewhere there is evidence that she planned to bring her old faithful servant Anna with her.

633. Hintock House was based on Turnworth House (several miles due east of *The Woodlanders* country) and its situation in a valley beneath a steep wooded slope.

can tell you all this when you come.

How strange that you should be so countrified at Highgate. If I were obliged to live close to London I should probably live up that way.[634]

I get very odd letters. A lady writes to-day begging me to write one more novel before I 'pass on'.

T. H.

634. Part of the letter has been excised here.
This is the last of the extant letters from Hardy to Mrs Henniker. Three later letters from her to Hardy survive, the last dated 21 December 1922. After this there is nothing except the entries in Hardy's notebook, which he transferred to his *Life* (p. 419):

April 5. In to-day's *Times*:
'Henniker. – on the 4th April 1923, of heart failure, the Honourable Mrs. Arthur Henniker. R.I.P.'
After a friendship of 30 years!
April 10. F. Henniker buried to-day at 1 o'clock at Thornham Magna, Eye, Suffolk.

In this parish stood Thornham Hall, the seat of the Lords Henniker and formerly of the Majors. A Tudor house, it eventually passed to Elizabeth Major, wife of the second Duke of Chandos, and then to her brother-in-law, the first Baron Henniker, of Worlingworth Hall, Suffolk. It was destroyed beyond restoration by fire in 1954.

The church at Thornham Magna contains many memorials to the families who lived at the Hall, including a brass to Major-General Henniker. Florence Henniker was buried next to her husband at the east end of the churchyard. Nothing 'stately' (as Hardy once imagined) marks the place of her interment; only a cross on a three-tiered base forms their joint memorial.

In Death Divided

I

I shall rot here, with those whom in their day
    You never knew,
And alien ones who, ere they chilled to clay,
    Met not my view,
Will in your distant grave-place ever neighbour you.

II

No shade of pinnacle or tree or tower,
    While earth endures,
Will fall on my mound and within the hour
    Steal on to yours;
One robin never haunt our two green covertures.

III

Some organ may resound on Sunday noons
    By where you lie,
Some other thrill the panes with other tunes
    Where moulder I;
No self-same chords compose our common lullaby.

IV

The simply-cut memorial at my head
    Perhaps may take
A rustic form, and that above your bed
    A stately make;
No linking symbol show thereon for our tale's sake.

V

And in the monotonous moils of strained, hard-run
    Humanity,
The eternal tie which binds us twain in one
    No eye will see
Stretching across the miles that sever you from me.

The Letters of the Hon. Mrs Henniker to Thomas Hardy(1906–22)

The extant letters of Florence Henniker to Thomas Hardy – less than forty in number[1] – invariably open with 'My dear friend' and close with 'Your affectionate friend', or 'Ever your affectionate friend', 'Always your friend', or 'Ever affectionately yours'. There are long gaps in the correspondence, especially between the years 1915 and 1920. It is obvious that it is not complete, whether from accident or intention. She wrote from various addresses, Hayling Island, Felpham in Sussex and Shoreham in Kent, as well as from London – 2 Hyde Park Square, which she let from time to time, Stratford Place and Sussex Place in the West End, and two addresses in Kensington. She was neither well-to-do nor strong in health, and moved about, sometimes abroad, in search of financial or physical benefit. But it was at Felpham and Shoreham that, as the letters show, she found the greatest happiness, since – like the Hardys – she was a great lover of gardens, birds and domestic animals. Towards the end of her life she moved to Highgate Hill.

Her letters reveal something of her character – not as much as one could wish – and of those interests which she and Hardy had in common, animal welfare and, above all, literature. Her compassionate heart was drawn towards anti-vivisection and the amelioration of all animal suffering. Florence Hardy lamented after her death that they had no one to assist them, as she had done, in this cause. Mrs Henniker was delighted

1. They are all at the Dorset County Museum. In addition to the thirty-five in the main collection, there are four congratulatory letters, one relating to the award of the O.M. to Hardy in 1910, and three to birthdays from 1920 to 1922. See C. and C. Weber, *Thomas Hardy's Max Gate Correspondence*, Colby College, 1968, where Mrs Henniker's letter of 28 May 1915 is not listed.

with the passage of the Plumage Bill in America and the rending of feathers from the hats of callous women. When Prince Arthur of Connaught opened a laboratory at Cambridge which she associated with vivisection, she wished some mad woman would burn it down. She had been very grateful to receive from Hardy a cheque for the relief of wounded war horses. If only a bill for their relief, and a Plumage Act, could be passed, 1921 would not be a bad year for England despite the strikes. Nor was she oblivious of human suffering. During the First World War she was occupied in sending parcels of books to wounded or captive soldiers in Egypt and Mesopotamia.

In her first extant letter there is a reminder, as late as 1906, of that interest in architecture by which Hardy had striven to bind her to him as a pupil in the 1890s. She had spirit and strong opinions of her own, and disagreed with him over the retention of Georgian pews in medieval churches. He had sent her his essay, 'Memories of Church Restoration', published in *The Cornhill Magazine* in the month in which she wrote to him:

> I ought to have thanked you, before this, for the address on ancient buildings, which was both interesting *and* amusing. ... I don't see the objection to restoration, when, for example you leave the *original* half window, or half arch ... intact? And as to the Georgian pews – I think they *had far better go,* in spite of some interesting associations. They would have greatly disgusted the first builders, and it seems to me are more of an eyesore than some other innovations would be?

Later she appealed to Hardy to prevent the destruction of some ancient buildings in the city:

> I wish you would write a *strong* protest against the wicked proposal to demolish Cloth Fair. It is really worse to pull down beautiful and interesting old buildings in time of *peace* than to burn them in the excitement of War. Surely those Smithfield houses should be kept as treasured *relics,* even if they are not supposed to be suitable to be lived in.

Sir Walter Besant had described these houses as 'very old ... with projecting stories and gable ends. Many of these have the bowed curve of old age resembling the curving back of an old man' (a comment that would have appealed to Hardy). '[Some] are covered with rough stucco and have bayed windows and gable ends. These are the fronts of those seen over the church-yard [of St Bartholomew's].'[2]

In other letters there are comments on the conduct of the First World War, on national prejudices; on the Coalition Government of 1915, and Lloyd George and the new government of 1922; more particularly on the Irish question, with which her brother, Lord Crewe, the former Lord-Lieutenant, was intimately concerned. She had little use for the nascent Irish Republic and the bitter struggle for independence. Parnell and Dillon, yes; but she found the resuscitation of the Gaelic names and tongue, which the English had cruelly suppressed, 'farcical', an attitude she could hardly escape since she belonged to the ruling English aristocracy of the period.

Literature was her predominant interest, but she was also fond of music and painting. Hardy sent her tickets for exhibitions and lectures that he could not, and she might not otherwise have been able to, attend. (In one letter she refers to straitened circumstances.) So, when thanking him, she comments on Royal Academy paintings and people, concerts at the Albert Hall and the public lectures of Sir Henry Newbolt, who spoke on Shakespeare and the poetry of Walter de la Mare, and of Professor Ernest de Selincourt, who lectured on John Keats. When the Keats memorial volume was being planned, she was asked to write her memories of her father's conversations on his favourite poet, but she regretted that she did not feel up to it. She is familiar with the current French novelists, and with the work of Thackeray and Dickens. When she is moving to Highgate she likes to think that her house is near the terrace where Steerforth and Rosa Dartle sat, just as with Hardy's novels she is anxious to see scenes and settings for the action of *Tess of the d'Urbervilles* and *The Woodlanders*. She reads a biography of Cavour with

2. E. V. Lucas thought that the best idea of old London was afforded by the sixteenth-century houses of Cloth Fair and Bartholomew Close, on the north side of St Bartholomew the Great (*A Wanderer in London*, London, 1906).

admiration of his character, and revels, in spite of herself, in
the romantic love-story told in two indiscreet volumes by Kitty
O'Shea after her marriage to Parnell. She receives Bret Harte's
grandson at Hyde Park Square with pleasure, Harte having
been one of her guests as well as her father's. Something of the
woman who her nephew says liked slang, and who in spite of
her devoutness was not given to mysticism, emerges in her
description of Blake's poetry as 'twaddly at times'.

Among the 'modern' poets, she is interested in W.B.
Yeats, and impressed by Julian Grenfell, Ralph Hodgson,
and Walter de la Mare, though she finds some of his work 'a
little too mystical and puzzling'. She must have appreciated
A Shropshire Lad, for she looks forward to Housman's new
volume of poetry in 1922. She recognizes cleverness in some
of the younger writers, but concludes they must be 'unwhole-
some young *decadents*'. The reactionary in her responds to
Newbolt's criticism of the cynical cast of writing towards the
end of the First World War period. Her conservatism makes
her averse to 'movies' ('so bad for the eyes'), and critical of
modern dress ('idiotic women in London who go to work on
wet days wearing transparent stockings and cardboard shoes
with high heels') and such eccentricities as Edith Sitwell's
hat – 'a bad specimen of – shall we say, Gothic architecture'.

Her criticisms of Barrie and Galsworthy are interesting,
proving that she was original enough not to be swayed by
current taste. She thinks it *absurd* that Barrie should have
been given the Order of Merit in 1922 – an honour awarded
to Hardy in 1910 – and considers his work overrated and
overpraised, 'an undue fuss' being made about him, his
writing, and his 'whimsical' humour. She finds Galsworthy's
style

almost too facile, – more a 'knack' – perhaps, than really
fine work. . . . The descriptions . . . are, of course charming.
But I *do* resent what has become a perfect obsession with
Mr. Galsworthy, viz. his detestation of what, for want of a
better word, one may describe as the 'respectable' and the
religious. Though he doesn't know it, he is quite as narrow-
minded in his way, as the Puritans of the 'Scarlet Letter'
were in theirs. He can't conceive the possibility of any
woman who has declined to leave her husband, and who

wishes to go to church, having *any* sort of fascination, or temptations, which shows that his experience is limited!

Elsewhere she writes that Galsworthy's 'curious fondness for the flagrantly immoral woman seems to be more marked than ever – as he now even condones their suffocating their children!' One wonders what the author of *Jude the Obscure* thought of that.

The tie between Hardy and Florence Henniker was strengthened by their interest in each other's work. Hers in his was unfailing. It is clear that she read everything he wrote as soon as she could get hold of it, and that she was as keenly interested in his verse as in his prose. Her criticisms were light but perceptive. It is significant, and to her credit, that she asked for a copy of Edmund Gosse's long and important essay on Hardy's poetry and its inception. She admired, she says, Hardy's lyric of which he himself was fond, 'When I set out for Lyonnesse', and thought that perhaps her favourite of all his poems was 'The Darkling Thrush' (another favourite of his, she had read in an article). Her conversations with Newbolt and de la Mare after their lectures, with Lady Ilchester and Lady St Helier, and with the Gosses and their guests, inevitably turned to Thomas Hardy.

When *Late Lyrics and Earlier* was published in 1922, Mrs Henniker describes the general impression of the volume as being 'much sadder in tone than you yourself are'. On another occasion she rightly remarks that there is as much in two or three lines of one of his poems 'as in a complete one by many people', an appraisal which would have been unacceptable to most of Hardy's readers, still not ready to rank him as a major poet. How deeply he valued her criticisms we do not know. But all writers need admiration and comfort. For him her responsive appreciation, especially in the dark years when he and his first wife were sealing off their hearts from each other, was stimulus and nourishment.

The letters are not literary masterpieces, but they complement Hardy's to her, in a measure, and transmit something of the essence of a brave, intelligent, warm-hearted woman with a restrained, intuitive nature, streaked like his with irony and humour.

The Hon. Mrs. Henniker

by
THOMAS HARDY[1]

Florence Ellen Hungerford Henniker, *née* Milnes, whose portrait is annexed, is the younger daughter of the first Lord Houghton and sister of the present Lord Lieutenant of Ireland and of the Hon. Lady Fitzgerald. The literary bias which has almost resulted in placing Mrs. Henniker on the list of professional authors may possibly be hereditary in her, for it manifested itself at an early age – a quaint devotional fervour, not uncommon in imaginative children, taking the form of an enthusiasm for the writing of hymns. Possibly also her having been surrounded through childhood and youth by literary personages of all classes and countries, whom her father was accustomed to entertain at Fryston Hall and in London, made her early familiar with the idea of putting her thoughts upon paper. But it was not until the last three or four years that she decided to publish as fiction the experiences of life gained in England and abroad by one who has certainly had good opportunities of observing it. Her first and wholly experimental novel, bearing the amateurish title of *Bid Me Good-bye*,[2] was followed by a tale of stronger characterization, called *Sir George*, which has lately been republished in one volume. Last year Mrs. Henniker issued a longer novel entitled *Foiled*, wherein the growing strength shown in character-drawing makes the reader indifferent to the absence of a well-compacted plot. A volume of short stories called *Outlines*, published this year, evidences a literary form and style sufficient to carry their author through more ambitious performances. Mrs. Henniker has also written tales for the *Cornhill*,

1. Published anonymously in *The Illustrated London News*, 18 August 1894.
2. Hardy's order is wrong: Mrs Henniker's first novel, *Sir George*, appeared in 1891, and her second, *Bid Me Good-bye*, in 1892.

Blackwood, English Illustrated, and other magazines, and has published some scattered translations of French and Italian verse. Her note of individuality, her own personal and peculiar way of looking at life, without which neither aristocrat nor democrat, fair woman nor foul, has any right to take a stand before the public as author, may be called that of emotional imaginativeness, lightened by a quick sense of the odd, and by touches of observation lying midway between wit and humour.

Published volumes of novels and short stories by the Hon. Mrs Henniker

Sir George, Richard Bentley and Son, 1891
Bid Me Good-bye, Richard Bentley and Son, 1892
Foiled, Hurst and Blackett, 1893
Outlines, Hutchinson, 1894:
    A Statesman's Love-Lapse
    The Major's Prodigal
    Our Neighbour, Mr. Gibson
    A Sustained Illusion
In Scarlet and Grey, John Lane, 1896:
    The Heart of the Colour-Sergeant
    Bad and Worthless
    A Successful Intrusion
    A Page from a Vicar's History
    At the Sign of the Startled Fawn
    In the Infirmary
    The Spectre of the Real (*in collaboration with Thomas Hardy*)
Sowing the Sand, Harper and Brothers, 1898
Contrasts, John Lane, 1903:
    Lady Coppinger's Perplexity
    The Butterfly
    A Brand of Discord
    In a Rhineland Valley
    Mr. and Mrs. Cartaret
    Maurice Ballantine's Friend
    Lady Gillian
    The Home-Coming of Job
    Three Corporals
    Ex-Trooper Tempany
    The Man who Waited

The Lonely House on the Moor
Glory
An Hour in October
Past Mending
After Thirty Years
Our Fatal Shadows, Hurst and Blackett, 1907
Second Fiddle, Eveleigh Nash, 1912
Stories and Play Stories, published in 1897 by Chapman and
Hall (from *Chapman's Magazine*), contained one short story by
the Hon. Mrs Arthur Henniker. This was 'Mrs. Livesey', but
Hardy's letters suggest that others were published only in
magazines. In March 1917 she expressed the hope that her
new story (a novel?), which she thought better than *Second
Fiddle,* would soon be published; it was to be dedicated to
Thomas Hardy. So far it has not been traced. She seems to have
attempted drama more than once; *The Courage of Silence*, a
four-act comedy, was published in 1905.

Bibliography of principal references in Notes

As frequent references have already been made to Hardy's works, it is superfluous to list them here. It may be helpful, however, to point out that the only complete edition of his poems is *The Collected Poems of Thomas Hardy*, London, 1930.

The following are the books to which abbreviated references are made throughout:

E. Charteris
The Life and Letters of Sir Edmund Gosse, London, 1931.

Evelyn Hardy
Thomas Hardy, A Critical Biography, London, 1954; New York, 1970.

Evelyn Hardy
Thomas Hardy's Notebooks, London, 1955.

Florence Hardy
The Life of Thomas Hardy, London, 1962.

Viola Meynell
Friends of a Lifetime (letters to Sydney John Cockerell), London, 1940, pp. 274–316.

Harold Orel
Thomas Hardy's Personal Writings, Kansas, 1966; London, 1967.

F. B. Pinion
A Hardy Companion, London and New York, 1968.

James Pope-Hennessy
Lord Crewe, London, 1955.

R. L. Purdy
Thomas Hardy, A Bibliographical Study, London, 1954.

T. W. Reid
The Life, Letters, and Friendships of Richard Monckton Milnes, First Lord Houghton (two vols), London, 1890.

W. R. Rutland
Thomas Hardy, A Study of his Writings and their Background, London, 1938; New York, 1962.

Carl Weber
'Dearest Emmie' (Hardy's letters to his first wife), London, 1963.

INDEX